# Written Text Becomes Living Word

## *The Vision and Practice*
## *of Sunday Preaching*

Stephen Vincent DeLeers

LITURGICAL PRESS
Collegeville, Minnesota

www.litpress.org

| 1 | 2 | 3 | 4 | 5 | 6 | 7 | 8 |
|---|---|---|---|---|---|---|---|

**Library of Congress Cataloging-in-Publication Data**

DeLeers, Stephen Vincent, 1958–
    Written text becomes living Word : the vision and practice of Sunday preaching / Stephen Vincent DeLeers.
        p. cm.
    Includes bibliographical references and index.
    ISBN 0-8146-2759-5 (pbk : alk. paper)
    1. Preaching. 2. Church year sermons. 3. Catholic Church—Sermons. I. Title.

BV4211.3.D45 2004
251—dc22

2004004871

# Contents

Preface   v

1   Repairing the "Accidents of History": Roman Catholic Restoration and Embrace of the Sunday Homily   1

2   The Evolution of the "Restored" Homily: 1963–1993   13

3   A Roman Catholic Contribution to the Vision of Sunday Preaching   45

4   The Homily as Personal Word: Responsibility, Faith, and Love   53

5   The Homily as Liturgical Word: The Assembly and Its Sacred Ritual   69

6   The Homily as Inculturated Word: Correlating Experience and Tradition   87

7   The Homily as Clarifying Word: One Good Point, Clearly Made   103

8   The Homily as Actualizing Word: Written Text Becomes Living Word   119

9   Arriving at the Sunday Message: Three Necessary Encounters with the Word   137

10   From Message to Homily: Content, Structure, and Delivery   157

11   Ten Suggestions for Becoming a Better Preacher   179

Appendix: Official Roman Catholic Documents Concerning Preaching, 1963–1994   195

Index   201

# Preface

Can anything good come out of Rome? When it comes to preaching, even the Pope had his doubts. I met Pope John Paul II in Rome in the fall of 1995. He asked me what I was doing in the city, and I told him, "Doctoral work." He asked about my field of study and I replied, "Preaching." The Pope did a double take and said, "Preaching? Here?" Even the Bishop of Rome apparently had his doubts about what his local church had to offer the preacher. I assured him that I was earning my degree in the United States and only doing some background research in Rome. "Oh, oh," he responded, seemingly reassured.

Can anything good come out of Rome? When it comes to preaching, I am happy to answer, "Yes." The central administrative agencies of the Roman Catholic Church have a great deal to offer all Christian preachers of God's Word. This book seeks to reveal and develop a significant Catholic contribution to the vision and practice of Sunday preaching.

Chapter 1 provides a brief historical context for the developing Catholic contribution to homiletics. It was just over forty years ago that the bishops constituting the Second Vatican Council began the process of rethinking the Catholic understanding of Sunday preaching. It was a radical rethinking, and the council's vision won the rapid embrace of churchgoing Catholics.

In chapter 2 I race through thirty years worth of documents issued by various persons and agencies of the Roman Catholic Church. Though the sources consulted vary widely—in time, authorship, and level of authority—they nonetheless provide a coherent vision of the nature and purpose of

Sunday preaching. This diachronic journey captures every significant reference to the homily that emerged from Rome from 1963 through 1993.

In chapter 3 I take a step back from the plethora of references to the homily and attempt to offer a synchronic description arising from the documents. I believe that this material invites preachers to understand the Sunday homily as *personal, liturgical, inculturated, clarifying,* and *actualizing* (that is, PLICA).

Chapters 4 through 8 take each of the PLICA characteristics in turn and explore the abilities necessary to preach in such a way. The vision of preaching and its practice are treated in an integrating way, since what we hope to accomplish in the pulpit must drive the choices we make in preparation and delivery.

Every preacher follows a routine in preparing a Sunday homily. Chapters 9 and 10 present a method for achieving a personal, liturgical, inculturated, clarifying, and actualizing Sunday homily. Chapter 11 goes on to suggest ten strategies for every preacher, from the beginning one to the most experienced, to improve the homily.

Throughout *Written Text Becomes Living Word,* I hold vision and practice together. While the very best preaching involves artistry, all preaching is first and foremost a craft. Principles can be learned and skills can be developed to put that craft into practice. It is my contention that certain documents issued by Rome provide very helpful contributions to the vision and practice of Sunday preaching for all Christians called to that ministry.

Allow me a couple of additional prefatory notes.

First, throughout this book I use the term "homily" to refer to the act of Sunday preaching. I do so because this is the term that Roman Catholic documents on liturgical preaching rapidly adopted in the early years during and after the Second Vatican Council. However, even a cursory look at the Christian homiletics of the second half of the twentieth century reveals that "sermon" and "homily" are not to be contrasted artificially. In 1963, when Vatican II first turned its attention to renewing Sunday preaching, it used both *sermo* and *homilia* to refer to that preaching (see Constitution on the Sacred Liturgy 35, 52). However, as will be seen in chapter 3, "homily" is the term used in all documents subsequent to the Constitution on the Sacred Liturgy, and so I use it as well. Nonetheless, Christian preachers more accustomed to the term "sermon" should feel free to make a mental translation to that more familiar term, especially if their understanding of "sermon" is that of the *Concise Encyclopedia of Preaching:* "an oral interpretation of scripture, usually in the context of worship."[1]

Second, especially in my first three chapters, I will be referring to a variety of documents that have come from Rome. On the one hand, it is important to understand that, for Catholics, these documents are not all of equal authority. The teaching authority of an ecumenical council of bishops united with the pope is highest, followed by official teaching done by the pope in his own name. Of lesser authority are those documents issued by the congregations and councils of the Roman Curia, the bureaucracy used by a pope in his day-to-day governing of the Catholic Church. On the other hand, though, my intention in this book is not to parse more or less authoritative statements, but rather to mine nuggets of wisdom from thirty years' worth of Roman writings, whatever their source or claim to authority. I invite any Western Christian reader, whether Reformed, Anglican, or Roman Catholic, to take these Roman insights into Sunday preaching on their own merit, judging them in terms of both fidelity to Christian experience and homiletic utility.

Forty years ago, the bishops at Vatican II had great hopes that Roman Catholic renewal would benefit all Christians, and they explicitly pointed to a renewal of preaching as a most promising area.

> Church renewal therefore has notable ecumenical importance. Already this renewal is taking place in various spheres of the Church's life: the biblical and liturgical movements, the preaching of the Word of God. . . . All these should be considered as promises and guarantees for the future of ecumenism.[2]

My hope is that *Written Text Becomes Living Word* might be a step toward ongoing ecumenical progress in the holy preaching of God's Word. For decades, Roman Catholic preachers have benefited greatly from the contributions to homiletics made by Protestants. I offer this book as a Roman Catholic contribution in turn.

---

1. David L. Bartlett, "Sermon," *Concise Encyclopedia of Preaching,* ed. William H. Willimon and Richard Lischer (Louisville: Westminster John Knox Press, 1995) 433.
2. Second Vatican Council, Decree on Ecumenism *(Unitatis Redintegratio)* 6. Accessed at <http://www.vatican.va/archive/hist_councils/ii_vatican_council/documents/vat-ii_decree _19641121_unitatis-redintegratio_en.html>.

CHAPTER 1

# Repairing the "Accidents of History": Roman Catholic Restoration and Embrace of the Sunday Homily

Four years after the close of the Second Vatican Council, in 1969, Pope Paul VI issued a revised ritual for the celebration of Mass. In introducing that ritual, he wrote that it would restore "to the tradition . . . 'elements that have suffered injury through the accidents of history,' . . . for example, the homily."[1] Following the decree of Vatican II, the Sunday homily was now to "not be omitted except for a serious reason."[2]

How did it come to pass that the Catholic Sunday homily became a victim of "the accidents of history" in the first place? What forces led to the restoration of the homily as an integral part of the liturgy? And how has that restoration been accepted by the Catholic faithful? These are the concerns of this chapter.

## Repairing the Accidents of History

In the centuries after the Protestant Reformation, it became a commonplace to observe that the "divorce" of Protestants and Catholics led to a

1. Paul VI, Apostolic Constitution Approving the Roman Missal *(Missale Romanum),* footnoting the Constitution on the Sacred Liturgy *(Sacrosanctum Concilium)* 50, in International Committee on English in the Liturgy, *Documents on the Liturgy: 1963–1979* (Collegeville: Liturgical Press, 1982) 459.

2. Second Vatican Council, Constitution on the Sacred Liturgy *(Sacrosanctum Concilium)* 52. Accessed at <http:www.vatican.va/archive/hist_councils/ii_vatican_council/documents/vat-ii _const_19631204_sacrosanctum-concilium_en.html>.

most unfortunate property settlement: Protestants got the Word, and Catholics got the sacraments. In the way of most pithy pronouncements, there is both truth and oversimplification here. It was in fact the case that post-Reformation Catholics celebrated more sacraments more frequently than Reformed Christians did. And it was also the case that Reformed Christians heard the Word of God preached more biblically and more frequently than Catholics did. Indeed, as the centuries rolled by, some Protestants celebrated the Lord's Supper only once a year, and some Catholics could go at least as long without hearing a scriptural sermon. How did the Church come to this skewed state of affairs, especially regarding the role of preaching?

The years just before and after Martin Luther's emergence as a Church reformer held no clue of the coming split of Word from sacrament. The early Reformers neither rejected Sunday Eucharist nor invented Sunday eucharistic preaching. As historian Hughes Oliphant Old notes, "The Church in which the Reformers were born and brought up loved preaching."[3] Luther, however, came to be convinced that much of Sunday preaching was lacking in efficacy, and his diagnosis was that late medieval sermons were insufficiently biblical and evangelical. He criticized the homiletic form he found far too common: "The preacher runs through the gospel superficially and then follows it up with a fable about Attila the Hun or a story about Dietrich of Bern, or he mixes in something from Plato, Aristotle, or Socrates."[4] Such preaching did not sufficiently release the saving power of the gospel of Jesus Christ. And so Luther, following his famous encounter with St. Paul's Letter to the Romans, began to preach the Good News as he had come to understand it: the gospel of salvation through faith in Jesus Christ. Old put it well: "The classical Protestant Reformation produced a distinct school of preaching. It was a preaching of reform, to be sure, but it was also a reform of preaching."[5]

There was, of course, a Catholic response to the preaching of reform and the reform of preaching. That response—the Council of Trent and its aftermath—both recognized the value of regular scriptural preaching and

3. Hughes Oliphant Old, *The Reading and Preaching of the Scriptures in the Worship of the Christian Church,* vol. 4: *The Age of the Reformation* (Grand Rapids: William B. Eerdmans Publishing Company, 2002) 1.

4. Ibid., 10–11.

5. Ibid., 1.

failed to act on that value. The bishops at Trent were well aware that a large part of the Reformers' popularity was due to their preaching. And so Trent decreed:

> But seeing that the preaching of the Gospel is no less necessary to the Christian commonwealth than the reading thereof; and whereas this is the principal duty of bishops; the same holy Synod hath resolved and decreed, that all bishops, archbishops, primates, and all other prelates of the churches be bound personally—if they be not lawfully hindered—to preach the holy Gospel of Jesus Christ. But if it should happen that bishops, and the others aforesaid, be hindered by any lawful impediment, they shall be bound . . . to appoint fit persons to discharge wholesomely this office of preaching. But if any one through contempt do not execute this, let him be subjected to rigorous punishment.
>
> Archpriests, curates, and all those who in any manner soever hold any parochial, or other, churches, which have the cure of souls, shall, at least on the Lord's days, and solemn feasts, either personally, or if they be lawfully hindered, by others who are competent, feed the people committed to them, with wholesome words, according to their own capacity, and that of their people . . . .[6]

One could scarcely imagine a more straightforward decree, backed up by no less than a demand for "rigorous punishment" for the failure to preach. The council adopted this decree in 1546, but by 1563 the council felt the need to repeat this decree, in almost the same words.[7] Perhaps the council fathers had noticed that this regular Sunday preaching of the gospel had not yet been achieved.

In the post-Tridentine Catholic Church, there were individual preachers of note, such as Robert Bellarmine and Francis de Sales. And there were a few periods in a few places where powerful Sunday preaching could be found, for instance Spain in the sixteenth century or France in the seventeenth. But in general,

> Catholic preaching went in a very different direction from the preaching of the Reformation. In fact, it is probably in regard to preaching more than anything else that the term "Counter-Reformation" is especially appropriate. Its preachers simply refused to move in the direction the Reformers moved in their reform of preaching.[8]

6. Council of Trent, Fifth Session, "Decree on Reformation," ch. 2, in *The Council of Trent: The canons and decrees of the sacred and oecumenical Council of Trent,* ed. and trans. J. Waterworth (London: Dolman, 1848) 27. Accessed at <http://history.hanover.edu/early/trent.html>.

7. Council of Trent, Twenty-Fourth Session, "Decree on Reformation," ch. 4, in Waterworth, *Council of Trent,* 211–212.

8. Old, *The Reading and Preaching of the Scriptures,* 160.

Instead, for the most part, the trajectory of Catholic Sunday preaching after the Reformation was increasingly doctrinal and decreasingly related to the scriptural texts being proclaimed at Mass. Already in the mid-sixteenth century, the Council of Trent had shown how deep had been the impact of preachers like Francis of Assisi when it characterized "preaching the holy Gospel of Jesus Christ" as

> teaching them the things which it is necessary for all to know unto salvation, and . . . announcing to them with briefness and plainness of discourse, the vices which they must avoid, and the virtues which they must follow after, that they may escape everlasting punishment, and obtain the glory of heaven . . . .[9]

This definition of Sunday preaching must have seemed to the Reformers to be Gnostic and Pelagian, and indeed right knowledge and right action as keys to salvation did mark Catholic post-Tridentine preaching.

In general, then, Reformed and Catholic Christian ministers took Sunday preaching in opposite directions. Protestants concentrated their preaching on the scriptural text proclaimed in Sunday worship; Catholics concentrated their preaching on doctrine and morality. Ironically, Catholic practice actually mirrored one of Luther's early innovations: explicitly catechetical preaching. In 1521 the Christian humanist Erasmus called for a revival of catechetical preaching, to catechize baptized children before their First Communion. Various localities warmed to this suggestion, and Martin Luther implemented it in Wittenberg. In 1528 Luther preached four two-week series of catechetical sermons, on weekday afternoons. By that time, "Reformers had essentially settled on the four-fold makeup of the catechism: namely, the Ten Commandments, the Apostles' Creed, the Lord's Prayer, and an explanation of baptism and the Lord's Supper."[10] Roman Catholics all the way up to the eve of the Second Vatican Council would recognize those sermon topics, as they came to provide much of the fare of Catholic Sunday preaching. Many dioceses issued preaching syllabi, covering a year's worth of Sundays. A three-year cycle of "Creed, Ten Commandments, and Sacraments" was quite common. What Luther implemented for the weekday instruction of children became the Catholic approach to Sunday preaching for adults.

---

9. Council of Trent, Fifth Session, "Decree on Reformation," ch. 2, in Waterworth, *Council of Trent,* 27.

10. Old, *The Reading and Preaching of the Scriptures,* 18.

It is worth noting a parallel to the history of preaching in the history of biblical scholarship. Protestants insisted on the scriptural nature of Sunday preaching, and so it is not surprising that come the nineteenth century, Protestants also took the lead in scientific study of the Scriptures. Biblical scholarship began to thrive in the schools of the Reformed Churches as the historical critical method emerged and developed. The Catholic Church, which was not doing much scriptural preaching, was unsurprisingly discomfited by the latest Protestant developments. Catholic scholarship was above all the clarifying of doctrinal and moral teachings, and interpretation of Scripture could only proceed in keeping with those teachings. In 1546 the Council of Trent had decreed:

> Furthermore, in order to restrain petulant spirits, . . . no one, relying on his own skill, shall,—in matters of faith, and of morals pertaining to the edification of Christian doctrine,—wresting the sacred Scripture to his own senses, presume to interpret the said sacred Scripture contrary to that sense which holy mother Church,—whose it is to judge of the true sense and interpretation of the holy Scriptures,—hath held and doth hold. . . .[11]

After a century of Protestant biblical scholarship, Pope Pius X reiterated this Tridentine stance in his attack on "modern" biblical criticism:

> The Modernists have no hesitation in affirming generally that these [biblical] books, and especially the Pentateuch and the first three Gospels, have been gradually formed from a primitive brief narration, by additions, by interpolations of theological or allegorical interpretations, or parts introduced only for the purpose of joining different passages together. This means, to put it briefly and clearly, that in the Sacred Books we must admit a vital evolution, springing from and corresponding with the evolution of faith. . . . We believe, then, that We have set forth with sufficient clearness the historical method of the Modernists. The philosopher leads the way, the historian follows, and then in due order come the internal and textual critics. And since it is characteristic of the primary cause to communicate its virtue to causes which are secondary, it is quite clear that the criticism with which We are concerned is not any kind of criticism, but that which is rightly called agnostic, immanentist, and evolutionist criticism. Hence anyone who adopts it and employs it makes profession thereby of the errors contained in it, and places himself in opposition to Catholic teaching.[12]

---

11. Council of Trent, Fourth Session, "Decree Concerning the Edition, and the Use, Of the Sacred Books," in Waterworth, *Council of Trent,* 19.

12. Pius X, encyclical On the Doctrine of the Modernists *(Pascendi Dominici Gregis)* 34. Accessed at <http://www.vatican.va/holy_father/pius_x/encyclicals/documents/hf_p-x_enc_19070908 _pascendi-dominici-gregis_en.html>.

In short, at the dawn of the twentieth century, Catholic Sunday preaching was optional (contrary to Trent), non-scriptural, and non-liturgical. When a sermon was given, it was doctrinal or moral and was often set apart from the action of the liturgy (by leaving the sanctuary to preach or removing the Mass vestments or even preaching after Mass). Furthermore, any Catholic preacher interested in the advances in biblical scholarship was told that such interest was "in opposition to Catholic teaching."

This brief survey of the "accidents of history" helps us understand how the Catholic Sunday homily withered away. But how did it come back from the grave?

Even as the witch hunts against "modernists" in Catholic universities and seminaries continued in the early twentieth century, new winds were blowing. Through their study of the biblical, theological, and patristic sources of the liturgy, members of the Benedictine Order in Europe planted the seeds for what would come to be known as the "liturgical movement." As described by Annibale Bugnini, himself one of the principal actors in the movement, the "liturgical movement was an effort to reunite rites and content . . . to restore as fully as possible the expressiveness and sanctifying power of the liturgy and to bring the faithful back to full participation and understanding."[13] From its formal organization in 1909, the liturgical movement spread rapidly throughout Europe and abroad, through publications, scholarly and popular meetings, and liturgical congresses.

By 1947 Pope Pius XII recognized and blessed the movement by issuing his encyclical *Mediator Dei* (On the Sacred Liturgy). While concerned by some perceived excesses of the liturgical movement, Pius XII made clear at the outset that "We derive no little satisfaction from the wholesome results of the movement just described."[14] The Pope's satisfaction led to concrete results, as Pius oversaw the reform of the Easter Vigil (1951) and the whole of Holy Week (1955). Before an ecumenical council was even on the horizon, then, Catholic reform of the liturgy was well underway.

In a parallel development, it was also Pope Pius XII who finally embraced the renewal of biblical studies. In his encyclical *Divino Afflante Spiritu* (On Promoting Biblical Studies), Pius commended those Scripture scholars who

---

13. Annibale Bugnini, *The Reform of the Liturgy 1948–1975,* trans. Matthew J. O'Connell (Collegeville: Liturgical Press, 1990) 6.

14. Pius XII, encyclical On the Sacred Liturgy *(Mediator Dei)* 7. Accessed at <http://www.vatican.va/holy_father/pius_xii/encyclicals/documents/hf_p-xii_enc_2011194>.

by the written word, have promoted and do still promote, far and wide, the study of the Bible; as when they edit the sacred text corrected in accordance with the rules of textual criticism or expound, explain, and translate it into the vernacular; or when they propose it to the faithful for their pious reading and meditation; or finally when they cultivate and seek the aid of profane sciences which are useful for the interpretation of the Scriptures.[15]

A more dramatic departure from Pius X's condemnation of the historical critical method could not be imagined.

When Pope John XXIII stunned the world in 1959 by calling the Second Vatican Council, then, much was already in place toward a restoration of the homily. A great deal of research into the liturgy had already been done, and a renaissance of Catholic biblical scholarship was underway. The importance of the Word of God, proclaimed and preached in the liturgical assembly, was already on the minds of many of the experts who had gathered to prepare for the council.

## The Restored Sunday Homily

The first action of the Second Vatican Council was a reform of Roman Catholic liturgy. The council's initial words to the world bear repeating:

> This sacred Council has several aims in view: it desires to impart an ever increasing vigor to the Christian life of the faithful; to adapt more suitably to the needs of our own times those institutions which are subject to change; to foster whatever can promote union among all who believe in Christ; to strengthen whatever can help to call the whole of mankind into the household of the Church. The Council therefore sees particularly cogent reasons for undertaking the reform and promotion of the liturgy.
>
> For the liturgy, "through which the work of our redemption is accomplished," most of all in the divine sacrifice of the eucharist, is the outstanding means whereby the faithful may express in their lives, and manifest to others, the mystery of Christ and the real nature of the true Church.[16]

For the council to achieve its aims, "reform and promotion of the liturgy" was job one. And as the Constitution on the Sacred Liturgy re-

---

15. Pius XII, encyclical On Promoting Biblical Studies *(Divino Afflante Spiritu)* 10. Accessed at <http://www.vatican.va/holy_father/pius_xii/encyclicals/documents/hf_p-xii_enc_3009194>.

16. Second Vatican Council, Constitution on the Sacred Liturgy *(Sacrosanctum Concilium)* 1–2, footnoting the Secret Prayer of the Ninth Sunday after Pentecost. Accessed at <http://www.vatican.va/archive/hist_councils/ii_vatican_council/documents/vat-ii_const_19631204_sacrosanctum-concilium_en.html>.

veals, there were three keys to that reform. The first key was the recognition of the fundamental role of Scripture in Christian worship.

> Sacred scripture is of the greatest importance in the celebration of the liturgy. For it is from scripture that lessons are read and explained in the homily, and psalms are sung; the prayers, collects, and liturgical songs are scriptural in their inspiration and their force, and it is from the Scriptures that actions and signs derive their meaning. Thus to achieve the restoration, progress, and adaptation of the sacred liturgy, it is essential to promote that warm and living love for scripture to which the venerable tradition of both eastern and western rites gives testimony.[17]

One notes that from the council's very first mention of the importance of Scripture, the proclamation and the preaching of Scripture are linked.

A second key to liturgical reform was a revision of the ritual action. The rites were to be reformed so as to be more comprehensible in and of themselves, and more clearly related to the proclamation of the Word. Once again, preaching was to play a role. Hence,

> The rites should be distinguished by a noble simplicity; they should be short, clear, and unencumbered by useless repetitions; they should be within the people's powers of comprehension, and normally should not require much explanation.

> That the intimate connection between words and rites may be apparent in the liturgy:

> 1) In sacred celebrations there is to be more reading from holy scripture, and it is to be more varied and suitable.

> 2) Because the sermon is part of the liturgical service, the best place for it is to be indicated even in the rubrics, as far as the nature of the rite will allow; the ministry of preaching is to be fulfilled with exactitude and fidelity. The sermon, moreover, should draw its content mainly from scriptural and liturgical sources, and its character should be that of a proclamation of God's wonderful works in the history of salvation, the mystery of Christ, ever made present and active within us, especially in the celebration of the liturgy.[18]

There is much more to be said about this first "definition" of the restored homily, but suffice to note here that the "sermon" is called a part of the liturgy, and as such is to be an address that is primarily biblical and liturgical, a "proclamation of God's wonderful works."

17. Ibid., 24.
18. Ibid., 34–35.

A final key to liturgical reform was the use of the vernacular language. Although Latin "is to be preserved,"

> the use of the mother tongue, whether in the Mass, the administration of the sacraments, or other parts of the liturgy, frequently may be of great advantage to the people, [hence] the limits of its employment may be extended. This will apply in the first place to the readings and directives, and to some of the prayers and chants. . . .[19]

Roman Catholic preaching was always in the vernacular language, even as the liturgical rites remained in Latin. But now the vernacular language could be used in other parts of the liturgy. Clearly, the council saw that a wider reading of Scripture would bear little spiritual fruit if the Word could not be understood. So, "in the first place" the vernacular was approved for the biblical readings.

These three keys to liturgical reform are apparent in the council's attention to the Mass, the eucharistic celebration.

> The rite of the Mass is to be revised in such a way that the intrinsic nature and purpose of its several parts, as also the connection between them, may be more clearly manifested, and that devout and active participation by the faithful may be more easily achieved.
>
> For this purpose the rites are to be simplified, due care being taken to preserve their substance; elements which, with the passage of time, came to be duplicated, or were added with but little advantage, are now to be discarded; other elements which have suffered injury through accidents of history are now to be restored to the vigor which they had in the days of the holy Fathers, as may seem useful or necessary.
>
> The treasures of the bible are to be opened up more lavishly, so that richer fare may be provided for the faithful at the table of God's word. In this way a more representative portion of the holy scriptures will be read to the people in the course of a prescribed number of years.
>
> By means of the homily the mysteries of the faith and the guiding principles of the Christian life are expounded from the sacred text, during the course of the liturgical year; the homily, therefore, is to be highly esteemed as part of the liturgy itself; in fact, at those Masses which are celebrated with the assistance of the people on Sundays and feasts of obligation, it should not be omitted except for a serious reason.[20]

The Second Vatican Council called for the restoration of the biblical, liturgical homily at the end of its first session in December 1963. At its

19. Ibid., 36.
20. Ibid., 50–52.

final session in the autumn of 1965, it asserted that "the liturgical homily must hold the foremost place" within "the ministry of the word."[21] Apparently the unfolding vision of the Church occasioned by the sessions of the council only burnished the importance of the restored homily.

And so it came to pass: the bishops of the Catholic Church gathered in council declared their intention to restore the biblical, liturgical homily to Catholic Sunday worship. By this action they sought to repair an important element of the liturgy that had clearly "suffered injury through accidents of history," and recognized once again that "the preaching of the word is needed for the very ministering of the sacraments. They are precisely sacraments of faith, a faith which is born of and nourished by the word."[22]

## The Reception of the Restored Homily

Theologians continue to debate the precise role in the development of doctrine played by the concept of "reception" of teaching by the people of God. Still, as eminent a Catholic theologian as Cardinal Avery Dulles states: "In contrast to Vatican I's strong emphasis on the autonomy and sufficiency of the papal magisterium, Vatican II again made room for the ancient concept of reception."[23] I happily leave that debate to systematic theologians, while at the same time making this claim: one of the best received teachings of the Second Vatican Council was its restoration of the biblical, liturgical homily as an obligatory part of Sunday worship.

In the early years of the implementation of the changes in Roman Catholic liturgy, especially, there were many voices raised in complaint: "How can you change the Mass?" "How can you get rid of Latin?" "What's with the guitars?" and so on. Certainly, more than a few who were used to "low Masses" on Sunday—undisturbed by preaching or music—were not initially thrilled that both music and preaching were now to be a part of every Sunday service. However, one rarely hears such voices anymore.

---

21. Second Vatican Council, Dogmatic Constitution on Divine Revelation *(Dei Verbum)* 24. Accessed at <http://www.vatican.va/archive/hist_councils/ii_vatican_council/documents/vat-ii_const_19651118_dei-verbum_en.html>. This marks the only use of the word "homily" outside the Constitution on the Liturgy.

22. Second Vatican Council, Decree on the Ministry and Life of Priests *(Presbyterorum Ordinis)* 4. Accessed at <http://www.vatican.va/archive/hist_councils/ii_vatican_council/documents/vat-ii_decree_19651207_presbyterorum-ordinis_en.html>.

23. Avery Dulles, *A Church to Believe In: Discipleship and the Dynamics of Freedom* (New York: Crossroad, 1982) 116.

Complaints rather center on the *quality* of preaching and the *quality* of music, backhanded confirmation of the importance that most Catholics now ascribe to those elements of Sunday worship.

Unfortunately, the sea change that I have just described has not been well documented. Catholic sociologist Andrew Greeley laments that he has "begged in vain for the last several decades for research on preaching."[24] A recent contact with Greeley confirmed for me that he laments still. However, at least one scholar has attempted to do statistically valid research on the reality of preaching in the United States. In 2000, *The Great American Sermon Survey* was published. In it, Dr. Lori Carrell, a professor of communications at the University of Wisconsin–Oshkosh, details the results of her survey work among Protestant and Catholic Americans, both preachers and congregants. Her research confirms the sea change in the Roman Catholic attitude toward preaching. Catholics and Protestants now agree on the "component of the church service [that] has the most important impact on your spiritual life," and that component is the sermon.[25] Interestingly, the second most important component for Catholics is music.[26] If this survey is to be believed, the avatars of the preconciliar "low Mass" with no music and no homily are all but extinct.

And most Catholic pastors and preachers would believe this survey. They know what I have come to know, anecdotally if not statistically: people hunger to hear the Word of God preached in a way that is relevant and saving. That hunger, most will also admit knowing, leads not a small number of Catholics to seek out parishes where the Sunday liturgy features what they value the most: good preaching and good music.

Truly, then, at least one of the most regrettable "accidents of history" in the Roman Catholic Church is well along in the process of repair. The biblical, liturgical homily moved in just a generation from seeming innovation to embraced expectation. In the next chapter I will examine more closely the exhilarating contribution of popes and their bureaucrats in implementing the Second Vatican Council's call for the restoration of the Sunday homily.

24. Andrew Greeley, "A Catholic Revival?" *America* (April 10, 1999) 8–14. Greeley does have one statistic at his fingertips though: "less than one out of five American Catholics think that the homilies they hear are excellent" (12).

25. Lori Carrell, *The Great American Sermon Survey* (Wheaton, Ill.: Mainstay Church Resources, 2000) 95.

26. Ibid.

# CHAPTER 2

# The Evolution of the "Restored" Homily: 1963–1993

The Second Vatican Council decreed the restoration of the homily to Roman Catholic Sunday worship. As we just saw, this decree represented a marked shift in the nature of Sunday preaching—a marked shift, but at the same time an embryonic shift. Vatican II gave only the barest outline of what this restored homiletic preaching would entail. Luckily for Catholic preachers, two popes and their collaborators spent the next thirty years reflecting on that conciliar shift and elaborating the nature of the restored homily. It is to that evolution that I now turn.

Both Pope Paul VI and Pope John Paul II issued documents referring to the homily. In addition, no fewer than twelve of the congregations and councils of the Roman Curia (those bodies that assist the pope in his governance of the Church) have issued such documents during the three decades after the opening of Vatican II. For purposes of analysis, I have divided these thirty years into five periods: the period of initial implementation from the Vatican II until 1969; the release of revised liturgical texts and ministerial directories (1969–1974); the "dueling popes" (1975–1980); the period of summary (1981–83); and finally documents from the papacy of John Paul II, dating from 1984 through 1993.

The current chapter presents the evolution of the homily by means of a diachronic analysis of Roman documents. I urge the reader with sufficient time and interest to journey with me through these thirty years, while also inviting those in a hurry to read at least the most important citations that head up each section. The next chapter will take a step back from this mass of material, offering a synchronic picture of the restored homily.

## 1. Initial Implementation of the Second Vatican Council: 1964–1969

The work of implementing the teaching of the Second Vatican Council on the homily fell first to Pope Paul VI and his Curia; it remained a task throughout the entire pontificate. The first five years after the Council saw a series of "occasional documents" whose intent was to address specific questions about the council's call for a biblical, liturgical homily.

❖    ❖    ❖

"A homily on the sacred text means an explanation, pertinent to the mystery celebrated and the special needs of the listeners, of some point. . . ."

(First Instruction on the Proper Implementation
of *Sacrosanctum Concilium,* 1964)

In 1964, while the Second Vatican Council was still in session, the Consilium released the First Instruction on the Proper Implementation of *Sacrosanctum Concilium* (that is, Vatican II's Constitution on the Sacred Liturgy). The Consilium was a newly created arm of the Sacred Congregation for Rites intended by Paul VI to aid in the implementation of liturgical reform. The First Instruction is noteworthy as the initial attempt to define the "homily" so recently called for by the council:

> A homily on the sacred text means an explanation, pertinent to the mystery celebrated and the special needs of the listeners, of some point in either the readings from sacred Scripture or in another text from the Ordinary or Proper of the day's Mass.
> Because the homily is part of the liturgy for the day, any syllabus proposed for preaching within the Mass during certain periods must keep intact the intimate connection with at least the principal seasons and feasts of the liturgical year (see *Sacrosanctum Concilium* art. 102–104), that is, with the mystery of redemption.[1]

Two items are noteworthy here. First, this description of the homily advances beyond the council by its claim that a homily must take into ac-

---

1. Consilium of the Sacred Congregation for Rites, First Instruction on the Implementation of *Sacrosanctum Concilium (Inter Oecumenici)* 54–55, in International Committee on English in the Liturgy, *Documents on the Liturgy: 1963–1979* (Collegeville: The Liturgical Press, 1982) 23.

count both the mysteries being celebrated and the needs of the listeners. The following year the Second Vatican Council itself, in its Decree on the Ministry and Life of Priests, would develop this point:

> But priestly preaching is often very difficult in the circumstances of the modern world. In order that it might more effectively move men's minds, the word of God ought not to be explained in a general and abstract way, but rather by applying the lasting truth of the Gospel to the particular circumstances of life.[2]

Second, the First Instruction reflects well some of the unsettled business that attended the council's move to restore the homily. There were bishops who felt that the doctrinal ignorance of their people demanded that Sunday preaching continue to be primarily doctrinal exposition. This position is reflected in the council's description of the homily as an act of expounding "the mysteries of the faith and the guiding principles of the Christian life."[3] On the other hand, as we have seen, those promoters of renewal of the liturgy felt strongly that the homily was first and foremost a "proclamation of . . . the mystery of Christ, ever made present and active within us, especially in the celebration of the liturgy."[4] The tension between these two positions was not overcome by the council. It seems clear that the First Instruction comes down on the catechetical side of the tension. Although this instruction does call the homily "a part of the liturgy" (indeed intimately connected to it), it is also clear in calling it an "explanation," finding no problem with dioceses continuing to issue syllabi of preaching topics.[5]

2. Second Vatican Council, Decree on the Ministry and Life of Priests *(Presbyterorum Ordinis)* 4. Accessed at <http://www.vatican.va/archive/hist_councils/ii_vatican_council/documents/vat-ii_decree_19651207_presbyterorum-ordinis_en.html>.

3. Second Vatican Council, Constitution on the Sacred Liturgy *(Sacrosanctum Concilium)* 52. Accessed at <http://www.vatican.va/archive/hist_councils/ii_vatican_council/documents/vat-ii_const_19631204_sacrosanctum-concilium_en.html>.

4. Ibid., 35.

5. The see-saw between homily as liturgical proclamation and homily as catechesis continued within the Consilium itself. The year after *Inter Oecumenici,* it published the following query and response:

*Query:* Does it go counter to the spirit of the Constitution art. 52 to provide in place of the homily a catechetical instruction of the faithful?

*Reply:* The Instruction *[Inter Oecumenici]* clarifies the Constitution art. 52 in the sense that if the competent authorities arrange a syllabus for preaching during Mass, this preaching must be so planned as to safeguard a close connection with at least the chief seasons and feasts of the liturgical year, that is, with the mystery of redemption *(Notitiae* 1 [1965]: 137 n4).

The response is carefully worded. While it does not directly answer the stated question and thus leaves the door open to replacing the homily with catechesis, it does insist on the *"intimus nexus"* between liturgical preaching and the liturgy.

❖   ❖   ❖

"Christ is present in the preaching of his Church."
(Paul VI, Encyclical on the Holy Eucharist, 1965)

In his second encyclical—On the Holy Eucharist *(Mysterium Fidei),* issued in 1965, near the end of the Second Vatican Council—Pope Paul VI signaled another advance in the Catholic theology of preaching. In compiling, as had Pius XII and the Second Vatican Council, a list of the various modes of the "presence" of Christ in the liturgy, Paul VI wrote:

> In still another very genuine way, He [Christ] is present in the preaching of his Church, since the Gospel which he proclaims is the word of God, and it is only in the name of Christ, the Incarnate Word of God, and by His authority and with His help that it is preached, so that there might be "one flock resting secure in one shepherd."[6]

There is theological development here. Pius XII's encyclical On the Sacred Liturgy (issued in 1947) had not mentioned "the Word" in its list of ways in which Christ is present in the liturgy.[7] Vatican II's Constitution on the Sacred Liturgy reformulates Pius XII's list to include: "[Christ] is present in his word, since it is he himself who speaks when the Holy Scriptures are read in Church."[8] Paul VI took a further step beyond Pius and the council: Christ is present in the preaching of the Church.

❖   ❖   ❖

"The people have a right to be nourished by the word of God proclaimed and explained."
(Instruction on the Worship of the Eucharist, 1967)

With 1967 came the Instruction on the Worship of the Eucharist from the Sacred Congregation for Rites (Consilium). This instruction is noteworthy on three counts. First, though it treats the presence of Christ in the liturgy, it does not repeat Paul VI's teaching on Christ's presence in preach-

---

6. Paul VI, encyclical On the Holy Eucharist *(Mysterium Fidei)* 36, alt. Accessed at <http://www.vatican.va/holy_father/paul_vi/encyclicals/documents/hf_p-vi_enc_03091965_mysterium_en.html>. The translation on the Vatican Web site weakens the sense of the Latin: *"praesens adest Ecclesiae suae praedicationi"* is not so much "present in the Church as she preaches" as "present in the preaching of his Church."

7. Pius XII, encyclical On the Sacred Liturgy *(Mediator Dei)* 20. Accessed at <http://www.vatican.va/holy_father/pius_xii/encyclicals/documents/hf_p-xii_enc_20111947_mediator-dei_en.html>.

8. Second Vatican Council, Constitution on the Sacred Liturgy *(Sacrosanctum Concilium)* 7.

ing enunciated in *Mysterium Fidei*. Instead, it reverts to the language of the council: "[Christ] is also present in his word, for it is he who is speaking as the sacred scriptures are read in the Church."[9] Though *Mysterium Fidei* is quoted later in the same section (entitled "The Different Modes of Christ's Presence"), its theological advancement regarding preaching is ignored.[10]

Second, the Instruction on the Worship of the Eucharist brings forward the council's concerns about preaching rather more effectively than had the First Instruction on Implementation. For instance, this instruction marks the first citation after the Second Vatican Council of a paragraph that will be frequently cited in the decades to come—Decree on the Ministry and Life of Priests *(Presbyterorum Ordinis)* 4: "The preaching of the word is necessary for the administration of the sacraments. For the sacraments are sacraments of faith and faith has its origin in the word." The Instruction on Worship continues:

> This is especially true of the celebration of the Mass, in which the purpose of the liturgy of the word is to develop in a specific way the close link between the proclamation and hearing of the word of God and the eucharistic mystery (cf. *Presbyterorum Ordinis* 4). . . . In this way the Church feeds upon the bread of life as it comes from the table of both the word of God and the body of Christ (cf. *Dei Verbum* 21).[11]

The phrase *intimus nexus* ("intimate connection") recurs, here referring to the link between Word and Eucharist, not between Word and liturgical year. Nonetheless, the phrase indicates in both documents the desire to ensure that the proclamation and preaching of the Word is understood as part of the liturgy itself, as opposed to a prelude or accompaniment to the liturgy.

Third, the Instruction on Worship clearly links the homily to the council's call for active participation by all in the liturgy. It states:

> To ensure that the celebration is conducted properly and that the faithful take an active part, the ministers should not only fulfill their role correctly according to the norms of liturgical laws, but their very bearing should communicate a sense of the sacred. The people have a right to be nourished by the word of God proclaimed and explained. Accordingly priests are not

---

9. Sacred Congregation for Rites (Consilium), Instruction on the Worship of the Eucharist *(Eucharisticum Mysterium)* 9, in *Documents on the Liturgy,* 179 (see note 1 above). This is an exact quote of *Sacrosanctum Concilium* 7, made without citation.

10. This omission is all the more surprising when one considers Paul VI's close involvement with the final text of *Eucharisticum Mysterium* (see Annibale Bugnini, *The Reform of the Liturgy 1948–1975* [Collegeville: The Liturgical Press, 1990] 851–852).

11. Consilium, Instruction on the Worship of the Eucharist *(Eucharisticum Mysterium)* 10.

only to give a homily whenever it is prescribed or seems advisable, but also to see to it that anything that their functions require them to pronounce is said or sung so distinctly that the people hear it clearly, grasp its meaning, and are thus drawn to respond and participate willingly (*Sacrosanctum Concilium* 11). To this end ministers should be prepared through the right kind of training, especially in seminaries and religious houses.[12]

The people's "right to be nourished by the word of God proclaimed and explained," as well as the desired outcome that they hear the Word "clearly, grasp its meaning, and are thus drawn to respond and participate willingly," are the reasons why priests are to preach a homily. Such preaching is to play an important role in fulfilling the council's wish for a liturgy that is not only conducted properly but also in which the faithful take an active part. In the reformed liturgy, the presider's very bearing is to "communicate a sense of the sacred," and all that the presider does—preaching being singled out as especially important—is to lead people to fuller participation.

During this initial period of implementation, then, the Roman congregations began to consider the general implications of the "supreme importance of preaching" (Paul VI) for the Church in the modern world, as well as the specific implications of the homily as "a part of the liturgy." Much of the vocabulary that would mark the postconciliar development was already in place by the end of this period: "part of the liturgy," "presence," "expound, explain," "announce, proclaim," "concrete," "active participation," "needs of the listeners."

## 2. The Council-Mandated Liturgical Books and Ministerial Directories: 1969–1974

As has just been seen, the first five years after the Second Vatican Council saw the release of closely focused instructions and responses by which the Curia intended to guide the beginnings of conciliar implementation. The second five years saw documents of another type: the liturgical books with their introductions and the directories that guided the preparation and service of priests and bishops. Each of these types reflected in its own ways the developing Roman Catholic understanding of the homily.

***The Revised Order of Mass.*** A complete review of the reformed rites of the liturgy is well beyond the scope of this chapter.[13] What will suffice is a

---

12. Ibid., 20 (alt.).
13. See Bugnini, *Reform of the Liturgy,* for a full commentary.

thorough look at the Mass and the Third Instruction on the Implementation of the Constitution on the Liturgy.

❖   ❖   ❖

"A living commentary on the word, that is the homily, . . . increases the word's effectiveness."

(General Instruction of the Roman Missal, 1969)

As was mentioned in the last chapter, the Roman Missal containing the revised rites of the Mass was promulgated by Paul VI in 1969. The General Instruction of the Roman Missal mentions the homily nine times. Development in the Church's understanding of the restored homily is evident.

In treating the different elements of the Mass, the General Instruction gives its most significant description of the homily and its place in the liturgy: "In the biblical readings God's word addresses all people of every era and is understandable to them, but a living commentary on the word, that is the homily, as an integral part of the liturgy (cf. *Sacrosanctum Concilium* 7, 33, 52), increases the word's effectiveness."[14]

In its next section the General Instruction outlines the Order of the Mass. The homily is mentioned briefly in the overview to the Liturgy of the Word and then is treated more extensively under its own title.

> Readings from Scripture and the chants between the readings form the main part of the liturgy of the word. The homily, profession of faith, and general intercessions or prayer of the faithful expand and complete this part of the Mass. In the readings, explained by the homily, God is speaking to his people (cf. *Sacrosanctum Concilium* 33), opening up to them the mystery of redemption and salvation, and nourishing their spirit; Christ is present to the faithful through his own word (cf. *Sacrosanctum Concilium* 7).[15]

> The homily is an integral part of the liturgy and is strongly recommended (*Sacrosanctum Concilium* 52): it is necessary for the nurturing of the Christian life. It should develop some point of the readings or of another text from the Ordinary or the Proper of the Mass of the day, and take into account the mystery being celebrated and the needs proper to the listeners (cf. *Inter Oecumenici* 54).[16]

> There must be a homily on Sundays and holydays of obligation at all Masses that are celebrated with a congregation. It is recommended on other days, especially on the weekdays of Advent, Lent, and the Easter season, as well as

14. Sacred Congregation for Divine Worship, General Instruction to the Roman Missal *(Institutio Generalis Missale Romanum)* 9, in *Documents on the Liturgy,* 208.

15. Ibid., 33.

16. Ibid., 41. A more accurate translation would read: "The homily is part of the liturgy . . ."; the Latin reads: *"Homilia est pars liturgiae . . ."*

on other feasts and occasions when the people come to church in large numbers (cf. *Inter Oecumenici* 53). The homily should ordinarily be given by the celebrant.[17]

These passages mark the most extended consideration to date of the preaching that is to occur at Mass. The Constitution on the Sacred Liturgy and the First Instruction on its proper implementation are the cited sources, but there are new elements here as well.

One such element emerges metaphorically. The Second Vatican Council had spoken of the sacred Scriptures as "nourishment" for God's people,[18] even extending this metaphor into that of people being nourished from the "one table" of God's Word and Christ's Body.[19] This metaphor is picked up in the General Instruction: "in the readings, explained by the homily, God . . . is nourishing their spirit."[20] Later, however, the same metaphor is invoked to describe the homily itself: "the homily is . . . necessary for the nurturing of Christian life."[21] According to the General Instruction, then, one can make the same claim for the homily as for the Scriptures themselves: both are "nourishment" *(nutrimentum)* for the spiritual life.

In summary, then, the General Instruction of the Roman Missal marks the first sustained attention given to liturgical preaching after the Second Vatican Council. It repeats the substance of the attention to the homily given by the Constitution on the Sacred Liturgy. It fails to repeat Paul VI's doctrine of the presence of Christ in preaching, although it sees the homily as necessary nourishment for the faith, just as the Scriptures themselves. Its most significant contribution to the understanding of liturgical preaching is its claim that "a living commentary on the word, that is the homily, as an integral part of the liturgy, increases the word's effectiveness."

❖   ❖   ❖

"The homily has as its purpose to explain to the faithful the word of God just proclaimed and to adapt it to the mentality of the times."
(Third Instruction on the Implementation of
the Constitution on the Sacred Liturgy, 1970)

17. Ibid., 42.

18. Second Vatican Council, Dogmatic Constitution on Divine Revelation *(Dei Verbum)* 21, 24; *Presbyterorum Ordinis* 4, 18.

19. *Dei Verbum* 21, cited and amplified in *Presbyterorum Ordinis* 18.

20. General Instruction of the Roman Missal, 33.

21. Ibid., 41.

Prior to any further release of liturgical books, the Congregation for Divine Worship issued in 1970 the Third Instruction on the Implementation of the Constitution on the Sacred Liturgy. The reference to the homily here is a brief but significant one, omitting some of what had come before, but also adding two new elements. The instruction notes:

> Of all the texts read in the liturgical assembly the books of sacred scripture possess the primacy of a unique dignity: in them God is speaking to his people; Christ, present in his own word, continues to proclaim his gospel (cf. *Sacrosanctum Concilium* 7, 33). Therefore:
> a) . . . The homily has as its purpose to explain to the faithful the word of God just proclaimed and to adapt it to the mentality of the times. The same, therefore, pertains to the bishop or priest; the congregation is to refrain from comments, attempts at dialogue, or anything similar.[22]

On the one hand, this third postconciliar definition of the homily is made without reference to the first two, that is, without reference to the First Instruction (54) or to the General Instruction of the Roman Missal (41). Consequently, it fails to refer to the homily as a part of the liturgy, fails to note its intimate connection to the mysteries being celebrated, and fails to evoke the "nourishing" character of the homily.

On the other hand, the Third Instruction adds two new elements to the understanding of the homily. First, this instruction states more concisely than ever before the central axis of preaching's concerns: the homiletic task is to make clear to the faithful the proclaimed Word of God and to make it fit the sensibility of our age. This marks the first postconciliar deployment of an important conciliar term and concept—that of "accommodation" or "adaptation." The Second Vatican Council's Pastoral Constitution on the Church in the Modern World had already said:

> For, from the beginning of her history she [the Church] has learned to express the message of Christ with the help of the ideas and terminology of various philosophers, and has tried to clarify it with their wisdom, too. Her purpose has been to adapt the Gospel to the grasp of all as well as to the needs of the learned, insofar as such was appropriate. Indeed this accommodated preaching of the revealed word ought to remain the law of all evangelization.[23]

22. Third Instruction on the Implementation of the Constitution on the Sacred Liturgy *(Liturgicae Instaurationes)* 2 (alt.), in *Documents on the Liturgy,* 52.

23. Second Vatican Council, Pastoral Constitution on the Church in the Modern World *(Gaudium et Spes)* 44. Accessed at <http://www.vatican.va/archive/hist_councils/ii_vatican_council/documents/vat-ii_cons_19651207_gaudium-et-spes_en.html>.

The Third Instruction applies that conciliar "law" to homiletic preaching: the homilist must adapt the Word of God to the sensibilities of the age. The First Instruction (54; repeated in the General Instruction of the Roman Missal, 41) had previously spoken of the homilist "taking into account the particular needs of the listeners." That "accounting" is here taken to the next level: the homiletic word is an accommodated word.[24]

***The Ministerial Directories.*** As the Constitution on the Sacred Liturgy of the Second Vatican Council occasioned revision of the liturgical books, so the Dogmatic Constitution on the Church and the decrees On the Pastoral Office of Bishops in the Church and On the Ministry and Life of Presbyters occasioned a number of documents on the training for and exercise of ordained ministry. Because Vatican II had repeated and strengthened the Council of Trent's doctrine of preaching as preeminent among the duties of bishops and priests, it is not surprising that the first wave of the postconciliar ministerial documents would also concern preaching.

❖   ❖   ❖

"Preaching the Word of God: [An] Act of Living Tradition"
(General Catechetical Directory, 1971)

The Decree on the Pastoral Office of Bishops in the Church occasioned two postconciliar directories. The first to be produced came in 1971, as the Congregation for Clergy released the General Catechetical Directory. Vatican II's decree had seen the teaching office of the bishop to entail "first of all, preaching and catechetical instruction, which always hold pride of place."[25] In keeping with that theological stance, the General Catechetical Directory presents a sustained treatment of the "ministry of the word" in general, and of preaching and the homily in particular. Three sections stand out.

---

24. In 1973 this concern for adaptation resurfaces. In *Eucharistae Participationem* (circular letter on the Eucharistic Prayers), the Congregation for Divine Worship says: "Among the elements favoring fuller adaptation that are within the power of individual celebrants may be mentioned the introductions, the homily, and the general intercessions . . ." (14, in *Documents on the Liturgy*, 248). "The homily must also be mentioned. It is 'a part of the liturgy' (*Sacrosanctum Concilium* 52) by which the word of God proclaimed in the liturgical assembly is explained to help the community present. It is given in a way that is suited to the community's capacity and way of life and that is relevant to the circumstances of the celebration" (15).

25. Second Vatican Council, Decree on the Pastoral Office of Bishops in the Church *(Christus Dominus)* 13. Accessed at < http://www.vatican.va/archive/hist_councils/ii_vatican_council/documents/vat-ii_decree_19651028_christus-dominus_en.html>.

The first section of importance is entitled "Ministry of the Word or Preaching of the Word of God: Act of Living Tradition." The entire section is a development of the Second Vatican Council's Dogmatic Constitution on Divine Revelation *(Dei Verbum)* 8, which it quotes extensively. This section holds that "tradition is bound up with things that have been said. In scope and depth, however, it is more than these sayings. It is a living tradition, since through it God continues his conversation" with the Church.[26] Given this understanding, "the ministry of the word can be considered as that which gives voice to this living tradition, within the totality of tradition."[27]

The Catechetical Directory then cites the passage from *Dei Verbum* 8 about the growth of understanding of revelation that comes, among other ways, through preaching. It notes the special grace that attends episcopal preaching and the leadership role of the magisterium. It concludes thus: "In this way the ministry of the word is not a mere repetition of ancient doctrine, but rather it is a faithful reproduction of it, with adaptation to new problems and with a growing understanding of it."[28] The metaphor ("living tradition") is thus extended in a way almost reminiscent of Darwin: not only does tradition live, but it reproduces with adaptation, thus remaining viable.

The second important section is entitled "Sacred Scripture." Its primary sources are *Dei Verbum* 8, 11, 21, 24–25; but once again, it ventures beyond those sources. The section says, in part:

> But if it takes its norm for thinking from the Sacred Scripture, the Church, inspired by the Spirit, interprets the same Scripture: "and the sacred writings themselves are more profoundly understood and unceasingly made active in her (*Dei Verbum* 8)." The ministry of the word, therefore, takes its beginning from Holy Writ and from the preaching of the apostles, as these are understood, explained, and applied in concrete situations by the Church.[29]

The ministry of the word, equated with preaching in the previous section, is in this section seen to accomplish what preaching accomplishes according to previously released documents: both interpret Scripture in such a

---

26. Congregation for the Clergy, General Catechetical Directory, 13. Accessed at <http://www.vatican.va/roman_curia/congregations/cclergy/documents/rc_con_cclergy_doc_11041971_gcat_en.html>.

27. Ibid.

28. Ibid.

29. Ibid., 14.

way as to make it live; both "explain" Scripture and "apply" it in a concrete way to life today. A previous section had already spoken of another
aspect of the Church's interpretative function: "the ministry of the word
. . . interprets human life in our age, the signs of the times, and the things
of this world, for the plan of God works in these for the salvation of men."[30]
In short, the "ministry of the word is the communication of the message
of salvation: it brings the Gospel to men."[31]

A final important section of the General Catechetical Directory concerns the preaching task of priests.

> [I]n individual parishes the preaching of the word of God is committed chiefly
> to priests, who are obliged to open the riches of Sacred Scripture to the faith-
> ful, and to explain the mysteries of the faith and the norms of Christian liv-
> ing in homilies throughout the course of the liturgical year (cf. *Sacrosanctum
> Concilium* 51, 52). Hence it is of great importance that a thorough catecheti-
> cal preparation be given students in seminaries. . . .[32]

❖   ❖   ❖

"As the bishop devotes himself to the task of preaching he . . .
speaks in a way that is filled with faith, redolent of the sacred scriptures, and expressive of pastoral love."
(Directory on the Pastoral Ministry of Bishops, 1973)

The second directory occasioned by Vatican II's Decree on the Pastoral Ministry of Bishops appeared in 1973. The Directory on the Pastoral
Ministry of Bishops was issued by the Congregation for Bishops, and it
insists upon the "Importance and the Obligation of Preaching." This is
the subheading for the first section of the chapter on the teaching office of
the bishop, listed first among his various ministries. This section considers preaching in general and the homily in particular.

The Directory quotes the Second Vatican Council, which itself was
quoting the Council of Trent: "Among the principal duties of bishops, the
preaching of the Gospel occupies an eminent place . . . ,"[33] and then goes
on to specify this duty:

30. Ibid., 11.
31. Ibid., 16.
32. Ibid., 115.
33. Second Vatican Council, Dogmatic Constitution on the Church *(Lumen Gentium)* 25. Accessed at < http://www.vatican.va/archive/hist_councils/ii_vatican_council/documents/vat-ii
_const_19641121_lumen-gentium_en.html>.

A bishop is bound to devote himself to the ministry of the word (cf. Acts 6:4), religiously meditating on it and proclaiming it boldly (*Dei Verbum* 1). Unless he is legitimately prevented, he personally preaches the word of God. His preaching is nourished and ruled by Sacred Scriptures (*Dei Verbum* 21), so that everyone may offer the obedience of faith to God who reveals (*Dei Verbum* 5). He makes his priests realize that preaching the word of God is the special and absolutely necessary duty of the pastor of souls.[34]

Having reminded the bishop of the types of preaching to which he is called, the Directory gives the first extended advice on how to go about such preaching:

As the bishop devotes himself to the task of preaching he is concerned not just about choosing arguments and having a good, elegant style, but he also speaks in a way that is filled with faith, redolent of the sacred scriptures, and expressive of pastoral love. His sermons are faithful to the mind of the Church and show an understanding of the many needs of modern man. He never forgets that it is his office—and the example of his own life lights the way—to proclaim the Gospel and make known to all men the greatness and the truth and the power of the Word of God (cf. I Corinthians 2:4) rather than to make an academic exposé of some thesis.[35]

The Directory devotes an entire section to the homily; it constitutes what might be counted as the fourth postconciliar definition of the homily. Though it makes only one citation, it resounds with echoes of previous documents. The paragraph is entitled *"De magisterio homiletico"* and it says:

The special form of preaching for a community that is already evangelized is the homily which the bishop gives at the celebration of the sacred liturgy, in a plain, familiar way suited to the understanding of all, as from the sacred text he recalls the wonderful works of God and the mysteries of Christ and instructs the faithful in the laws of Christian living.

Since the homily comes after the sacred readings in the liturgy—which is the summit and source of the entire life of the Church (*Sacrosanctum Concilium* 10)—it excels all other forms of preaching and in a certain way embraces them, especially catechizing. If the bishop himself can but rarely and with difficulty perform this task of catechizing in a formal way, the homily does give him an effective opportunity briefly and very pointedly to draw from the liturgy of the day—unless pastoral reasons suggest something else—the principal truths of the Christian faith.

34. Congregation for Bishops, Directory on the Pastoral Ministry of Bishops *(Ecclesiae Imago)* (Ottawa: Canadian Catholic Conference Publications Service, 1973) 55.

35. Ibid., 57. This passage has many elements in common with *Evangelii Nuntiandi* 43, released two years later. See below.

That he may more easily move the hearts of the faithful and draw them to the truth, the bishop should above all understand the mentality, customs, conditions, dangers and prejudices of the individuals and groups to whom he speaks and he should constantly adapt his method of teaching to their capacity, character and needs so that each one may be able to draw water joyfully from the springs of salvation (cf. Isaiah 12:3) and the treasury of sacred doctrine.[36]

The Directory's consideration of the homily is completed several paragraphs later: "The *homily* should never be omitted at Masses which are celebrated on Sundays and feasts when people are present (*Sacrosanctum Concilium* 52) . . . so that the paschal mystery of Christ re-presented in the Eucharist may become known to all and celebrated with faith."[37]

What emerges from the Directory on the Pastoral Ministry of Bishops, then, is a faithful summation of the Second Vatican Council's understanding of preaching and an application of that understanding to the pastoral ministry of bishops today. The conciliar texts and the Scriptures are quoted often. This Directory incorporates much of the postconciliar development as well, although always without citation. Finally, it contributes its own notes to the developing understanding of the homily. Four contributions are noticeable.

First, the Directory returns to *Sacrosanctum Concilium* 35 for the first time since the Council. Previous documents have been content to describe the homily as an explanation; this Directory understands it first as an act of proclamation of the wonderful works of God. It rephrases and develops this thought beautifully, borrowing also from *Sacrosanctum Concilium* 52; thus the homiletic preacher proclaims from the sacred text the wonderful works of God, both tilling anew the mysteries of Christ and planting (in) the faithful the laws of Christian life (an elegant agricultural metaphor missed by the translator).[38]

Second, the Directory sees one of the purposes of the homily to be that "the paschal mystery of Christ re-presented in the Eucharist may become known to all and celebrated with faith." The Constitution on the Sacred Liturgy (35) had suggested the link between preaching and liturgical participation; the 1967 Instruction on the Worship of the Eucharist (20) had also hinted at it; this Directory makes it clear. One of the main ways

36. Ibid., 59.
37. Ibid., 64.
38. Ibid., 59. The original says, *"pronuntiat e textu sacro mirabilia Dei ac mysteria Christi recolens et vitae christianae legibus fideles instituens."*

in which the homily is "part of the liturgy" is that it enables participation in the liturgy.

Third, the Directory recalls but goes beyond *Dei Verbum* 24. *Dei Verbum* says that in the ministry of the Word the liturgical homily holds pride of place. The Directory goes further: the homily "excels all other forms of preaching and in a certain way embraces them, especially catechizing."

Finally, the Directory spends more effort than ever before describing just what preaching should sound like today. It is not "an academic exposé of some thesis"; it is less about "arguments" and "elegant style" than it is about speaking "in a way that is filled with faith, redolent of the sacred scriptures, and expressive of pastoral love." The homily is delivered in a plain and familiar way and is accommodated to those present. The necessity of accommodation to the hearers, heard before in other documents, is reiterated in this Directory. Episcopal preaching is to "show an understanding of the many needs of modern man"; the need "to adapt . . . to their capacity, character and needs" is dictated by preaching's goal: to "move the hearts of the faithful and draw them to the truth."[39]

The period from 1969 through 1974, then, was remarkably fruitful in its repeated consideration of the homily. Through both the liturgical books and the ministerial directories, the shape and substance of the homily came into sharper focus. By the end of the period, the homiletic task had been made clear: to increase the scriptural Word's effectiveness by means of accommodating it to the concrete circumstances of those gathered in worship. Though the catechetical slant on the homily emerged occasionally, the documents of this period repeatedly insisted that there is a distinction between catechesis and liturgical preaching. The homily not only clarifies but also applies, adapts, accommodates, makes alive God's Word, and in that increases the capacity of the faithful for active liturgical participation.

## 3. The "Dueling Popes": 1975–1980

In the course of just four years, two popes gave extended consideration to the nature of the homily. To compare these two papal documents is to dis-

---

39. Given this extensive and ebullient treatment of preaching and the homily, it is perhaps shocking to find this later: "Since the homily and other traditional forms of preaching are not adequate for the needs of our times . . .," along with a suggestion to create preaching syllabi (64). The tensions of "homily as catechesis" and "homily as proclamation" found in the Second Vatican Council itself continue to become visible from time to time.

cover the shift in emphasis regarding the nature and role of liturgical preaching from Paul VI to John Paul II, a shift from the evangelical emphasis of *Sacrosanctum Concilium* 35 to the catechetical emphasis of *Sacrosanctum Concilium* 24 and 52.

❖   ❖   ❖

The homily must be "simple, insightful, direct, well-adapted, . . . animated and balanced by apostolic ardor coming from its own characteristic nature, full of good hope, nourishing belief, and begetting peace and unity."

(Paul VI, 1975)

Eleven years after the Second Vatican Council, in 1975, Pope Paul VI looked back at the council and claimed that its objectives "are definitively summed up in this single one: to make the Church of the twentieth century ever better fitted for proclaiming the Gospel to the people of the twentieth century. . . ." With such thoughts Paul VI begins his magnum opus, the apostolic exhortation on Evangelization in the Modern World *(Evangelii Nuntiandi)*. Not since the Second Vatican Council had the theme of the preaching of God's Word been addressed in such detail. This exhortation contains the most sustained reflection on the homily ever to emerge from the magisterium.

Paul VI found in the homily "an important and very adaptable instrument of evangelization." He then continued:

> Of course it is necessary to know and put to use the exigencies and the possibilities of the homily, so that it can acquire *the fullness of*[40] its pastoral effectiveness. But above all it is necessary to be convinced of this and to devote oneself to it with love. This preaching, inserted in a unique way into the Eucharistic celebration, from which it draws special force and vigor, certainly has a particular role in evangelization, to the extent that it expresses the profound faith of the sacred minister and is *deeply imbued* with love. The faithful assembled *so as to form* a Paschal Church, celebrating the feast of the Lord present in their midst, expect much from this preaching, and *experience its joyful fruits* provided that it is simple, *insightful,* direct, well-adapted, profoundly *positioned in and fixed upon* Gospel teaching and *equally adhering* faithfully to the magisterium *of the Church,* animated and balanced by apostolic ardor coming from its own characteristic nature, full of *good* hope, *nourishing* belief, and *begetting* peace and unity. Many parochial

---

40. Italicized words are words omitted in the official English translation of the original Latin.

or other communities live and *are strengthened through* the Sunday homily, when it possesses these qualities.

Let us add that, thanks to the liturgical renewal, the Eucharistic celebration is not the only appropriate moment for the homily. The homily has a place and must not be neglected in the celebration of all the sacraments, at paraliturgies, and in assemblies of the faithful. It will always be a privileged occasion for communicating the Word of the Lord.[41]

The claims made for the homily in this passage are great. First, the homily expresses the *faith* of the preacher. Later in the apostolic exhortation, Paul VI expands upon this insight:

It is often said nowadays that the present century thirsts for authenticity. . . . Either tacitly or aloud—but always forcefully—we are being asked: Do you really believe what you are proclaiming? Do you live what you believe? Do you really preach what you live? The witness of life has become more than ever an essential condition for real effectiveness in preaching.[42]

Second, the homily must also reflect the *love* of the preacher, who must be devoted to preaching with love. Paul VI expands upon this later:

That model evangelizer, the Apostle Paul, wrote these words to the Thessalonians, and they are a program for us all: 'With such yearning love we chose to impart to you not only the gospel of God but our very selves, so dear had you become to us' (1 Thessalonians 2:8). What is this love? It is much more than that of a teacher; it is the love of a father; and again, it is the love of a mother. It is this love that the Lord expects from every preacher of the Gospel.[43]

Finally, the homily, like the broader evangelization it serves, is found on the "axis" of fidelity to message and fidelity to people.[44] This means that the homily is at once rooted in the Gospel, faithful to Tradition and accommodated to the hearers—a privileged means of proclaiming the Word. The fruits of the well-preached homily are many: hope, belief, peace, unity, community. In all this, Paul VI reflected the evangelical understanding of the homily seen in *Sacrosanctum Concilium* 35—the homily as proclamation of God's work and the presence of Christ.

---

41. Paul VI, apostolic exhortation on Evangelization in the Modern World *(Evangelii Nuntiandi)* 43. Accessed at <http://www.vatican.va/holy_father/paul_vi/apost_exhortations/documents/hf_p-vi_exh_19751208_evangelii-nuntiandi_en.html>.

42. Ibid., 76; cf. 41.

43. Ibid., 79.

44. Ibid., 4.

❖   ❖   ❖

"The homily takes up again the journey of faith put forward by catechesis. . . . Preaching, centered upon the Bible texts, must then in its
own way make it possible to familiarize the faithful with the whole of
the mysteries of the faith and the norms of Christian living."

(John Paul II, 1979)

In 1978 John Paul II became pope. One of his early documents was
the apostolic exhortation Catechesis in Our Time *(Catechesi Tradendae)*.
Like Paul VI just four years earlier, John Paul II devotes an entire paragraph of his exhortation to the homily. In this paragraph the shift to a
more catechetical understanding of the homily is reflected.

John Paul II's paragraph shares a common structure with that of Paul
VI: (a) the designation of the homily as an instrument of evangelization or
catechesis, (b) notice of the liturgical character of the homily, (c) a description of the homily in the form of a list of words and phrases, and (d) notice that the homily is preached not only at Eucharist but also in other
liturgies. *Evangelii Nuntiandi* 43 opens by saluting the homily as one of
the fruits of the Second Vatican Council; *Catechesi Tradendae* 48 closes
with such a salute. This common structure makes the differences in the
two paragraphs all the more noticeable. John Paul II wrote:

> This remark [regarding the variety of occasions at which catechesis is ap-
> propriate] is even more valid for the catechesis given in the setting of the liturgy,
> especially at the Eucharistic assembly. Respecting the specific nature and proper
> cadence of this setting, the homily takes up again the journey of faith put forward
> by catechesis, and brings it to its natural fulfillment. At the same time it encour-
> ages the Lord's disciples to begin anew each day their spiritual journey in truth,
> adoration and thanksgiving. Accordingly, one can say that catechetical teaching
> too finds its source and fulfillment in the Eucharist, within the whole circle of the
> liturgical year. Preaching, centered upon the Bible texts, must then in its own way
> make it possible to familiarize the faithful with the whole of the mysteries of the
> faith and the norms of Christian living. Much attention must be given to the
> homily: it should be neither too long nor too short; it should always be carefully
> prepared, rich in substance and adapted to the hearers, and reserved to ordained
> ministers. The homily should have its place not only in every Sunday and feast-
> day Eucharist, but also in celebrations of baptisms, penitential liturgies, mar-
> riages and funerals. This is one of the benefits of the liturgical renewal.[45]

45. John Paul II, apostolic exhortation Catechesis in Our Time *(Catechesi Tradendae)* 48. Accessed at <http://www.vatican.va/holy_father/john_paul_ii/apost_exhortations/documents/hf
_jp-ii_exh_16101979_catechesi-tradendae_en.html>.

Paul VI and John Paul II agree on three key elements: the homily occurs within the liturgy, it is based on Scripture, and it is to be accommodated to the hearers. Beyond that, the differences are rather striking. Where Paul VI had hoped for the evangelical fruits of homiletic preaching (faith, hope, love, peace, unity), John Paul II hopes for catechetical fruits: familiarity with mysteries and norms. Paul VI saw the homily as addressed to and productive of Christian community; John Paul II sees it as "encouragement" for disciples to begin their day "in truth, adoration and thanksgiving." Paul VI calls homiletic preachers to express their own faith and love in a way animated by ardor; John Paul II does not mention the preacher's faith, but instead urges preachers to carefully prepare a message rich in substance. The shift to a more catechetical understanding of the homily is clear. In addition, it must be mentioned that John Paul II introduced something not previously held by the magisterium in the sixteen years from the time when the homily was restored to the liturgy: the homily is reserved to sacred ministers.

Pope John Paul II introduces another term new to the magisterium in this exhortation—"inculturation." I mention it here because he will later apply it explicitly to preaching, although at this point it is applied to "catechesis [and] evangelization in general." Having earlier said of catechesis what Paul VI had said of evangelization, namely, that it needs to be accommodated to the hearers of today, John Paul II goes on to write:

> As I said recently to the members of the Biblical Commission: "The term 'acculturation' or 'inculturation' may be a neologism, but it expresses very well one factor of the great mystery of the Incarnation." We can say of catechesis, as well as of evangelization in general, that it is called to bring the power of the Gospel into the very heart of culture and cultures. For this purpose, catechesis will seek to know these cultures and their essential components; it will learn their most significant expressions; it will respect their particular values and riches. In this manner it will be able to offer these cultures the knowledge of the hidden mystery (cf. Romans 16:25; Ephesians 3:5) and help them to bring forth from their own living tradition original expressions of Christian life, celebration and thought.[46]

---

46. Ibid., 53. The dependence upon *Evangelii Nuntiandi* (especially 20 and 63) is clear though uncited. This passage is also reminiscent of the Second Vatican Council's conviction that "the Church has . . . utilized the resources of different cultures in preaching" (*Gaudium et Spes* 58) and that the "Tradition that comes from the apostles makes progress in the Church" (*Dei Verbum* 8), and yet it goes beyond.

The term "inculturation" is new, as is the strength of the statement that successful inculturation yields "original expressions of Christian life, celebration and thought" brought forth from various cultures' "own living tradition." Inculturation as a concept, then, combines the task of accommodation of the Gospel with an explicit statement of its intended result—original expressions of Christian life.

What might this "accommodation" sound like? John Paul describes what he has in mind for the effective minister of the Word, whether in catechetical works or, one presumes, in homilies:

> a) they must be linked with the real life of the generation to which they are addressed, showing close acquaintance with its anxieties and questionings, struggles and hopes;
> b) they must try to speak a language comprehensible to the generation in question;
> c) they must make a point of giving the whole message of Christ and his Church, without neglecting or distorting anything, and in expounding it they will follow a line and structure that highlights what is essential;
> d) they must really aim to give to those who use them a better knowledge of the mysteries of Christ, aimed at true conversion and a life more in conformity with God's will.[47]

The next year, 1980, John Paul II issued his letter to bishops, On the Mystery and Worship of the Eucharist. Here he briefly supplements his former comments on the homily.

> The reading of Scripture cannot be replaced by the reading of other texts, however much they may be endowed with undoubted religious and moral values. On the other hand such texts can be used very profitably in the homily. Indeed the homily is supremely suitable for the use of such texts, provided that their content corresponds to the required conditions, since it is one of the tasks that belong to the nature of the homily to show the points of convergence between revealed divine wisdom and noble human thought seeking the truth by various paths.[48]

This addition is clearly in keeping with the Pope's developing theology of inculturation.

---

47. Ibid., 49.

48. John Paul II, On the Mystery and Worship of the Eucharist *(Dominicae Cenae)* 10. Accessed at < http://www.vatican.va/holy_father/john_paul_ii/letters/documents/hf_jp-ii_let _24021980_dominicae-cenae_en.html>.

## 4. Two Summaries of the Conciliar Implementation: 1981–1983

At the beginning of the period of the implementation of the Second Vatican Council, all that had been said about the homily could be repeated in a sentence or two. By the end of the period, a great deal more of the homily's character had emerged. Indeed, enough had been written to allow it to be gathered and summarized. It is to those summaries that I now turn.

❖   ❖   ❖

"From this living explanation [the homily], the word of God proclaimed in the readings and the Church's celebration of the day's liturgy will have greater impact."

(Revised Introduction to the Lectionary for Mass, 1981)

In 1981 the Congregation for Sacraments and Divine Worship rectified a problem arising from the haste of the renewal of the liturgy. When the Lectionary for Mass was first released in 1969, it had a minimal introduction, with almost nothing of the theological depth found in other liturgical books.[49] That problem was solved by the 1981 revision of the Lectionary's introduction. The revised introduction gives an extensive theology of the Word of God and, with it, a summary of much of what had been written about liturgical preaching up to that point.

49. Complementing the promulgation of the Roman Missal in 1969 was the promulgation of the Lectionary for Mass *(Ordo Lectionum Missae)*. It is clear that the bulk of the Consilium's effort went into the principles of selection and arrangement, and into the choice of the readings themselves, for the introduction is relatively slight. The homily is mentioned only twice. The first is a combination of a slight paraphrase and a direct quote of the General Instruction of the Roman Missal 33: "By means of sacred Scripture, read during the liturgy of the word and explained during the homily, 'God is speaking to his people, opening up to them the mystery of redemption and salvation, and nourishing their spirit; Christ is present to the faithful through his own word'" (1). The second is also a passing reference in the section called "Celebrant's Choice of Texts." The celebrant is instructed, when choosing between two readings, to favor the one that is "more closely related to the day's gospel or is more helpful in presenting an organized and unified instruction over a period of time or that permits a semicontinuous reading of a book of the Bible" (8a). When choosing between the long and short form of a reading, celebrants are to consider "the capacity of the hearers to listen to the longer or shorter reading with profit, their ability to understand difficult texts correctly, and their appreciation of a more complete text that will be explained in the homily" (8b).

These two rubrics suggest an understanding of the homily as catechetical. Indeed, this introduction goes on to say that the priest "should choose the readings systematically for a number of Sundays in order to present his catechesis logically and coherently" (8a). Though the Lectionary itself is profoundly influenced by the liturgical year, its introduction—at least as regards the homily—is not. The homily appears as less a part of the liturgy than an instruction within the liturgy. These problems are corrected in the 1981 revision of the introduction.

The revised introduction speaks powerfully of the intimate connection of Word and sacrament:

> The more profound our understanding of the liturgical celebration, the higher our appreciation of the importance of God's word. Whatever we can say of the one, we can in turn say of the other, because each recalls the mystery of Christ and each in its own way causes that mystery to be ever present.[50]

> . . . The Church has honored the word of God and the eucharistic mystery with the same reverence, although not with the same worship, and has always and everywhere intended and endorsed such honor. . . . "The preaching of the word is necessary for the sacramental ministry. For the sacraments are sacraments of faith and faith has its origin and sustenance in the word (*Presbyterorum Ordinis* 4)." . . . The celebration of Mass in which the word is heard and the eucharist offered and received forms but one single act of divine worship (cf. *Sacrosanctum Concilium* 56).[51]

That theological groundwork having been laid, the revised introduction gathers together much of what had been written about the homily from the time of the Second Vatican Council onward.

> Through the course of the liturgical year the homily sets forth the mysteries of faith and the standards of the Christian life on the basis of the sacred text. Beginning with the Constitution on the Liturgy, the homily as part of the liturgy of the word (cf. *Sacrosanctum Concilium* 52; *Inter Oecumenici* 54) has been repeatedly and strongly recommended and in some cases it is obligatory. As a rule it is to be given by the one presiding (cf. General Instruction of the Roman Missal 42). The purpose of the homily at Mass is that the spoken word of God and the liturgy of the eucharist may together become 'a proclamation of God's wonderful works in the history of salvation, the mystery of Christ' (*Sacrosanctum Concilium* 35). Through the readings and homily Christ's paschal mystery is proclaimed; through the sacrifice of the Mass it becomes present (cf. *Sacrosanctum Concilium* 6, 47). Moreover Christ himself is also always present and active in the preaching of his Church (cf. *Mysterium Fidei* 36, *Ad Gentes* 9, *Evangelii Nuntiandi* 43).
> Whether the homily explains the biblical word of God proclaimed in the readings or some other text of the liturgy (cf. *Sacrosanctum Concilium* 35; General Instruction of the Roman Missal 41), it must always lead the community to celebrate the eucharist wholeheartedly, 'so that they may hold fast in their lives to what they have grasped by their faith' (*Sacrosanctum Concilium* 10). From this living explanation, the word of God proclaimed in

---

50. Congregation for Sacraments and Divine Worship, Revised Introduction to the Lectionary *(De Verbo Dei)* 5, in *The Liturgy Documents: A Parish Resource,* 3rd ed. (Chicago: Liturgy Training Publications, 1991) 128.

51. Ibid., 10, in *The Liturgy Documents,* 130.

the readings and the Church's celebration of the day's liturgy will have greater impact. But this demands that the homily be truly the fruit of meditation, carefully prepared, neither too long nor too short, and suited to all those present, even children and the uneducated (cf. *Catechesi Tradendae* 48).[52]

This remarkable summary misses almost nothing of what had come before; even more amazing, it harmonizes elements that had sometimes appeared in conflict. For instance, the tension between the proclamatory and the catechetical views of the homily is lessened. The revised introduction to the Lectionary, following the lead of the General Instruction of the Roman Missal, makes clear that any exposition is to be a living one—any explanation must lead to participation and faith.

❖     ❖     ❖

"Among the forms of preaching the homily is preeminent; it is a part of the liturgy itself and is reserved to a priest or to a deacon; in the homily the mysteries of the faith and the norms of Christian living are to be expounded from the sacred text throughout the course of the liturgical year."

(Code of Canon Law, 1983)

When Pope John Paul II promulgated the new Code of Canon Law in 1983, he stated:

Indeed, in a certain sense, this new Code could be understood as a great effort to translate this same doctrine, that is, [the Second Vatican Council's] ecclesiology, into canonical language. If, however, it is impossible to translate perfectly into canonical language the conciliar image of the Church, nevertheless, in this image there should always be found as far as possible its essential point of reference.[53]

As regards the conciliar theology of preaching, the Code can be considered a moderately successful effort at translation; as regards the homily, a less successful effort.

Book Three of the Code is entitled "On the Teaching Office of the Church." It consists of a general introduction and five titles (on the ministry

---

52. Ibid., 24, in *The Liturgy Documents,* 133. Original textual references replace the footnotes supplied by the editors.

53. John Paul II, Promulgation of the Revised Code of Canon Law *(Sacrae Disciplinae Legis)* xiv. Accessed at <http://www.vatican.va/holy_father/john_paul_ii/apost_constitutions/documents/hf_jp-ii_apc_25011983_sacrae-disciplinae-leges_en.html>.

of the Word, missionary action, Catholic education, social communication, and profession of faith). The first of these titles, "On the Ministry of the Divine Word," consists of an introduction and two chapters: one on preaching and the other on catechetics.

The Code's chapter on preaching discusses the homily (can. 767), the content of preaching ("those things which one must believe and do for the glory of God and the salvation of humanity"—can. 768), the need for preaching to be "accommodated to the condition of the listeners and in a manner adapted to the needs of the times" (can. 769), a call for "spiritual exercises and sacred missions" or other forms of preaching adapted to the needs of today (can. 770), a call to preach to those alienated or outside the Church (can. 771), and a reminder that the bishop's norms regarding preaching are to be observed by all (can. 772).[54] Except for the medieval sound of canon 768, this is a fairly accurate summary of the postconciliar theology and discipline of preaching.

Canon 767 concerns the homily, although whether it refers to the eucharistic homily only or to all homilies, is not clear. The canon reads:

§1. Among the forms of preaching the homily, which is part of the liturgy itself and is reserved to a priest or deacon, is preeminent; in the homily the mysteries of the faith and the norms of Christian life are to be explained from the sacred text during the course of the liturgical year.

§2. A homily must be given at all Masses on Sundays and holy days of obligation which are celebrated with a congregation, and it cannot be omitted except for a grave cause.

§3. It is strongly recommended that if there is a sufficient congregation, a homily is to be given even at Masses celebrated during the week, especially during the time of Advent or Lent or on the occasion of some feast day or a sorrowful event.

§4. It is for the pastor or rector of a church to take care that these prescripts are observed conscientiously.[55]

Sections 2 and 3 are straightforward codifications of the Second Vatican Council (*Sacrosanctum Concilium* 52) as strengthened by the First Instruction on Implementation (53). Section 4 envisions the pastor in his parish as being analogous to the bishop in his diocese, in the sense that he has overall responsibility for the homiletic preaching in his church.

---

54. John Paul II, Code of Canon Law, in *Code of Canon Law: Latin-English Edition,* trans. Canon Law Society of America (Washington, D.C.: Canon Law Society of America, 1998) 250.
55. Ibid., 251.

Section 1 is the most significant because it strives to "translate into canonical language" the theology of the homily. It makes five assertions. First, the homily is preeminent among the forms of preaching; this is a paraphrase of *Dei Verbum* 24 ("the liturgical homily must hold the foremost place" among the forms of "the ministry of the Word"). Second, the homily is part of the liturgy itself; this is an exact quote of *Sacrosanctum Concilium* 52. Third, the homily is reserved to a priest or a deacon. Fourth, the homily expounds the mysteries of faith and the norms of Christian living; this too is an exact quote of *Sacrosanctum Concilium* 52. Finally, the homily is drawn from the sacred text and related to the liturgical year, another exact quote from *Sacrosanctum Concilium* 52.

This translation of theology into canonical language misses much of the postconciliar development. One need only contrast this canon with the paragraph on the homily in the revised introduction to the Lectionary to see that canon 767 §1 contains the bare minimum—the full theological story of the homily is not captured by this paraphrase and quote of the Council.

## 5. Other Documents from the Papacy of John Paul II: 1984–1993

After the two major summaries just noted, five additional documents offered some advances in the understanding of the homily, even as the signs of some retrenchment became clear.

❖   ❖   ❖

"Since the Liturgy is totally permeated by the word of God, any other word must be in harmony with it, above all in the homily. . . ."
                                                                (John Paul II, 1988)

The homily again occupies John Paul II's attention in 1988, as he issues the apostolic letter On the Twenty-Fifth Anniversary of *Sacrosanctum Concilium*. There he renews his call for "careful preparation of the homily through study and meditation," [56] and his insistence upon the scriptural basis of the homily: "Since the Liturgy is totally permeated by the word of God, any other word must be in harmony with it, above all in the

---

56. John Paul II, On the Twenty-Fifth Anniversary of *Sacrosanctum Concilium (Vicesimus Quintus)* 8. Accessed at < http://www.vatican.va/holy_father/john_paul_ii/apost_letters/documents/hf_jp-ii_apl_04121988_vicesimus-quintus-annus_en.html>.

homily. . . . [T]he words of men must be at the service of the word of
God without obscuring it. . . ."[57] Most importantly, though, John Paul devotes section 7 of the letter to his own list of the "presences" of Christ in
the liturgy, following the path trod by Pius XII, the Second Vatican Council, and Paul VI. He wrote:

> In order to re-enact his Paschal Mystery, Christ is ever present in his Church,
> especially in liturgical celebrations (cf. *Sacrosanctum Concilium* 7; *Mysterium
> fidei* 36). . . . Christ is present in the Church assembled at prayer in his name.
> . . . Christ is present and acts in the person of the ordained minister who
> celebrates (cf. *Eucharisticum mysterium* 9). The priest is not merely entrusted
> with a function, but in virtue of the Ordination received he has been conse-
> crated to act *"in persona Christi."* To this consecration there must be a corre-
> sponding disposition, both inward and outward, also reflected in liturgical
> vestments, in the place which he occupies and in the word which he utters.
>   Christ is present in his word as proclaimed in the assembly and which,
> commented upon in the homily, is to be listened to in faith and assimilated
> in prayer.[58]

For Paul VI, Christ is present in preaching. John Paul II backs off from
this position, returning instead to the conciliar statement of Christ's presence in the Word. While somewhat reducing the status of the homily to a
"commentary," John Paul does understand Christ to be present in the words
of the priest (presumably including the homily), a presence attributable to
the fact that the priest acts *in persona Christi,* "in the person of Christ"—
a key to John Paul's theology.

❖   ❖   ❖

"The Bible exercises its influence down the centuries. A constant
process of actualization adapts the interpretation to the contemporary mentality and language. . . . [I]n order for it to have a profound effect, there must be inculturation according to the genius
proper to each people. . . ."

(John Paul II, 1993)

In 1990 Pope John Paul II issued his eighth encyclical, On the Permanent Validity of the Church's Missionary Mandate. In this encyclical John
Paul restates for the Church the priority of evangelization, and within it,

57. Ibid., 10.
58. Ibid., 7.

preaching.[59] This encyclical shows some further development of the concept of inculturation. John Paul wrote:

> Through inculturation the Church makes the Gospel incarnate in different cultures and at the same time introduces peoples, together with their cultures, into her own community (cf. *Catechesi tradendae* 53; *Slavorum apostoli* 21). She transmits to them her own values, at the same time taking the good elements that already exist in them and renewing them from within (cf. *Evangelii nuntiandi* 20). Through inculturation the Church, for her part, becomes a more intelligible sign of what she is, and a more effective instrument of mission.
>
> Thanks to this action within the local Churches, the universal Church herself is enriched with forms of expression and values in the various sectors of Christian life, such as evangelization, worship, theology and charitable works. She comes to know and to express better the mystery of Christ, all the while being motivated to continual renewal.[60]

Inculturation is here seen as a part of the whole Church's own self-realization and not only as an instrument of evangelization. Further, John Paul makes a very strong statement about the fruits of inculturation: better knowledge of the gospel, better expression of the gospel, enriched worship, enhanced theology, deepened charity.

The direct application of this developed theology of inculturation to preaching comes in a 1993 papal address, as John Paul II received and commended a document of the Pontifical Biblical Commission. This document develops the application at length (see below); the papal address merely makes the application explicit. Hence:

> The Bible exercises its influence down the centuries. A constant process of actualization adapts the interpretation to the contemporary mentality and language. . . . [I]n order for it to have profound effect, there must be inculturation according to the genius proper to each people. . . . In our day, a great effort is necessary, not only on the part of scholars and preachers, but also those who popularize biblical thought: they should use every means possible . . . so that the universal significance of the biblical message may be widely acknowledged and its saving efficacy may be seen everywhere. . . .[61]

59. John Paul II, On the Permanent Validity of the Church's Missionary Mandate *(Redemptoris Missio)* 44, citing *Evangelii Nuntiandi* 15, 45. Accessed at <http://www.vatican.va/edocs/ENG0219/_INDEX.HTM>.

60. Ibid., 52.

61. John Paul II, Address to the Pontifical Biblical Commission, The Interpretation of the Bible in the Church (Boston: St. Paul Books and Media, 1993) 15.

Actualization and inculturation are here denominated as among the means by which preachers release the power of the Word.[62] The document of the Pontifical Biblical Commission itself explains these processes in some depth and shows them to be at the heart of preaching.

❖   ❖   ❖

"The *liturgy of the Word* is an integral part of sacramental celebrations. To nourish the faith of believers, the signs which accompany the Word of God should be emphasized: the book of the Word . . . , its veneration (procession, incense, candles), the place of its proclamation (lectern or ambo), its audible and intelligible reading, the minister's homily which extends its proclamation, and the responses of the assembly. . . ."

(Catechism of the Catholic Church [no. 1154] 1992)

The Catechism of the Catholic Church was promulgated in 1992, with the release of the French-language original text, and was definitively revised when the Latin text was released in 1997. The Catechism is most noteworthy, not for furthering the Second Vatican Council's understanding of preaching and the homily, but rather for unfortunate retrenchment.

Of the Second Vatican Council's 125 references to preaching, the Catechism refers to six. In articles on episcopacy and priesthood, the Catechism does not mention the Council's teaching on preaching as the primary duty of the ordained (*Lumen Gentium* 25, 28; *Presbyterorum Ordinis* 4), reserving that for the section on magisterium and infallibility.[63] Pope Paul VI's teaching on the presence of Christ in preaching (*Mysterium Fidei* 36) is not mentioned either. Neither do the Catechism's articles on the sacraments and on the Eucharist mention the Council's renewed emphasis on the biblical, liturgical homily (*Sacrosanctum Concilium* 35, 52).

Although the Catechism does cite *Dei Verbum* 24 ("The ministry of the Word, too—pastoral preaching, catechetics and all forms of Christian instruction, among which the liturgical homily should hold pride of place— is healthily nourished and thrives in holiness through the Word of Scrip-

---

62. By contrast, however, in the general audience talk of April 21, 1993, the most John Paul is able to say about the role of adaptation in preaching is that it is "not opposed" to "authentic and complete proclamation" (7).

63. John Paul II, Catechism of the Catholic Church, no. 888. Accessed at <http://www.scboromeo .org/ccc/para/888.htm>. This web site has the complete text of the Catechism and a search engine. It is the basis of the Vatican web site containing the Catechism in English.

ture"),[64] this quotation near the beginning is not a fair indicator of the coming treatment of the homily. Rather than appearing "preeminent," the homily is called an accompaniment to the Word of God (listed along with book, candles, and ambo).[65] The homily's conciliar status as "a part of the liturgy itself" is not mentioned, nor is its identity as a "proclamation of the wonderful works of God in the history of salvation, the mystery of Christ" (*Sacrosanctum Concilium* 35). Rather, the homily is called an "extension" of the proclamation,[66] or "an exhortation to accept this Word as what it truly is, the Word of God."[67] The homily is otherwise noted only in passing.[68]

❖    ❖    ❖

"In principle, the liturgy, and especially the sacramental liturgy, . . . brings about the most perfect actualization of the biblical texts, for the liturgy places the proclamation in the midst of the community of believers. . . . Written text thus becomes living word. . . . The homily, which seeks to actualize more explicitly the Word of God, is an integral part of the liturgy."

(The Interpretation of the Bible in the Church, 1993)

The final document of the period under consideration is also the most significant. In 1993 the Pontifical Biblical Commission[69] issued its work entitled The Interpretation of the Bible in the Church. As was seen above, this work was warmly received by Pope John Paul II, who noted specifically the connection between the work of modern exegesis and the mission of preaching. The document itself develops this connection in a way that captures much of what had come before. Two principles are of great importance: actualization and inculturation.

Actualization of the Scriptures can be seen "within the Bible itself. . . : very early texts have been re-read in the light of new circumstances and applied to the contemporary situation of the People of God. The same

---

64. Ibid., no. 132.
65. Ibid., no. 1154.
66. Ibid.
67. Ibid., no. 1349.
68. Ibid., no. 1100 (quoting *Sacrosanctum Concilium* 24), no. 1346, no. 1482, no. 1688.
69. The Pontifical Biblical Commission is not in itself "an organ of the teaching office" but is nonetheless organized under the auspices of the Congregation for the Doctrine of the Faith and "enjoys the confidence of the teaching office" (Joseph Cardinal Ratzinger, preface, Interpretation of the Bible in the Church, 28).

basic conviction stimulates believing communities of today to continue the process of actualization."[70]

Inculturation is another way of looking at this same task. The first stage of inculturation is translating the Scripture into another language. "Translation has to be followed by interpretation, which should set the biblical message in more explicit relationship with the ways of feeling, thinking, living and self-expression which are proper to the local culture."[71] The process continues from there, leading to implantation of the Church and permeation of culture itself; further, "the treasures contained in diverse cultures allow the Word of God to produce new fruits."

Having laid these foundations, Interpretation of the Bible goes on to apply them to liturgical preaching.

> In principle, the liturgy, and especially the sacramental liturgy, the highpoint of which is the Eucharistic celebration, brings about the most perfect actualization of the biblical texts, for the liturgy places the proclamation in the midst of the community of believers, gathered around Christ so as to draw near to God. Christ is then "present in his word, because it is he himself who speaks when Sacred Scripture is read in Church" (*Sacrosanctum Concilium* 7). Written text thus becomes living word. . . . The homily, which seeks to actualize more explicitly the Word of God, is an integral part of the liturgy.[72]

"[P]reaching . . . should draw from the ancient texts spiritual sustenance adapted to the present needs of the Christian community." With catechesis and the rest of the biblical apostolate, "the presentation of the Gospels should be done in such a way as to elicit an encounter with Christ. . . . The word of the prophets and that of the 'ministers of the Word' (Luke 1:2) ought to appear as something addressed to Christians now."[73]

The document goes on to explain something of how such preaching is to be done.

> The explanation of the biblical texts given in the course of the homily cannot enter into great detail. It is, accordingly, fitting to explain the central contribution of texts, that which is most enlightening for faith and most stimulating for the progress of Christian life, both on the community and individual level. Presenting this central contribution means striving to achieve

70. The Interpretation of the Bible in the Church, 117.
71. Ibid., 122–123.
72. Ibid., 124–125.
73. Ibid., 128.

its actualization and inculturation, in accordance with what has been said above.[74]

The Biblical Commission ends this section with a word of caution. It warns that "good hermeneutical principles are necessary," as is adequate preparation. Indeed,

> want of preparation in this area leads to the temptation to avoid plumbing the depths of the biblical readings and to being content simply to moralize or to speak of contemporary issues in a way that fails to shed upon them the light of God's word. . . . Preachers should certainly avoid insisting in a one-sided way on the obligations incumbent upon believers. The biblical message must preserve its principal characteristic of being the good news of salvation freely offered by God. Preaching will perform a task more useful and more conformed to the Bible if it helps the faithful above all to "know the gift of God" (John 4:10) as it has been revealed in Scripture; they will then understand in a positive light the obligations that flow from it.[75]

The treatment of the homily in The Interpretation of the Bible in the Church thus provides the technical, theological shorthand to describe what has developed since the Second Vatican Council as the Catholic understanding of the nature of liturgical preaching: the homily, which seeks to actualize more explicitly the Word of God, is an integral part of the liturgy. The preacher must strive to achieve the actualization and inculturation of the biblical texts.

I bring my consideration of preaching documents to a close with the excellent Interpretation of the Bible in the Church. Unfortunately, the following decade of documents from the papacy of John Paul II does not offer any advances in understanding the Second Vatican Council's restoration of the biblical, liturgical homily. Indeed, as was foreshadowed by the Catechism, some of the documents tend to take away from the developments described in this chapter.[76]

---

74. Ibid., 128–129.

75. Ibid., 129.

76. Let me note an example of the regression. The Directory on the Ministry and Life of Priests was issued in 1994 by the Sacred Congregation for Clergy (and can be accessed at <http://www.vatican.va/roman_curia/congregations/cclergy/documents/rc_con_cclergy_doc _31011994_directory_en.html>). This Directory is much more concerned with insisting upon the authoritative nature of priests' preaching than with preaching well. What little is said about how to preach takes the form of warnings. For instance, the Directory cites *Presbyterorum Ordinis* 4. However, the reference is to the admonition "not to teach his own wisdom but the Word of God and to issue an urgent invitation to all men to conversion and holiness" (*Presbyterorum Ordinis* 4;

cf. *Pastores Dabo Vobis* 26). This sounds a theme to which the Directory warms, as it urges priests in their preaching to avoid "falsifying, reducing, distorting or diluting the content of the divine message"; they must preach "'without duplicity and without any dishonesty, but rather manifesting with frankness the truth before God' (2 Corinthians 4:2)" (45). Further, "preaching, therefore, cannot be reduced to the presentation of one's own thought, to the manifestation of personal experience, to simple explanations of a psychological (cf. John Paul II, *Catechesi,* 21 April 93), sociological or humanitarian nature; nor can it excessively concentrate on rhetoric, so often found in mass-communication" (45).

The Directory concludes its section on preaching with a paragraph about the homily. In its content and in its sources, it stands in stark contrast with the treatment of the homily in the Directory for Bishops (57, 59) issued twenty-one years before. Whereas that earlier document developed the insights of the Second Vatican Council, the Directory for Priests returns to a more patristic and scholastic approach. Indeed, it seems innocent of most of the developments regarding the homily, and of most of the sources, with the exception of Canon Law. Thus:

> [T]he priest must feel personally bound to cultivate, in a particular way, a knowledge of Holy Scripture with a sound exegesis, principally patristic, and meditated on according to the various methods supported by the spiritual tradition of the Church, in order to obtain a living understanding of love (cf. Aquinas, *Sum. Theo.* I, q. 43, a. 5). Seen in this light, the priest will feel the duty of paying particular attention to the preparation, be it remote or proximate, of liturgical homilies, to their content, to the balance between theoretical and practical aspects, to the manner of teaching and to the technique of delivery, even to good diction, respectful of the dignity of the matter and of the listeners (cf. c. 769) (46).

# CHAPTER 3

# A Roman Catholic Contribution to the Vision of Sunday Preaching

In the last chapter I took a diachronic approach to document the development in the official Roman Catholic understanding of the homily, from its embryonic appearance in the Second Vatican Council's first document through thirty years of restatement, evolution, and occasionally, devolution.

In the present chapter I intend to take a synchronic approach, backing off from the trees to see the forest itself. After thirty years of insight, what might Roman Catholics have to contribute to the vision of Sunday preaching? To answer that question, I will describe the major themes that have emerged throughout the period under consideration. In turn, these themes will ground an extended description of liturgical preaching. In keeping with this purpose, I generally will not utilize direct quotations in this chapter.

## Overview of Major Themes

If one considers only those claims about the homily made three or more times in the official documents, then five major themes emerge. In turn, these themes serve as categories that embrace the vast majority of other words and phrases used to describe the homily. Let me begin, then, by presenting and briefly describing these major themes.

The most frequent claim made about the homily is that it is a *liturgical word*. In various forms, this claim is made about thirty-six times. The homily's liturgical nature emerges in five ways. First, it is directly called a

part of the liturgy. Second, the homily is called highly desirable or obligatory for liturgical celebrations. Third, the homily leads to greater participation in the liturgy. Fourth, the homily is grounded in both Scripture and
the wider liturgy. Finally, the homily serves the intimate connection between word and ritual action.

The second most frequent claim made about the homily is that it is
an *actualizing word.* This claim is made about twenty-five times and emerges
in several forms. One form uses the word *living:* the homily is a living commentary on the Word, is itself a living word, and is an act of living tradition. Another form uses the concept of *efficacy:* the homily renders faith
efficacious, increases the efficacy of the Word and of the entire liturgy. A
final form uses the concept of *activity:* the homily makes Scripture active,
actualizes the Word, indeed manifests Christ's presence and action.

The third most frequent claim made about the homily is that it is a
*clarifying word.* This claim appears, in one form or another, about twenty-
four times. In the homily the readings or other liturgical texts are explained;
the mysteries of the faith and principles of Christian life are expounded.
The homily is concerned with both gospel and tradition, which are expli-
cated in their fullness. Given this character, the homily's language is simple,
direct, and clear.

The fourth most frequent claim made about the homily is that it is an
*inculturated word.* This claim is made about twenty-three times. Early on,
this claim appears as *adaptation* or *accommodation* (taking into account
the needs of specific listeners). Later the favored term is *inculturation.* Although each of these terms has its own nuances, their shared significance
is clear: the homily does not just repeat the ritual texts but rather interprets them. This interpretation is not generic but specific to an assembly,
not timeless but rooted in the present, not abstract but concrete, its language not arcane but familiar. The culture of the gathered assembly provides the raw material for the homily; in turn, the homily contributes to
that culture new ways of appropriating the gospel.

Finally, the documents see the homily as a *personal word.* This claim
is made about fifteen times and emerges in three ways. First, the homily is
carefully prepared, the fruit of the preacher's own study and meditation.
Second, the faith of the preacher affects the efficacy of the homily. Sometimes this point is made by insisting that, in St. Augustine's phrase, the effective preacher of the Word must first be a hearer of the Word. At other

times, it is made by insisting that the preacher be a witness, giving authentic testimony. While there is some reticence shown on this point (a caution against the preaching of self), nonetheless the call to speak one's own faith is clear. Third, the love of the preacher contributes to the homily's effect. The homily manifests the love that the preacher has for the gathered assembly. All in all, the homily is a personal act, not only consisting of the preacher's own words but also constituting a loving gift of self.

In short, then, official Roman Catholic documents understand the homily as a part of the liturgy that actualizes the Scriptures, inculturating and clarifying them for the gathered assembly. This actualization flows from the faith-filled love and preparation of the preacher.

## The *Via Negativa:* What the Homily Is Not

In light of these five themes, how might the homily be described? What is supposed to occur when the preacher stands to break the silence following the scriptural proclamation?

Reflecting insights from the documents, perhaps it would be good to begin with what the homily is not. The homily is not a mere exercise in eloquence or rhetoric (although rhetorical techniques are helpful). It is not an academic exposé of some thesis nor a protracted exegesis (although liturgical texts are clarified by the homily). It is not general and abstract. The homily is not mere repetition of doctrine (although it is faithful to tradition). The homily does not present Jesus as an object (but rather, as a person present and active now). The homily does not moralize (although it enables listeners to understand better the obligations that flow from the gift of salvation). Homilists can never be the servants of any human ideology or party, nor do they preach themselves. Homilists cannot preach effectively without first being hearers of the Word.[1]

Continuing down the *via negativa,* one might seek to describe the homily by contrasting it with other seemingly similar speech events, that is, with events that, like the homily, involve a single person speaking monologically to a gathered group.

---

1. The U.S. Bishops' *Fulfilled in Your Hearing: The Homily in the Sunday Assembly* (Washington, D.C.: USCCB Publishing, 1982) substantially agrees on what the homily is not: not theological speculation, painstaking exegesis, nor oratorical flamboyance (15); not a platform for personal doubts, anxieties or problems (15); not a call to conversion from radical unbelief (a homily presupposes faith) (17); not primarily educational (18).

One venerable example of the monologue is the soliloquy spoken by an actor in a play. The actor, portraying a character, speaks the words of the playwright in hopes of moving the audience in some way. For example, if well delivered, the speech that begins "To be or not to be" still has the power to move its listeners to sorrow in face of the "slings and arrows of outrageous fortune" in each life. Those words can still evoke the despair with which many are familiar. There are preachers who model their approach on the dramatic soliloquy, and yet that model is not on balance a helpful analogy to the homily. It is true that both are speeches that seek a reaction in their hearers. But actors speak the words of another, whereas homilists must speak their own words. The homily has a personal quality that even the best drama does not.

A much more familiar example of the monologue is that given by late-night talk show hosts at the beginning of their shows. This nightly monologue is an attempt at trenchant and humorous observation on the day's events. There are preachers who model their approach on the talk show host, and yet that model is not on balance a helpful analogy to the homily. It is true that both must be topical to be effective; relevance to current culture is crucial. But the talk show host seeks solely to entertain, whereas the homilist does not. The homily is a liturgical moment, part of a ritual whose goal is communal worship, not diversion.

Another familiar monologist is the university lecturer, who stands before the gathered students and speaks. The lecturer intends to transmit knowledge to those students. There are preachers who model their approach on the university professor, and yet that model is not on balance a helpful analogy to the homily either. It is true that the homilist must know what he or she is talking about—indeed must know the larger tradition and how to hand it on. But the lecturer's intent is to remedy ignorance by telling students what they do not yet know, whereas the homilist testifies to what is already known. The Christian assembly is not a Gnostic gathering for the transfer of arcane facts. The homilist speaks about the reality which gathers those present and which the liturgy itself celebrates and actualizes—salvation in Jesus Christ.

What of the political candidate, another well-known monologist? The candidate stands before the potential voters and speaks with the intention of persuading them of the rightness of his or her position, but even more of the rightness of the person for the job. There are preachers who model their approach on the stump speech, and yet that model is not on balance a helpful analogy to the homily. It is true that communicating personal credibility is necessary for a homilist; insincerity serves neither politician nor preacher. Nonetheless, the candidate is selling himself or herself, whereas the homilist is "selling" neither self nor stance. The homilist shares personal faith with the intention of supporting and nurturing the faith of others.

Even the other monologues within the liturgy itself do not provide the perfect analogy. There are plenty of ritual moments in which one person stands before the assembly and speaks, most notably the proclaiming of the Scripture passages and the praying of the Eucharistic Prayer. But these and all other obligatory ritual monologues involve speaking the words of others, the words of the ritual text. Only in the homily does the ritual demand that one speak in one's own words.

In short, the homily is *sui generis.* The homilist is neither actor nor comedian, neither professor nor politician, nor is the homilist some hybrid of these other monologists. How, then, might we describe a preacher of the homily?

## A Roman Catholic Contribution to the Vision of Sunday Preaching

The *via negativa* having led to a dead end, the only remaining route is a circular one: the preacher of the homily does what preachers have done since preaching was invented. Like Ezra, homilists through the centuries have "opened the book in the sight of all the people, and . . . read from book, from the law of God, with interpretation. They gave the sense, so that the people understood the reading" (Neh 8:6, 8). Like Jesus, homilists pronounce God's Word and follow it with their own words: "You have heard it said . . . But I say to you . . ." (Matt 5:21-48). This personal word, endowed with faith, redolent of love, allows written text to become living word.

The homily is the act that, beyond all odds, allows an ancient text from a foreign culture to be received as God's Word today, relevant and powerful. Homiletic preaching transcends mere repetition of sacred formulas to become the means for God to act today; like Jesus, homilists "speak with *exousia,* not like the scribes" (Matt 7:29)—they speak with the power of personal faith, pastoral love, liturgical sensitivity, cultural awareness, and intellectual clarity.

In short, the Sunday homily is PLICA: personal, liturgical, incultur-ated, clarifying, and actualizing.

The homilist speaks a *personal word.* Though the homily is a part of the Church's liturgy and speaks the Church's faith, it does this by being a personal statement of faith. The homilist has experienced God anew through encounter with a text and wishes, out of love for the assembly, to commu-nicate that encounter in a way that evokes for them an experience of God.

The homilist speaks a *liturgical word.* He or she uses the verbal re-sources of the liturgy, its vocabulary and symbols, in preaching. The homilist also utilizes the visual resources of the liturgy: vesture, liturgical furnishings, and ritual space. The homily, as a part of the liturgy, shares with the greater liturgy the goal of enabling the faithful "to express in their lives and manifest to others the mystery of Christ and the real nature of the true Church"; in the liturgy, the "work of our redemption is accomplished."[2]

The homilist speaks an *inculturated word,* manifesting deep under-standing of the anxieties and questionings, struggles and hopes, of the gathered community. The homily is crafted using the symbols and vocabu-lary of today's people so that God's Word might speak to them. As such, the inculturated homily is always an act of interpretation—the preacher's attempt to make sense of the world in light of a ritual text and to make sense of a ritual text in light of the world.

The homilist speaks a *clarifying word,* a word that addresses head as well as heart. Conceptual language is not foreign to the homily. Indeed, for a homily to have effect beyond the moment, it must provide the hearer with the means to name the experience generated and to carry it beyond the liturgy into life. The clarifying of the ritual text, expressed in conceptual language, allows a "portability" to the liturgical experience: grace having been named, it can be carried into the world.

Above all, the homilist speaks an *actualizing word.* To the extent that the faith underlying a ritual text lives for the preacher—and in turn through the preacher's words lives for the hearer—to that extent is a homily suc-cessful. Like the Scriptures themselves, the homily is "written so that you may come to believe that Jesus is the Messiah, the Son of God, and that through believing you may live in his name" (John 20:31). Preachers today,

---

2. Second Vatican Council, Constitution on the Sacred Liturgy *(Sacrosanctum Concilium)* 2. Accessed at <http://www.vatican.va/archive/hist_councils/ii_vatican_council/documents/vat-ii_const_19631204_sacrosanctum-concilium_en.html>.

having experienced that faith, are moved to share it with and actualize it for their listeners, believers in this time and this place. The homilist is the voice which allows the tradition to live.

What, then, is a homily? A homily is a verbal act by which, after the proclamation of God's Word, a minister speaks in his or her own words to the assembly. Having had an experience of faith in a personal encounter with the text, the preacher now produces an address whose intention is evoking an analogous experience in the listener. Thus, the preacher's words intend to actualize a ritual text, that is, to endow it with life, with power, with dynamism. What is sought is an encounter with Christ, which happens most often when the message of the ritual text is experienced as "good news" by those gathered. A principal by-product of the homiletic experience is increased clarity about the text of the day, a clarity which renders that experience portable. The means employed by the homilist are several: the preacher's experience of the text (via head and heart), the preacher's knowledge of the listeners and their world, the preacher's personal faith and love for the assembly, and the preacher's efforts to speak in words not only understood but also felt by the gathered assembly. As such, the homily shares with much of the Scriptures the character of direct address to and from people of faith; it is less a commentary than a message in its own right.

Pope Paul VI described preaching as "the genuine art of proclaiming the Word of God," and he called upon the Church to "search for the principles which make for simplicity, clarity, effectiveness and authority, and so overcome our natural ineptitude in the use of this great and mysterious instrument of the divine Word."[3] In the next chapters, I take up Paul VI's challenge to "search for the principles" of the preaching art. What patterns, convictions, and behaviors might support and develop the vision of the homily arising from the Roman documents? If the homily is to be a personal, liturgical, inculturated, clarifying, actualizing word, then what abilities are necessary for a preacher, what knowledge is essential, what approaches are effective?

---

3. Paul VI, encyclical On the Church *(Ecclesiam Suam)* 90–91. Accessed at <http://www .vatican.va/holy_father/paul_vi/encyclicals/documents/hf_pvi_enc_06081964_ecclesiam_en.html>.

# CHAPTER 4

# The Homily as Personal Word: Responsibility, Faith, and Love

The twin truths stare unblinkingly at the preacher. First, the Sunday morning expectations of the people of God are high indeed. Second, it is not easy to preach well. Those Sunday morning expectations are, I think, well captured by the PLICA vision of the homily unfolded in the last two chapters. In this chapter and the following four, I will take each of the PLICA characteristics and discuss very concrete behaviors that will enable the preacher to give voice to the vision. It is not easy to preach well, but it most certainly can be done. I begin, then, at what I believe to be the very beginning—the homily as personal word.

## The Homily as Personal Word

We declare to you what was from the beginning, what we have heard, what we have seen with our eyes, what we have looked at and touched with our hands, concerning the word of life—this life was revealed, and we have seen it and testify to it, and declare to you . . . what we have seen and heard . . . (1 John 1:1-3).

Before it is anything else, the Sunday homily is the word of a person of faith, the word of a person who has experienced the Lord and who wishes to share that experience. To be able to speak this personal word, one must have the ability to present effectively oneself and one's message to the hearers. Five indicators would reveal a preacher with this personal ability. Such a preacher engages listeners by means of verbal and non-verbal communication skills. The personal preacher takes responsibility for choices made in preaching.

The personal preacher manifests genuineness, faithfulness, and pastoral love for the listeners. Let's take a closer look at each of these indicators.

## The Personal Preacher Engages the Listeners by Means of Verbal and Non-Verbal Communication Skills

The Sunday homily is a species of oral communication and as such is bound by all of its rules. At the most basic, if the people in the pews cannot hear us clearly, then we have appreciably increased the demands on the Holy Spirit in making our preaching meaningful! This seems so fundamental, and so obvious, that it continues to take my breath away at how often I hear—or don't hear—preachers whose lack of communication skills hobble the homily. The skills I have in mind are all able to be learned, and all able to be improved upon with practice. There are three inter-related sets: verbal skills, non-verbal skills, and composition skills.

*Verbal Communication Skills.* It would be redundant for me to give a mini-treatise on the skills of oral communication, as others have done much more complete and helpful treatments of the topic.[1] However, this much must be said: as oral communication, the homily demands of the preacher the ability to be heard. We must fill our lungs with sufficient air, and manipulate our voice boxes with sufficient precision, and open our mouths with sufficient breadth and shape, to allow our words to emerge whole and accessible. And in most church buildings, this coordination of lungs and voice box and mouth must be further coordinated with an amplification system. None of this comes naturally. These skills come about through conscious effort, practice, and most importantly, feedback from the hearers. The conscientious preacher asks the people in the pews—especially those in the back pews and the older folks whose hearing may be challenged—whether or not the homily is being heard. I cannot tell you the number of times that an older person has come up to me after I preached in a new parish, and said, "Thank you so much. I could actually hear you!" Such comments I always understand as a subtle statement of an awful fact: on most Sundays, the homily was not heard there.

---

1. See, for instance, Mitties McDonald de Champlain, "What to Do While Preaching," in *Best Advice for Preaching,* ed. John S. McClure (Minneapolis: Fortress Press, 1998) 99–116; Joseph M. Webb, *Preaching Without Notes* (Nashville: Abingdon Press, 2001) 97–118. On speaking skills in general, see Morton Cooper, *Change Your Voice, Change Your Life* (New York: Macmillan Publishing Company, 1984).

So practice your breathing. Practice your articulation. Develop your ear to listen to yourself preach. If you can hear your voice bouncing off the back wall and coming back to you, you are projecting effectively. If not, some people are probably not hearing your words. Tape yourself and listen for bad habits, like dropping your voice at the end of a sentence, or losing contact with the microphone when you look down at your notes or turn your head, or pacing yourself either too slowly (a recipe for boredom) or too quickly (a recipe for confusion). But above all, ask your parishioners after the service: Could you hear me?

When this irreplaceable foundation is laid—they can hear me—then preachers can turn their attention to other oral resources, like tone of voice, rhythm, and variety in volume and pace.

***Non-Verbal Communication Skills.*** Different communication experts will give different percentages, but none will deny that an important part of human communication consists of the bodily signals that accompany our speaking. Our eyes and the rest of our face, our hands and arms and the rest of our body—all these have tales to tell. For instance, a preacher with a "deer in the headlights" look in the eyes will find that his or her message is compromised by the fear that everyone can read. "Trust God in all things" is less than reassuring when delivered by a person whose body says "I'm afraid." So too for the finger-wagging that communicates the attitude of a disciplinarian or the looking down one's nose that communicates assumed superiority—there are gestures and stances aplenty that take away from the messages we are trying to communicate.

Most preachers are not consciously or intentionally choosing to adopt unhelpful bodily personas. But bad habits can develop. The best way to discover whether our non-verbal gestures are enhancing or damaging our homilies is to have ourselves videotaped while preaching so that we can see ourselves as others see us, and to watch that tape in the company of others willing to be honest with us. We may not discover a non-verbal nightmare, but we may well be amazed at the number of times we adjust our glasses or our vesture, or how many laps we make back and forth across the sanctuary. Effective use of our bodies enhances communication, and such effective use can be learned and practiced.

***Language Structured for Orality.*** The third aspect of effective communication is the words we use and the way we put them together. I will have much more to say on the question of structure in chapter 10, but several introductory comments will serve us here.

The first thing for preachers to remind themselves of is the oral nature of the homily, from beginning to end. Even when sitting in front of our computers or with legal pad in hand, we are ministers of sound. Recall that what sets the alphabet apart from pictographs or other forms of writing is that each character represents a sound. For the preacher, this is especially significant, since the letters we write are always intended to be reconstituted into sound. As we write, we should hear the sounds echoing in our minds. Even better, we should speak aloud as we write. Remember, up through the Middle Ages, the norm in written composition was for the author to dictate to a secretary: the sound came first, and then the writing.[2] We need to keep the sounds ever at play in our minds.

Second, effective oral communication differs in one principal way from effective written communication, and that is the need to say something more than once for it to be understood. In a text, one well-written sentence can communicate a world of meaning; in a homily, one well-spoken sentence can easily be lost if its message is not elaborated. Upon reading one boffo sentence on a page, the reader can stop and ponder and absorb. But one great sentence in a homily is always followed immediately by another sentence, and another. If what follows does not enhance, support, illustrate, or restate the message of the great sentence, then that sentence will be forgotten.

I would argue that in ten or fifteen minutes of preaching, a most reasonable goal is to communicate one main message, expressible in a fairly simple, declarative sentence. I will say more about this below. But as we discuss the oral nature of preaching, let me note that the task of the Sunday preacher is to choose that message and to structure a series of spoken sentences that will develop and illustrate that message. Any sentence spoken that does not relate directly to the message will take away from the message. Non sequiturs and off-the-cuff additions will almost always make the hearer's job harder.

## The Personal Preacher Takes Responsibility for Choices Made Regarding the Content of Preaching

Jesus must have seemed audacious in his preaching, daring to start with the Holy Scriptures and then say more: "You have heard it said. . . . But I

2. See Walter J. Ong, *Orality and Literacy: The Technologizing of the Word* (London and New York: Routledge, 1982) 95.

say to you . . ." (Matt 5:21-22). The Sunday preacher is called to a similar audacity. We preachers are those designated by the Church to be so bold as to add our own words to the proclamation of God's Word. We are only human, yes; we are subject to error, yes; yet we are called to reflect upon the scriptural word and then craft a message inspired by that Scripture and yet undeniably our own. The homily is a personal word, and as such the person who chooses and speaks those words must take responsibility for the choices made.

My experience confirms for me that many preachers shy away from this responsibility. Such avoidance emerges in two principal ways. The first is an exclusive reliance on first person plural speech, sentence after sentence of locutions like "*We* believe that *our* faith is what binds *us* together." Many of us were probably taught to preach this way, and yet there is a problem here. A homily whose entire voice is plural—"we," "we," "we"— is a homily in which the "I" of the preacher remains hidden in the crowd.[3] Of course, some think that is precisely where the preacher should be. David Buttrick, the dean of American homiletics, famously wrote: "Preaching prefers a language of 'we' and 'our' and 'us.' . . . 'I' alone is *always* a dangerous word. . . ."[4] I, for one, could not disagree more. It is the lack of "I" that is dangerous. The Sunday homily is the personal word of the preacher to the rest of the assembly, so it is most artificial to suppress any mention of what "*I* have experienced in *my* hearing of God's Word, and the impact it has had on *me*." Further, it strikes me as the height of presumption to think that every word I craft and speak is immediately "owned" by the assembly, that is, that my every word is truly "our" word. No, the homily is a personal word, and it demands the verbal presence of the preacher.

There are several roles in Sunday preaching for the first person singular.[5] At times the preacher may adopt the person of the "verifying I," testifying to some important reality. For example: "The newspaper says that unemployment is getting worse, and I for one believe it." Contrast that (unfavorably) with: "We all know that unemployment is getting worse." Or the preacher might adopt the person of the "biographical I," sharing

3. Rudolph Boren, *Predigtlehre* (Munich, 1974) 409, in Hans van der Geest, *Presence in the Pulpit: The Impact of Personality on Preaching*, trans. D. W. Stott (Atlanta: John Knox Press, 1981) 40.

4. David Buttrick, *Homiletic: Moves and Structures* (Philadelphia: Fortress Press, 1987) 219.

5. These various "I"s are the categories of Manfred Josuttis. See van der Geest, *Presence in the Pulpit*, 40.

something of his or her life. This should be used sparingly, and yet can have great effect. For instance: "When I was growing up, my family attended a church just like this one." In simple remarks like this, a real person emerges. Again, the preacher may adopt the person of the "confessional I," confessing personally held belief—"This is Easter Sunday, and I am here for one reason only: I believe that Jesus was raised from the dead." Or again, the preacher might speak as the "representative I," speaking in the singular but inviting identification. This "representative I" works very effectively when the preacher is broaching a delicate topic of morality. Contrast the typical plural approach with that of the "representative I": "We are all racists" versus "When I drive through certain neighborhoods, I automatically reach over to lock my car doors. Each time I do, though, I catch sight of my face in the mirror and wonder: 'Am I a racist'?" The typical plural is brusque and universalizing, tarring all with the same harsh brush. The latter is personal, gentler, and yet an effective invitation for the listener to ponder and perhaps identify with the preacher: "Yeah, I do that too." Finally—let's admit the truth—the preacher sometimes utilizes the "fictional I." As we illustrate our homilies, we may well so alter an anecdote as to cross into fiction. But there, too, first person singular may still be effective: "I was in the mall yesterday, and . . . ." Perhaps you were in the mall weeks ago, but the immediacy is demanded to make your illustration work. A little fiction in service of the gospel is fine. In all these examples, I am not calling for exclusive use of "I," "me," and "my." This misunderstands the nature of the homily just as much as the exclusive use of the first person plural does. However, since the homily is a personal word, there must be room for me.

The second common way in which preachers evade responsibility for choices made is by use of such commonplace formulae as, "In today's readings we hear that . . ." and "Jesus is telling us that . . ." and "God's Word is saying that . . . ." Unless these formulae are introducing a direct quotation from the Bible, they are false and misleading. Preachers use them—mostly unconsciously, I trust—to avoid having to take responsibility for the message they are delivering. Contrast these two locutions from an Advent homily:

> Today's readings tell us that it is the love of God, accepted in our own hearts and shared with others, that repairs our personal "potholes."

> It is the love of God, accepted in our own hearts and shared with others—it is the love of God that repairs our personal "potholes."

The first preacher has decided to cloak his choice of a message in the mantle of Scripture's authority. However, it is simply not the case that any of the texts proclaimed on the Second Sunday of Advent (Year C) actually say that the love of God "repairs our personal potholes." This is the preacher's metaphor for expressing his understanding of the readings in their Advent context. What he has spoken is "homily," not "readings." In addition, this preacher has *written* a perfectly lovely complex sentence, featuring an adjectival dependent clause. However, such a sentence in its very elegance is not good oral communication. The key phrase "love of God" would quite likely be lost as the hearers' brains sought to process "accepted in our own hearts and shared with others."

The second preacher, by contrast, has taken personal responsibility for his message. He looks his hearers in the eyes and expresses to them his conviction: "It is the love of God that repairs our personal potholes." This may seem an insignificant difference, but it is not. In the first instance, the preacher hides behind the day's readings; in the second, he speaks a word of faith directly to the rest of the assembly. In addition, the second preacher shows a better awareness of the oral nature of the homily, as he repeats the key phrase "love of God." On paper, the second preacher's sentence is less than elegant; from the pulpit, it is much more effective. The homily is first a personal word, and our word choices must reflect our conscious ownership of our message.

## The Personal Preacher Manifests Genuineness

A third aspect of the homily as personal word is that of genuineness. People want to know that the preacher is a "real person" and not some alien visitor with no lived knowledge of real human life. For such genuineness to manifest in our preaching, we must come across as sincere and transparent.

***Genuineness Demands Sincerity.*** When I commend the virtue of sincerity to my fellow preachers, I am not speaking of some internal disposition. What is important is that we come across as sincere in preaching. Communication theorists tell us that sincerity is manifested by a congruence of word, gesture, and affect. The person who appears sincere is the person whose bodily gestures and emotional affect match the content of the words being spoken. Let me give an example. If my message one Sunday is that "the love of God is overwhelming," then I must manifest certain behaviors which match that message if I am to be experienced as sincere. The love of which I speak must be seen in my gentle face and resonate in my tone of voice. My eyes must be wide open and excitement must be communicated in my gesture and volume—in other words, I should come across as someone overwhelmed. To deliver this message with downcast eyes, folded hands, and a voice wounded by depression will result in my sincerity being doubted. Again, the call to sincerity is not about merely internal disposition as much as it is about external congruence. Some mornings we may well be feeling like we'd rather be someplace else. But since the gospel demands sincere preachers, we muster all our strength to overcome our own internal drags and match our voices, faces, and bodies to our message.

***Genuineness Demands Transparency.*** A second aspect of being perceived as a "real person" is the willingness to be transparent, that is, to name our own experience as part of our preaching. I will say more about this next, when we consider the preacher as a person of faith. But at this point it is important to note that a willingness to share aspects of our real lives is a crucial element in being experienced as genuine. Now there are many caveats here. Preachers preach Jesus Christ, not themselves. As usual, David Buttrick expresses tartly his concern about transparency: "If a sermon is too much an expression of private experience, however, the gospel may be turned into an alien eccentricity that is all but unintelligible."[6] Nonetheless, as I tried to argue above, there is room in the homily for the "confessing I" or the "verifying I" or even the "biographical I." It is when we speak in the first person of our own lives that we burnish the hearer's acceptance of us as genuine preachers of the Word.

Transparency is not an end in itself, but rather a means to an end. And as a homiletic tool, it is governed by rules. The principal rule for self-disclosure is the same for the preacher as it is for the psychotherapist: one self-discloses when the purpose of the activity is advanced by such disclosure. When the homilist judges that sharing a personal experience of life or faith will help the gospel come alive, then the homilist shares that experience. The transparent preacher is always cautious, knowing that narcissism has no place in preaching and that the pulpit is not to be used as the preacher's own therapy couch. But such cautions do not annul the need for the preacher to emerge in the homily as a real human being, and then, even more, a real person of faith.

6. Buttrick, *Homiletic,* 195.

## The Personal Preacher Manifests a Deeply Held Faith

Recall that the Donatist controversy in the early Church settled the question once and for all—the personal sanctity of the minister has no effect on the sacraments. Sacraments make Christ present by the power of Christ, and even a minister who has lost his faith can validly perform a sacrament. I suppose most of the ordained are happy with this resolution, knowing as we do that we are sinners and often weak in faith. However, before we get too comfortable being "let off the hook" by the Church, it is good to be reminded of the intimate connection between the preacher's faith and the power of the homily. The Holy Spirit empowers the homily's effect, to be sure, but the faith of the preacher is an important contribution.

The Second Vatican Council sounded this theme when it quoted St. Augustine on the importance in the preacher's own life of praying with God's Word:

> Therefore, all the clergy must hold fast to the Sacred Scriptures through diligent sacred reading and careful study, especially the priests of Christ and others, such as deacons and catechists who are legitimately active in the ministry of the word. This is to be done so that none of them will become "an empty preacher of the word of God outwardly, who is not a listener to it inwardly" since they must share the abundant wealth of the divine word with the faithful committed to them, especially in the sacred liturgy.[7]

Those who do not nurture their own faith risk becoming "empty preachers."

Almost a decade later, Pope Paul VI reflected on the homily, as we saw in chapter 2. Recall how he began his analysis: "This preaching, inserted in a unique way into the Eucharistic celebration, from which it draws special force and vigor, certainly has a particular role in evangelization, to the extent that it expresses the profound faith of the sacred minister and is deeply imbued with love."[8] Preaching's role is dependent on the "profound faith" of the preacher.

Later in the same document, Pope Paul said of the twentieth century what is even truer today:

7. Second Vatican Council, Dogmatic Constitution on Divine Revelation *(Dei Verbum)* 25. The quotation cited is Augustine, *St. Augustine Sermons,* 179, 1: PL 38:966. Accessed at <http://www.vatican.va/archive/hist_councils/ii_vatican_council/documents/vat-ii_const_19651118_dei-verbum_en.html>.

8. Paul VI, apostolic exhortation on Evangelization in the Modern World *(Evangelii Nuntiandi)* 43. Accessed at <http://www.vatican.va/holy_father/paul_vi/apost_exhortations/documents/hf_p-vi_exh_19751208_evangelii-nuntiandi_en.html>.

It is often said nowadays that the present century thirsts for authenticity. . . . Either tacitly or aloud—but always forcefully—we are being asked: Do you really believe what you are proclaiming? Do you live what you believe? Do you really preach what you live? The witness of life has become more than ever an essential condition for real effectiveness in preaching.[9]

Lived faith as "an essential condition for real effectiveness in preaching"! This is no anti-Donatist solution by any means.

Pope John Paul II continued the development of this thought. He wrote: "A loving knowledge of the word of God and a prayerful familiarity with it are specifically important for the prophetic ministry of the priest. They are a fundamental condition for such a ministry to be carried out suitably . . . ," going on to quote the Second Vatican Council and St. Augustine's warning about becoming an "empty preacher."[10]

"Fundamental condition," "essential condition"—it could not be clearer that in contemporary Roman Catholic thought, the preacher must be a person of faith, preaching only that which is personally held and actively manifested. So how ought the preacher's faith be manifested on Sunday morning?

To a great extent, what has come before in this chapter has provided much of the answer to that question. The preacher emerges as a person of faith first by emerging as a real person, not fearful of speaking in the first person singular. This "real person" must be manifest, for the Sunday homily is at its core a person of faith speaking in the midst of people of faith. The preacher also emerges as a person of faith in taking explicit responsibility for the message being communicated—not "Today's readings tell us that God loves us," but "God loves us." The preacher emerges as a person of faith by a willingness to be transparent. The preacher shares his or her deeply held faith and very real doubts and struggles when such sharing advances the proclamation of the Good News. So as to avoid being perceived as an "empty preacher," homilists let people know that they themselves have first heard the Word that they now preach. We preachers are witnesses, giving testimony to what "we have heard, what we have seen with our eyes, what we have looked at and touched with our hands, concerning the word of life"

9. Ibid., 76; cf. 41.

10. John Paul II, post-synodal apostolic exhortation On the Formation of Priests in the Circumstances of the Present Day *(Pastores Dabo Vobis)* 47. Accessed at <http://www.vatican.va/holy_father/john_paul_ii/apost_exhortations/documents/hf_jp-ii_exh_25031992_pastores-dabo-vobis_en.html>.

(1 John 1:1). Finally, the preacher emerges as a person of faith by manifesting the love of God which is at the heart of our faith.

## The Personal Preacher Manifests Pastoral Love

Recall the poetic reflection of Pope Paul VI on the words of St. Paul:

> That model evangelizer, the Apostle Paul, wrote these words to the Thessalonians, and they are a program for us all: "With such yearning love we chose to impart to you not only the gospel of God but our very selves, so dear had you become to us" (1 Thessalonians 2:8). What is this love? It is much more than that of a teacher; it is the love of a father; and again, it is the love of a mother. It is this love that the Lord expects from every preacher of the Gospel.[11]

The final aspect of the homily as a personal word is the requirement that it manifest the preacher's love for the rest of the assembly. This pastoral love typically emerges in three ways.[12]

***Pastoral Love Demands Manifest Care for the Assembly.*** Our Sunday morning words on the Good News of our salvation have greater effect when spoken with a manifest care for God's people. In our bearing, in our tone of voice, we must assure our hearers that we care for them, that we stand before them because we love them. Naturally, this care is enfleshed throughout the week as we minister to our people in a variety of ways. But most parishioners will experience us only on Sundays. This means that the pastoral care exercised during the week on behalf of the few must be communicated to the many on Sundays.

***Pastoral Love Demands Respect for God's People.*** Our people need to feel not only cared for but also respected. Preachers must respect the dignity of those created in God's image and likeness; we do not preach to worms. Preachers must respect the freedom of conscience that God implants in each of us; we do not preach like a commandant barking orders. Above all, preachers must respect the faith of the people of God. As a committee of the United States Catholic bishops so succinctly put it: "A homily presupposes faith."[13]

11. Paul VI, On Evangelization in the Modern World, 79.

12. In this analysis of the behaviors that manifest pastoral love, I am influenced by the work of Carl Rogers on the conditions for relational health. See Emory A. Griffin, *A First Look at Communication Theory* (New York: McGraw-Hill, 1991) 170.

13. Bishops' Committee on Priestly Life and Ministry, United States Conference of Catholic Bishops, *Fulfilled in Your Hearing: The Homily in the Sunday Assembly* (Washington: USCCB Publishing, 1982) 17.

Indeed, the "fact that the homily is addressed to a congregation of believers gathered to worship indicates that its purpose is not conversion from radical unbelief to belief."[14] We respect what God has already accomplished in creating, redeeming, and giving faith to those who gather to hear us preach.

***Pastoral Love Demands Acceptance.*** Finally, our love for our people is made manifest by words that communicate our fundamental acceptance of them. Effective preachers have learned that fundamental lesson about human relating: we take people where they are at. Every member of our congregation is at a different place on the faith journey, and that's okay. The ebb and flow of sin and grace is a permanent condition among God's people, and that's okay. This realization is not to say that preachers can never challenge their people to greater fidelity, integrity, and sanctity. But it is to say that for any such challenge to be effective, our people must first realize that we accept them. It is only if our people first know that we love them, that we care for them, respect them, accept them, that we can possibly challenge them with any hope for effect.

## An Example of a Homily Reflecting
## Personal Characteristics

Sixteenth Sunday in Ordinary Time, Year C
[Revised Common Lectionary, Proper 11]
Luke 10:38-42

[OPENING]

After the 8:30 Mass next Sunday, I'm heading off for a week's retreat, and I have to tell you, I am dreading being beaten over the head with this morning's gospel. I dread it because I am most certainly a Martha, busy and anxious about many things. And I don't want some retreat director to talk to me like Jesus and tell me that only one thing is necessary. That's a fear partly because I'm worried I couldn't do the "one thing," but also, I'll be honest, because I doubt there really is just "one thing."

[FIRST MOVEMENT[15]]

Let me reiterate what might be on some of your minds: I doubt there is any "one thing" that is necessary. As best as I can understand this

---

14. Ibid.

15. I will discuss in chapter 10 my use of the term "movement" to describe the main sections of a homily. Let me note here, though, my partial debt to David Buttrick, who speaks of "moves" (see *Homiletic*, 23f.). His immediate model is oral communication; mine is a symphony.

story, Jesus must have been exaggerating. He must have been using overstatement to make his point to Martha. She was indeed busy to the point of distraction and needed a calming word. But his word about the one thing must be an overstatement, because otherwise, what exactly would that one thing be? Is the "one thing" we are called to faith, hope, or love? Is it repentance, or prayer? Is it listening to the Word or doing good deeds? How, O Lord, can you say there is only one thing we need?

[SECOND MOVEMENT]

Well, that's my confusion about this gospel, but I'm not using that confusion to run away from this story. I can't run away because I find so much to identify with in Martha. Martha was a person busy about many things, and so am I. And, I'd guess, so are the majority of you. It's not just adults in the workplace or adults who are home-makers who are busy, busy, busy; it's the teenagers, and even the younger kids. I never had a calendar when I was a kid, but I know many kids who have one these days, or whose parents keep one for them. High school students juggle school and work and homework and organized activities. Even young children can have schedules these days that mirror that of any adult workaholic: nursery school, nap, Japanese class, supper, soccer practice, and bedtime!

We're headed for the day when no person of any age will leave the house without a Palm Pilot. In fact, my latest cell phone has a built-in calendar and to-do list. Apparently the engineers thought that every time I make a call I should be reminded of everything I've already got to do!

Make no mistake: Martha felt herself busy, and Jesus perceived her as anxious and worried about many things. In her worry, Martha could be a symbol for twenty-first-century American life. We do, and do, and do; we spend and buy and have; and then we do some more.

[THIRD MOVEMENT]

Well, it's into that maelstrom of activity that I can imagine the voice of Jesus bellowing: "There's more to life than doing, buying, and having!" I can hear him saying to Martha and saying to us: "The many things that preoccupy you are not necessarily bad, but they are not the summit and source of your life. No, you've forgotten that in the midst of those many things, there is only one thing that is really necessary. Only one thing."

So, I go back to my earlier question: What is that one thing? Well, I've got an idea. I think that the one necessary thing that Jesus calls us to is whatever we need, at a given point in our lives, to remind us of the reality of God's love. The necessary thing is whatever I need now to better know God's love. That one necessary thing will vary from person to person, and at different points in our lives, but its object will always be God.

So, for Bob, the one necessary thing might be spending some quality time in prayer. For Anne, that one necessary thing might be volunteering to serve the poor. For José, it might be regular meditation on the Word. And for Kim it might be reconnecting with an estranged friend. At different moments in our lives, there are different paths to God. But I believe that at every moment in our lives, we are on one of those paths. We need only embrace our particular journey into God's saving love.

Jesus was right to tell Martha that no one works and worries one's way to God. Even in the midst of the many things we do, it is necessary that our focus remain on God, however that may happen.

[CLOSING]

That's my latest theory anyway. So, as I prepare for my retreat, I'd ask your prayers that I may discover the one necessary thing I need, right now, to help me know God better. And I promise to pray for you as well—Marthas all—that you might discover the one thing needed in your own life, to bring you closer to God.

❖      ❖      ❖

In this homily I tried to utilize many of the strategies mentioned in this chapter. You will have to take my word on the verbal and nonverbal communication skills, but I hope that some of the attempts to structure language for orality were clear. Among them are the use of repetition ("one necessary thing"), the use of contractions, which sound more conversational ("I've," "don't"), and the effort to enhance my "good sentence." In this homily, one of my favorite sentences is: "In her worry, Martha could be a symbol for twenty-first century American life." Such a sentence would lose much of its effect, however, had I not followed it up with a development, and then referred back to it as I began the next movement: "We do, and do, and do; we spend and buy and have; and then we do some more. Well, it's into that maelstrom of activity that I can imagine . . . ."

My strategy for taking responsibility for the choices I made in preaching this message consisted of using both first person singular language and explicit statements of responsibility. The "biographical I" emerges immediately in the opening, as I spoke about my retreat and my worry. The "representative I" appears twice—once in the First Movement and once in the Second. In each case I made the function of that "I" explicit by inviting the listeners to identify with me. The first instance: "Let me reiterate what might be on some of your minds: I doubt there is any 'one thing' that is necessary." The second instance: "Martha was a person busy about many things, and so am I. And, I'd guess, so are the majority of you." In each instance, I speak of my own experience and invite people's identification with me. This structure is much more personal, much more accurate, and much less coercive than the use of first person plural: "We are all busy about many things."

Several times I took explicit responsibility for my message. In the First Movement I said: "As best as I can understand this story . . ." In the Third Movement, not coincidentally the most crucial, I took responsibility twice: "I can imagine the voice of Jesus bellowing . . ." and "I think that the one necessary thing . . ." In this movement I also made use of the "confessional I," further signaling that I stood before my listeners sharing what I truly believed: "But I believe that at every moment in our lives, we are on one of those paths."

In terms of manifesting genuineness, the manuscript reveals the level of transparency that I felt was adequate for getting my message across effectively. I did not lapse into "true confessions" or "therapy-speak," but I did acknowledge that I found that Sunday's gospel passage both confusing and worrisome. Real people will sometimes find the Scriptures to be so, and I believe there are times when preachers are right to locate themselves with such real people.

I manifested my faith in several ways. I spoke very directly of my belief in the love of God and of praying and being prayed for. I stood as a witness to someone struggling with the Word of God and emerging from that struggle closer to God. And as just noted, the "confessional I" is willing to stand in the midst of the faithful and declare: "I believe."

Finally, I hope that my pastoral love for the rest of the assembly was clear. I empathized with the busyness that so many experience and with the confusion that Christians feel when they realize their similarity to Martha. This was non-judgmental empathy, most clear in that I included myself in the situation. As preacher, I took my people where they were at and suggested a way forward. In this I respected their faith; in fact, I honored their faith by asking for their prayers.

## The Response to a Homily Reflecting Personal Characteristics

The preacher choosing to utilize the strategies I have just illustrated is the preacher who believes that the Sunday homily is first of all a personal word, a word of faith from a person of faith. What kind of response from the assembly might such a preacher be hoping for?

Preachers manifesting effective communication skills will find their listeners reporting that they were engaged by the homilist and that they felt spoken to. Those preachers lacking such skills might hear reports of boredom, distraction, and feeling read to.

Preachers who take responsibility for their message will find listeners experiencing conviction, as opposed to hesitation or uncertainty. Preachers who are genuine will hear their listeners describe the homilist as sincere and real.

Preachers who come across as people of deeply held faith will hear comments that their homilies are faith-filled. And preachers who manifest pastoral love will hear their listeners speak of feeling cared for, respected, connected with, and accepted. But preachers who cannot communicate this requisite love will instead hear their people complain of being neglected, condescended to, and rejected.

Overall, the preacher of the Sunday homily who embraces the vision and utilizes the strategies discussed in this chapter will enjoy this judgment by the assembly: this is a "personal" preacher, a real person of faith who speaks to us with conviction and love.

# CHAPTER 5

# The Homily as Liturgical Word: The Assembly and Its Sacred Ritual

> The scribe Ezra stood on a wooden platform that had been made for the purpose. . . . And Ezra opened the book in the sight of all the people, for he was standing above all the people; and when he opened it, all the people stood up. Then Ezra blessed the LORD, the great God, and all the people answered, "Amen, Amen," lifting up their hands. Then they bowed their heads and worshiped the LORD with their faces to the ground. . . . So they read from the book, from the law of God, with interpretation. They gave the sense, so that the people understood the reading (Neh 8:4-8).

This scene from fifth century B.C.E. Jerusalem is iconic, setting a pattern that continues for Jews and Christians to this very day. Scholars still debate whether "the law of God" that Ezra proclaimed was a part or all of the recently redacted Pentateuch, but the status of that question does not change three fundamental realities. First, as soon as the conversion of the Torah from oral creature to written creature had begun, the People of God recognized the need to reconstitute the ink on the scrolls into sound. The Word of God is a spoken word.

Second, this Word was originally spoken to the chosen people, and so it is to the people gathered that it is proclaimed. Even if "private Bible reading" had been possible, it would have made no existential sense. Furthermore, this gathering is precisely a liturgical gathering (note the ritual elements of pulpit platform, common posture in standing and bowing, and prayer and response).

Third, this proclamation of ancient text demanded "interpretation . . . so that the people understood the reading." Preaching was invented out of necessity, now that God's Word, as the proclamation of written text, lacked the oral immediacy of its initial emergence. The preacher proclaims out loud what had become a fixed text, and then through preaching allows those words to live anew in the midst of the assembly.

Twenty-five hundred years later, these three realities perdure. The "people of the Book"—Jews and Christians alike—continue to read aloud from that book in a liturgical assembly and continue to depend on preachers to give the sense so that the people understand. The Pontifical Biblical Commission extracts from this historical reality a principle of biblical interpretation:

> In principle, the liturgy, and especially the sacramental liturgy, the high-point of which is the Eucharistic celebration, brings about the most perfect actualization of the biblical texts, for the liturgy places the proclamation in the midst of the community of believers, gathered around Christ so as to draw near to God.[1]

As we saw in chapter 2, the insistence of the Second Vatican Council on the homily being a part of the liturgy echoed throughout the next thirty years. This insistence recognized the pattern of worship that goes all the way back to Ezra: proclamation of sacred text in the midst of a liturgical assembly and preaching on that proclamation. In this chapter I will delve into the implications of the liturgical nature of the homily and look at strategies for preaching that recognize that nature and so allow the Word to live more fully in the midst of the gathered believers.

To begin, the overall ability that the liturgical nature of the homily demands that the preacher be able to speak and act as a minister of the liturgy. Such ability is manifest to the extent that the preacher communicates a sense of the sacred, speaks on behalf of the assembly, reinforces the listeners' experience of themselves as Church, encourages lively participation in the liturgy, and infuses the homily with the spirit of the liturgy. Let's take a closer look at each of these elements.

## The Liturgical Preacher Communicates a Sense of the Sacred

"Liturgy" probably came into use in English as a synonym for the celebration of the Eucharist, perhaps via the Eastern Churches. Its meaning broadened after the Reformation to include any "public worship con-

---

1. Pontifical Biblical Commission, The Interpretation of the Bible in the Church (Boston: St. Paul Books and Media, 1993) 124.

ducted in accordance with a prescribed form."[2] It is with that sense that the word is used in much of Christianity today.

Liturgy, then, is the public act of the Church gathered to worship God in ritual, both word and action. As worship, the liturgy seeks to place believers in the presence of God, that we might give praise and thanks. Therefore, it is incumbent upon the leader of worship (presider) to communicate a sense of that divine presence in all that is said and done. That duty extends as well to the preacher. For the homily is a part of the liturgy and so shares the nature of the liturgy: the homily, too, is an act of worship. The homilist, too, in word and gesture, must communicate a sense of the sacred. Two important means to this end are effective proclamation of Scripture and appropriate ritual presence.

***Effective Proclamation of the Scripture Passages.*** Even the most novice preacher soon discovers that a homily is helped when the passage being preached upon is proclaimed well and that a homily is harmed when the reading is butchered. Beyond the demands of the liturgy itself, then, it is in the preacher's own self interest to assure that the biblical passages are effectively proclaimed! This is easiest, of course, when the preacher proclaims the text that will be preached on. That happens frequently enough. However, it is often enough the case that the readers of Scripture and the preacher are not the same; indeed, the Catholic norm is to distinguish between those charged with reading and those charged with preaching. Either way, though, proclaiming publicly the Word of God demands careful preparation and determined use of voice and body.

Others have described the path to effective proclamation of the Scriptures.[3] Any preacher would do well to review the fundamentals of oral interpretation. In addition, though, pastors should make it a priority to work with those ministers charged with Sunday Scripture proclamation. This is "remote" preparation for Sundays, to be sure, and is therefore often lost in the more immediate demands of pastoral ministry and preparing to preach. But the importance of proclaiming the Scriptures well cannot be underestimated, and such proclamation does not happen spontaneously. The Introduction to the Lectionary for Mass says it well:

2. *Oxford English Dictionary,* 2nd ed., s.v. "liturgy."

3. Jack C. Rang, *How to Read the Bible Aloud: Oral Interpretation of Scripture* (New York: Paulist Press, 1994). This is a fully revised edition of the classic in the field, Charlotte I. Lee, *Oral Reading of the Scriptures* (Boston: Houghton Mifflin Company, 1974).

"It is necessary that those who exercise the ministry of reader . . . be truly qualified and carefully prepared so that the faithful may develop a warm and living love for Scripture from listening to the sacred texts read."

Their preparation must above all be spiritual, but what may be called a technical preparation is also needed. The spiritual preparation presupposes at least a biblical and liturgical formation. The purpose of their biblical formation is to give readers the ability to understand the readings in context and to perceive by the light of faith the central point of the revealed message. The liturgical formation ought to equip the readers to have some grasp of the meaning and structure of the liturgy of the word and of the significance of its connection with the liturgy of the Eucharist. The technical preparation should make the readers more skilled in the art of reading publicly, either with the power of their own voice or with the help of sound equipment.[4]

A large part of all Christian Sunday worship is the Liturgy of the Word—the proclamation of Scripture, the homily, and the attendant hymns and prayers. Such liturgies will have difficulty communicating a sense of the sacred apart from effective reading of the sacred text.

***Effective Liturgical Functioning (Ritual Presence).*** A second important component in communicating a sense of the sacred is the way in which the preacher behaves before and after the homily. I'm guessing that most of us have seen preachers who just don't look at home in the worship space; such preachers begin their homilies with one strike already against them. Our credibility as witnesses to the love and mercy of God suffers when our liturgical actions communicate our discomfort with public worship. Let me be concrete. Our credibility—and thus our homilies—suffer when our liturgical vesture is disheveled or in poor taste. Our credibility—and thus our homilies—suffer when we can't sit still while the readings are proclaimed, or fail to give the readers our fullest attention, manifest in eye contact and bodily posture. Our credibility—and thus our homilies—suffer when we bumble about the worship space, seemingly ignorant of the ritual in which we are taking part or even leading. Any action that communicates a lack of respect and love for the worship at hand will work to the detriment of our preaching. Conversely, though, a thoughtful and prayerful ritual presence—to space and assembly—predisposes our listeners to attend to our words as the words of a fellow worshiper of God.

4. Sacred Congregation for the Sacraments and Divine Worship, Introduction to Lectionary for Mass (Rome, 1981) 55, quoting The General Instruction of the Roman Missal, 66. In *The Liturgy Documents: A Parish Resource,* 3rd ed. (Chicago: Liturgy Training Publications, 1991) 138.

## The Liturgical Preacher Identifies with the Listeners and Speaks on Behalf of the Assembly

The most common language of liturgy is first person plural: "Let us pray," "Our Father," "Hear our prayer," "We believe in one God." As strenuously as I argued in the last chapter that the homily has a place for first person *singular* language, here I will insist with equal vigor that the homily must also speak in the language of the liturgy of which it is a part. The preacher stands before the liturgical assembly and speaks a message of his or her own choosing, it is true. But the preacher also stands as a member of that assembly, not an alien import. The effective preacher, as a human being, identifies with the members of that assembly, knowing and understanding the joys and sorrows that comprise the human story. Armed with such knowledge, and the self-reflection it entails, effective preachers are able to speak on behalf of those gathered with them to worship. They name shared experiences and shared beliefs.

"We" language is very powerful, though, and must be used appropriately. It took me a long time to figure this out, but I am convinced that Christian preachers are addicted to "we," out of control in their use of this language. In the last chapter I already pointed out one of the problems with the first person plural: used exclusively, it allows the preacher to "hide," subsumed completely into the rest of the assembly. But there is another, more insidious problem: many of the things preachers attribute to "us" are not universally true. Debaters are taught to avoid sweeping, universal statements, as they tend to be traps on cross-examination. Preachers would be smart to heed the same advice.

Let me give an example, and here I'll pick on David Buttrick, whom I admire greatly. We have already heard his dictum, "Preaching prefers a language of 'we' and 'our' and 'us.'" Buttrick follows this dictum too completely, I think, and in that he is not alone. Here is a section of one of his sermons:

> Have you noticed? Lately, on the TV screen, we've seen pictures of hunger. There they are, the hungry children of Ethiopia. We see them cradled, listlessly, in someone's bony lap. . . . From the television screen their black eyes stare up at us. So we walk over and switch channels, searching for sports or a half-hour sitcom. What are we doing? Perhaps we're evading ourselves. We don't want to feel guilty for what we've got. After all, we don't want to feel responsible. Down deep, we don't want to change our lives because of them.[5]

5. David Buttrick, *Homiletic: Moves and Structures* (Philadelphia: Fortress Press, 1987) 130.

This is a representative example of the "we"-addicted preacher, and on analysis, the use of first person plural here is simply not justified. It is simply not the case that everyone in church that morning had seen the hungry children of Ethiopia. Further, among those who did, it is simply not the case that all of them switched channels. Further still, among those who did see the pictures of hunger, undoubtedly some of them did feel responsible, and perhaps even a few changed their lifestyle in response. All these likelihoods are denied by the insistent use of "we." Those in the assembly who did not look away from the awful face of hunger are rendered invisible by the "we," indeed rendered "other" than the "we" of the assembly that the preacher claims to be speaking on behalf of.

"We" language is very powerful and so must be used appropriately. My rule of thumb is this: only fashion "we" statements that can be made with theological or scientific certitude. Under this rule, it is appropriate to note that "we are all sinners" or that "we have been saved by Jesus Christ." It is appropriate to say that "the Holy Spirit dwells in us" and that "we are created in the image and likeness of God." These are true statements and therefore appropriate uses of the first person plural. But that is not the case with a common statement like "we are all invited to the eucharistic table. . . ." In most churches there is a minimum age for taking communion; to say "we are all invited" is to exclude from the preacher's "we" at the very least many of the children present. So, too, when reflecting on particular sins, as Buttrick did in the example above, preachers must be cautious not to tar every listener with the same brush. It is theologically certain that "we are all sinners"; it is not certain that "we are all greedy" or "we are all racists."

So the liturgical preacher does identify with the rest of the assembly and speak on its behalf. Such a preacher names the beliefs and human experiences shared by all who gather on Sunday. The liturgical preacher uses the most common language of the liturgy—first person plural—with great intentionality and care.

Liturgical language also uses direct address, an "I" speaking to a "you": "The Lord be with you." "Lift up your hearts." "May Almighty God bless you." Direct address can also play a role in our Sunday preaching. When used sparingly and carefully, direct address by the preacher of the rest of the assembly can be quite powerful. I remember asking a preacher friend of mine what homily he had given that seemed to have the most effect. He said it was one given to a group of high school students preparing for confirmation. My friend was a typical "we"-addicted preacher, but at the last moment the Spirit moved him. Rather than his usual "God loves us," he looked the kids in their faces and told them, "God loves you." In retrospect, my friend marveled at how the change in grammatical person had strengthened the power of his message.

So, while first person plural is the most common language of the liturgy, and so of our homilies, the direct address of the liturgy can also be used, carefully, to great effect.

## The Liturgical Preacher Reinforces the Assembly's Identity as Church

Preachers identify with the rest of the assembly. But even more, effective preachers recognize that the identity of that assembly is precisely "Church." It is the Church of Jesus Christ that gathers in a million places each Sunday. The "we" of the liturgy, then, is not only "we humans," but "we, the sinful and yet redeemed followers of the Christ." Effective preaching reminds listeners often of this "we," reinforcing the listeners' experience of themselves as Church.

At least among Roman Catholics, one of the great ecclesiological leaps forward came in the wake of the Second Vatican Council. Especially in the second chapter of its Dogmatic Constitution on the Church, the council reminded Christians over and over again that the Church is "the people of God." At one point, the text equates the two terms explicitly: "the Church or people of God."[6] For typical Roman Catholics, this theological fact came as quite a surprise, for in common usage "church" referred first to the neighborhood building where worship took place, and second, to the pope and bishops. But the council insisted that the Church is all the people of God, and furthermore, that that identity was most clear on Sunday mornings. For the liturgy "is the outstanding means whereby the faithful may express in their lives, and manifest to others, the mystery of Christ and the real nature of the true Church."[7]

6. Second Vatican Council, Dogmatic Constitution on the Church *(Lumen Gentium)* 13. Accessed at <http://www.vatican.va/archive/hist_councils/ii_vatican_council/documents/vat-ii_const_19641121_lumen-gentium_en.html>.

7. Second Vatican Council, Constitution on the Sacred Liturgy *(Sacrosanctum Concilium)* 2. Accessed at <http://www.vatican.va/archive/hist_councils/ii_vatican_council/documents/vat-ii_const_19631204_sacrosanctum-concilium_en.html>. See Pope John Paul II, "For [the Risen

For most Catholics, awareness of their identity as Church came through preaching. It was preachers who took the reminders of the council and made them real, Sunday after Sunday. And reminding the gathered assembly that they are Church remains a part of liturgical preaching. At times the people's identity as Church will be at the heart of homilies, for instance when preaching on 1 Peter 2:9 ("But you are a chosen race, a royal priesthood, a holy nation, God's own people"—second reading on the Fifth Sunday of Easter, Year A). But other techniques can be used much more frequently and easily. For instance, preachers can expand any "we" to "we the Church" or make statements like "we are the Church, and as Church we. . . ," followed by whatever point is being made. Or again, a simple phrase like "sisters and brothers in Christ" affirms and renews our baptismal unity, and as such finds a home in our Sunday preaching. St. Augustine said of eucharistic communion: "Receive who you are." So, too, in our homiletic communion, the rest of the assembly hears anew who we are, in Christ. Consistent attention to the assembly's identity as Church will help them grow more deeply into that identity.

## The Liturgical Preacher Encourages
## Fully Conscious and Active Participation in the Liturgy

In reforming the liturgy of the Catholic Church, the Second Vatican Council had as its principal goal drawing the people of God more deeply into the words and actions of the liturgy. The Constitution on the Sacred Liturgy put it plainly and well:

> Mother Church earnestly desires that all the faithful should be led to that fully conscious and active participation in liturgical celebrations which is demanded by the very nature of the liturgy. Such participation by the Christian people as "a chosen race, a royal priesthood, a holy nation, a redeemed people" (1 Pet. 2:9; cf. 2:4-5), is their right and duty by reason of their baptism.
>
> In the restoration and promotion of the sacred liturgy, this full and active participation by all the people is the aim to be considered before all else; for it is the primary and indispensable source from which the faithful are to de-

---

Christ's] presence to be properly proclaimed and lived, it is not enough that the disciples of Christ pray individually. . . . It is important therefore that they come together to express fully the very identity of the Church, the *ekklesia,* the assembly called together by the Risen Lord. . . ." Apostolic letter On Keeping the Lord's Day Holy *(Dies Domini)* 31. Accessed at <http://www.vatican.va/holy_father/john_paul_ii/apost_letters/documents/hf_jp-ii_apl_05071998_dies-domini_en.html>.

rive the true Christian spirit; and therefore pastors of souls must zealously strive to achieve it, by means of the necessary instruction, in all their pastoral work.[8]

As we saw in chapter 2, one of the early documents issued to help implement the council's liturgical reform recognized that all the words and actions of the presider/preacher play an important part in deepening people's participation.

> To ensure that the celebration is conducted properly and that the faithful take an active part, the ministers should not only fulfill their role correctly according to the norms of liturgical laws, but their very bearing should communicate a sense of the sacred. . . . [A]nything that [priests'] functions require them to pronounce [must be] said or sung so distinctly that the people hear it clearly, grasp its meaning, and are thus drawn to respond and participate willingly (*Sacrosanctum Concilium* 11).[9]

Or as the Introduction to the Lectionary puts it, the homily "must always lead the community of the faithful to celebrate the eucharist wholeheartedly. . . ."[10]

There are both direct and indirect ways in which the homilist can lead the rest of the assembly into fuller and more active participation in the liturgy. Directly, we will sometimes preach about our common prayer—homilies whose chief purpose is to draw people more deeply into the worship of the day or season. By reflecting on the liturgical mystery, by better explaining it, by correlating it with our daily lives, the preacher encourages the fuller participation of the Sunday assembly. More indirectly, but as important, is the homilist's own "bearing" during preaching and the rest of the liturgy. For instance, our own bodily attention to the readings encourages those who see us to attend. Our own response in song to the liturgical texts encourages song in the rest of the assembly. If the preacher is also the presider, then brief invitations to pray or to listen or to sing are always a possibility for encouraging more active participation. And although the homily is a monologue, African American preachers and others have taught us all that both preacher and listener can grow in active

8. Ibid., 14.

9. Sacred Congregation for Rites (Consilium), Instruction on the Worship of the Eucharist *(Eucharisticum Mysterium)* 20, in International Committee on English in the Liturgy, *Documents on the Liturgy: 1963–1979* (Collegeville: The Liturgical Press, 1982) 179.

10. Introduction to the Lectionary 24, in *The Liturgy Documents,* 133.

engagement in preaching when call and response seem appropriate. Let the Church say "Amen!"

## The Liturgical Preacher Infuses the Homily with the Spirit of the Day's Liturgy

A final implication of the homily's identity as a part of the liturgy is the need for preachers to infuse their preaching with the spirit of the liturgy being celebrated. For the majority of the year, the very nature of Sunday itself sets the tone. In other seasons of the year (principally Advent/Christmas and Lent/Easter), the mystery of Sunday is further specified. Let me take a look at those two broad categories of liturgy and their implications for preaching.

For most of year, the homily is a "Sunday word." The Church gathers each week on the day of the Resurrection to experience anew the presence of the Risen One. Our scriptural readings, music, and other liturgical texts and actions meditate on and celebrate in one way or another our participation in the death and resurrection of Jesus—and so, too, must our homilies.

As a preacher, I have found helpful the reflections on the nature of Sunday found in the 1998 apostolic letter On Keeping the Lord's Day Holy. Pope John Paul II's sustained theological and pastoral analysis of Sunday can be an inspiration to preachers as we prepare to preach each week. I see four ways in which our understanding of Sunday can be infused in our preaching.[11]

***The Sunday Homily Is an "Easter Homily."*** Sunday was a workday for the first Christians, not a part of "the weekend." It was a most inconvenient day to gather, which is why the gatherings were most often held in the evening or very early in the morning. Christians met on that day because it was the day of the week that God raised Jesus from the dead. Every Sunday is a commemoration of the Resurrection, and so every Sunday homily is in some sense an Easter homily. We preach Christ crucified and raised, the pledge of our own future glory. The Resurrection was the defining event that influenced the telling of the story of Jesus; each pericope has as its subtext that Jesus is alive and with us. Our homilies must have the same character. If a preacher always speaks of Jesus in the past tense,

---

11. These reflections on the relationship between Sunday and the homily are based on my "Homily as Sunday Word," *New Theology Review* (August 2001) 76–78.

for instance, the preacher risks consigning Jesus to the ranks of interesting historical characters. But, "Sunday is not only the remembrance of a past event: it is a celebration of the living presence of the Risen Lord in the midst of his own people."[12] Jesus is risen and lives among us, and our Sunday preaching must reflect that.

***The Sunday Homily Names the Week's Struggles and Graces.*** What John Paul II says about the Sunday Eucharist in general is a great prescription for our Sunday preaching:

> The rhythm of the week prompts us to gather up in grateful memory the events of the days which have just passed, to review them in the light of God and to thank him for his countless gifts. . . . The truth that the whole community shares in Christ's sacrifice is especially evident in the Sunday gathering, which makes it possible to bring to the altar the week that has passed, with all its human burdens.[13]

As preachers strive to make the gospel come alive, we, too, gather up what has passed, view it in the light of God, and name the grace that abounds. Sunday preachers are in tune with the way God's grace is at work in homes and schools, at work and in the public square during the week, and we name that in our preaching on the Lord's Day.

***The Sunday Homily Expresses Christian Joy.*** John Paul reminds us that Sunday, as the day of Resurrection, is "the day of joy in a very special way." He quotes the *Disdiscalia:* "On the first day of the week, you shall all rejoice."[14] He then quotes Pope Paul VI's exhortation On Christian Joy. Pope Paul concluded that exhortation by asking that "on the Lord's Day, the Church should witness powerfully to the joy experienced by the Apostles when they saw the Lord on the evening of Easter. To this end, he urged pastors to insist 'upon the need for the baptized to celebrate the Sunday Eucharist in joy.'"[15]

If the baptized are to rejoice on Sundays, we preachers must do our part to ensure that the news we proclaim is *good* news, worthy of joy. Homilies that leave people guilty and dispirited conflict with the nature of Sunday itself. Sundays proclaim the Good News of the Resurrection and of

12. John Paul II, On Keeping the Lord's Day Holy, 31.
13. Ibid., 42, 43.
14. Ibid., 55.
15. Ibid., 58.

our inclusion into Christ through baptism. Sunday preachers proclaim the Good News of a world charged with the grandeur of God. We proclaim Good News, and so we celebrate the Day of Joy.

***The Sunday Homily Expresses Christian Love.*** John Paul takes an important step beyond joy when he writes:

> To experience the joy of the Risen Lord deep within is to share fully the love which pulses in his heart: there is no joy without love!. . . The Sunday Eucharist, therefore, not only does not absolve the faithful from the duties of charity, but on the contrary commits them even more "to all the works of charity, of mercy, of apostolic outreach. . . ."[16]

As homilists, we serve this aspect of Sunday preaching by keeping foremost in our minds the commandment of love. Our priority is love, for that is our identity: to love as we have been loved. The Sunday homily is not an occasion to slap people into submission, but to emphasize the gift of God's love, a gift we are called to share.

Sunday preachers suggest ways of living lives of love only in light of the freely given gift God has already bestowed upon us. When our preaching reflects the theology of Sunday itself, it not only makes the Word of God come alive but also enlivens and empowers Christian response to the Word, in worship and service. Indeed, John Paul notes that if love is experienced as central to the Sunday mystery, then "not only the Sunday Eucharist but the whole of Sunday becomes a great school of charity, justice, and peace."[17] Preachers serve that vision by the words we speak on Sunday.

So, in those four ways at least, our homilies on the Lord's Day are to be true "Sunday words." But what of those times in the Church's liturgical year with a special focus? In Advent and the Christmas season, in Lent and the Easter season, the liturgical preacher is especially attuned to the context of the homily in the wider seasonal liturgy. During these seasons it is even clearer that, in the apt expression of Dianne Bergant, the scriptural readings have been de-contextualized from the Bible and re-contextualized by the wider liturgy. A scriptural passage read on an "ordinary" Sunday takes on new tones and reveals new insights when proclaimed in the context of a liturgical season, and the preacher must attend to that. In addition, the prayers and songs of the season often provide wonderful

16. Ibid., 69.
17. Ibid., 73.

sources of homiletic imagery. Preachers in those Churches with developed ritual books will find a treasure trove of imagery and insight among the prayers available in a given season.

## An Example of a Homily Reflecting Liturgical Characteristics

Third Sunday of Advent, Year B
(Isaiah 61:1-2a, 10-11; Luke 1:46-48, 49-50, 53-54;
1 Thessalonians 5:16-24)

[OPENING]

"Life, liberty and the pursuit of happiness"—so does our Constitution speak of our most basic rights. "The pursuit of happiness": is this the American way of talking about the joy which emerges from our readings? Are happiness and joy the same thing?

[FIRST MOVEMENT]

The Third Sunday of Advent has traditionally been called "Gaudete" Sunday, that is, "Rejoice!" Sunday, and many of the texts of this morning's Mass evoke the emotion of joy:

• "I rejoice heartily in the Lord, in my God is the joy of my soul" (Isa 61:10).
• "My spirit finds joy in God my savior" (Luke 1:46).
• "Rejoice always!" (1 Thess 5:16).

Perhaps the most provocative text of all, though, is the opening prayer, wherein we prayed that "we may . . . experience the joy of salvation."

We prayed to experience an emotion—imagine that! This is the point where cognitive people start to get a little uncomfortable, and "feelings people" finally start to feel at home in our dogma-heavy Church. May we experience the joy of salvation!

[SECOND MOVEMENT]

Joy: what is it? It is an emotion, a feeling, but one that goes far beyond passing happiness. I'd like to give you the first definition of "joy" from the Oxford English Dictionary, and I'd ask you to close your eyes, go deep into your heart, use the gift of memory and imagination, and re-experience a joy that you have known. Joy is: "a vivid emotion of pleasure arising from a sense of well-being or satisfaction; the feeling or state of being highly pleased or delighted; exultation of spirit; gladness; delight."

• "A vivid emotion of pleasure arising from a sense of well-being or satisfaction": Imagine this emotion, so high-flying and yet so grounding, an experience of pleasure that takes your breath away and yet leaves you feeling secure with yourself and the world. Joy!

• "The feeling of being highly pleased or delighted": Remember that emotion that accompanies an action of which you've been intensely proud or that feeling of delight that attends your receiving the perfect gift from someone you love. Joy!

• "Exultation of spirit": Call to heart that emotion that soars on eagles' wings and carries your spirit, what is most you, to the highest planes of consciousness, to communion with another or even with God. Joy!

[THIRD MOVEMENT]

This is joy, and on this Sunday we remind ourselves that "joy" is a fitting symbol of salvation, of God's love, of our eternal destiny. We the Church pray with a special intensity during Advent to experience the joy of salvation.

This day gets its name of "Rejoice Sunday" from St. Paul. A line from his letter to the Philippians forms the opening chant of the Mass: "Rejoice in the Lord always! Again I say, rejoice!" We hear similar sentiments from Paul in today's second reading, wherein he writes to the Thessalonians: "Rejoice always." Now lest anyone get sidetracked here by the realization that we don't always feel joyful, let's remind ourselves what was going on in Paul's life when he wrote these words. Paul was at the height of his church-founding missionary travels when he wrote today's second reading. The church in Thessalonica needed a word of encouragement, and Paul was happy to oblige— "Rejoice always," he wrote to them. Now jump ahead about seven or eight years. Paul is confined after one of his many arrests, probably in Ephesus. It is from prison that he writes to the church at Philippi: "Rejoice always! Again I say, rejoice!"

Paul's joy, joy that is rooted in the experience of Christ, is clearly not identical with the passing happiness of the world, the happiness dependent upon circumstance, temperament, or material security. If joy were like that fickle emotion, Paul could hardly have written "Rejoice always" while in chains.

Our U.S. Constitution speaks of the right of the "pursuit of happiness." Our culture has taken that right, it would seem, to the nth degree. Much of our consumer economy is about products and services that are supposed to make us "happy." But salvation in Christ is not about the pursuit of happiness, it is about the gift of joy—joy that is given, not pursued; joy that is rooted so deeply in God that no passing circumstance of this world can wipe it out.

[CLOSING]

An ancient legend tells us that Jesus had a nickname as boy, and that name was "Hilaros" in Greek, or "Hilaritas" in Latin. The word means "cheerful" or "joyful." What a beautiful legend, so full of insight into who Jesus was and is. His playmates as a youth saw in him a joy so deeply rooted that it seemed to characterize him. As children, they did not yet appreciate the meaning of his given name: "Jesus," which means "God saves." But with youthful insight they saw into his heart nonetheless, and called him Hilaritas, the Joyful One.

This Advent morning we look at Jesus anew, we look into his eyes and see the joy that surpasses any happiness, and together we pray that in this holy season we might experience his joy, the joy of salvation.

❖   ❖   ❖

In this homily I employed many of the practices discussed in this chapter. My intention was to lead my listeners into a deeper appreciation of the joy that marks the Advent season; my basic approach was to contrast the American "pursuit of happiness" with the "pure gift of joy." In doing so, I did identify with the assembly and speak on its behalf. My "we" language passes my test of theological certainty; most of the usage reflects "our" identity as a liturgical assembly: "we pray," "we hear." I also used direct address, in the Second Movement when "I" the preacher asked the "you's" of the rest of the assembly to re-experience a joy you have known. Because each of us has different experiences of this emotion, it seemed fitting that my language respect that fact—hence the direct address.

In this homily I also tried to reinforce the assembly's identity as Church. In one sense, the very structure of the homily accomplished this, as it was a sustained contrast between us as Americans and us as Church—happiness versus joy. But at one point, in the Third Movement, I employed the simple technique of the expanded "we": "we the Church."

Further, I encouraged fully conscious and active participation in the liturgy. My hope was that the spirit of Gaudete Sunday would resonate in the hearts of my listeners as they remembered joys that they had experienced and correlated them with the joy of which the readings spoke. By this correlation I hoped to bring people into deeper participation, both in that Sunday and in the whole of the Advent season.

Finally, I certainly did infuse my preaching with the spirit of the day's liturgy. I briefly revisited three of the day's Lectionary readings, bringing out the shared theme of joy. My efforts in this area were further enhanced by using other texts of the liturgy, in this case the opening prayer (First Movement) and the opening chant (Third Movement; the chant of course is itself a Bible verse).

## The Response to a Homily Reflecting Liturgical Characteristics

The preacher choosing to utilize the strategies I discussed in this chapter is the preacher who has embraced the implications of the homily being a part of the liturgy. What sort of reaction might the preacher expect from the hearers of a homily that reflects its liturgical nature?

First, preachers who communicate a sense of the sacred in all that they say and do during worship will hear their fellow worshipers echo back feelings of having participated in something sacred. They will comment on the care and manifest comfort of the preacher in the sanctuary and on the liveliness of the scriptural proclamation.

Preachers who successfully identify with the rest of the liturgical assembly and speak on their behalf will hear their listeners say things like: "I recognized myself in that homily" or "I felt included." Preachers who do not master the liturgical "we," however, are likely to face the harsh judgment: "I just couldn't identify."

When we preachers reinforce our listeners' identity as Church, we are likely to hear feedback like: "I felt a part of the community," or "I experienced the reality of fellowship," or "I felt in communion with God and others." The converse reactions might include feelings of isolation or alienation—guaranteed results when preachers paint with the "we" brush too broadly, leaving various individuals alone.

Preachers who succeed in encouraging active participation in the liturgy will find assembly members reporting that they felt "involved" in a true "celebration," as opposed to passive attendance at a lecture. Such preachers will also have the evidence of their own eyes and ears during the liturgy, as the communal responses and song fill the space with praise.

Finally, preachers who infuse their homilies with the spirit of the day's liturgy will likely hear approving comments like: "Everything fit together so well this morning" or "You've given me a new way of approaching Lent."

Overall, preachers of the Sunday homily who embrace the vision and utilize the strategies discussed in this chapter will enjoy the knowledge that they are liturgical preachers, ministers of the Word, who fully appreciate that "the liturgy . . . brings about the most perfect actualization of the biblical texts, for the liturgy places the proclamation in the midst of the community of believers."[18]

18. Interpretation of the Bible in the Church, 124.

CHAPTER 6

# The Homily as Inculturated Word: Correlating Experience and Tradition

When the day of Pentecost had come, they were all together in one place. And suddenly from heaven there came a sound like the rush of a violent wind, and it filled the entire house where they were sitting. Divided tongues, as of fire, appeared among them, and a tongue rested on each of them. All of them were filled with the Holy Spirit and began to speak in other languages, as the Spirit gave them ability.

Now there were devout Jews from every nation under heaven living in Jerusalem. And at this sound the crowd gathered and was bewildered, because each one heard them speaking in the native language of each. Amazed and astonished, they asked, "Are not all these who are speaking Galileans? And how is it that we hear, each of us, in our own native language? . . .—in our own languages we hear them speaking about God's deeds of power" (Acts 2:1-8, 11).

From the beginning of the Church, the Holy Spirit has been at work empowering preachers to preach God's power in language that can be understood by their hearers. On the day of Pentecost, admittedly, the apostles seemed to have enjoyed a rather easy time of it; preachers today labor mightily to cooperate with the Spirit in making their homilies understandable. But such a goal is irreplaceable.

Helpful shorthand for this process of rendering the gospel intelligible is "inculturation." Without using the word, the Second Vatican Council set the stage for a renewed apprehension of Pentecost, recognizing the role of human culture in, and setting a "law" for, preaching:

[T]he Church herself knows how richly she has profited by the history and development of humanity.

The experience of past ages, the progress of the sciences, and the treasures hidden in the various forms of human culture, by all of which the nature of man himself is more clearly revealed and new roads to truth are opened, these profit the Church, too. For, from the beginning of her history she has learned to express the message of Christ with the help of the ideas and terminology of various philosophers, and has tried to clarify it with their wisdom, too. Her purpose has been to adapt the Gospel to the grasp of all as well as to the needs of the learned, insofar as such was appropriate. Indeed this accommodated preaching of the revealed word ought to remain the law of all evangelization.[1]

Appropriate "adaptation" and "accommodation" are the tools by which the ancient Word releases its power today. Less than a decade after the council, Rome declared that the bishop, as a homiletic preacher, "should above all understand the mentality, customs, conditions, dangers and prejudices of the individuals and groups to whom he speaks and he should constantly adapt his method of teaching to their capacity, character and needs."[2] The purpose of this homiletic adaptation was clear: "That he may more easily move the hearts of the faithful and draw them to the truth."[3]

As reflection upon the task of evangelization continued, "accommodation" gave way to the fuller concept of "inculturation." We saw in chapter 2 that Pope John Paul II introduced the term "inculturation" into Catholic teaching and later applied it specifically to preaching. His comment in 1993 could not have been any more forceful. Addressing biblical scholars and preachers, he said: "[I]n order for [the Bible] to have profound effect, there must be inculturation according to the genius proper to each people. . . ."[4]

The document of the Pontifical Biblical Commission, The Interpretation of the Bible in the Church, gave a concise theological rationale for inculturation.

The theological foundation of inculturation is the conviction of faith that the Word of God transcends the cultures in which it has found expression

1. Second Vatican Council, Pastoral Constitution on the Church in the Modern World *(Gaudium et Spes)* 44. Accessed at <http://www.vatican.va/archive/hist_councils/ii_vatican_council/documents/vat-ii_cons_19651207_gaudium-et-spes_en.html>.

2. Congregation for Bishops, Directory on the Pastoral Ministry of Bishops *(Ecclesiae Imago)* (Ottawa: Canadian Catholic Conference Publications Service, 1973) 59.

3. Ibid.

4. John Paul II, address to the Pontifical Biblical Commission, in The Interpretation of the Bible in the Church (Boston: St. Paul Books and Media, 1993) 15.

and has the capability of being spread in other cultures, in such a way as to be able to reach all human beings in the cultural context in which they live.[5]

When inculturated preaching occurs, every Sunday is the Day of Pentecost. As the apostles themselves, today's preachers are called to present the Good News in a fashion that is intelligible to a specific group of hearers. Preachers draw from the real lives of the assembly words, images, and experiences that can be used to bring the gospel to those gathered. This act of inculturation is no less than the correlation of the Scriptures with present experience and their mutual interpretation. Inculturating preachers use language easily understood by the listeners and illustrate their homilies with relevant imagery. Inculturation is further served by preachers who manifest an empathic knowledge of the real life of the gathered people of God. With these tools in place, the inculturating preacher interprets Scripture in terms of today's world and interprets today's world in the light of Scripture. Let's take a closer look at each of these aspects of inculturated preaching.

## The Inculturating Preacher Uses Language Easily Understood by the Listeners

Homiletic language exhibits a preference for the simple, plain, conversational speech of the gathered assembly.

We've already seen that the Roman Catholic vision of the homily suggests such straightforward and accessible language, but we preachers can take a hint from philology as well. Those who preach in English are preaching in the language with the largest vocabulary ever. Written English has about 1.5 million words! A giant tome like Webster's Third Dictionary contains about 450,000 words. According to David Buttrick, the average vocabulary of a theological school graduate is about 12,000 words. Now that might not seem too impressive until one recalls that the average American vocabulary is about 7,500 words. But even that number overstates the case, for that average includes the technical terms that belong to our own jobs and our own local idiom. Subtracting those sets of words, the philologists tell us that the average vocabulary shared by English-speaking Americans is about 5,000 words.[6]

5. Pontifical Biblical Commission, The Interpretation of the Bible in the Church, 122.
6. David Buttrick, *Homiletic: Moves and Structures* (Philadelphia: Fortress Press, 1987) 187–188.

There are two things to note about this number. First, please note that the average preacher with a Master of Divinity degree knows about 7,000 more words than the average parishioner. This in itself could clearly be a problem. As enamored as we theology buffs might be with our "eschatology" and "soteriology," as transported as we might be by the "circumincession" of the Trinity, as passionate as we might be about debating "transubstantiation" and "transignification,"our theological flashes pale in comparison to the eyes glazing over as we preach. The content of our faith must be spoken of and celebrated with language that is accessible to our hearers if it is to help them grow closer to the Lord. A good rule of thumb for the Sunday preacher: If you can't talk about it without resorting to twenty-dollar words, save the topic for an adult education series.

There is a second thing to note about the 5,000-word vocabulary of many of those in our assemblies. No preacher should feel hamstrung in the least by this simple vocabulary, for it closely resembles in size the vocabulary of the New Testament itself.

Ponder the glorious height and breadth and depth of the New Testament, one of the most enduring works of religious literature and a cornerstone of the Church. And then ponder all that has been accomplished with a mere 5,436 different words. But the story is even more startling. Eighty percent of the verses of the New Testament are composed of only 314 words, each used about fifty times. Imagine, 314 words and yet the depth of faith conveyed! The preacher's task is to do what the evangelists did, to do what Jesus did, namely, to use creatively the simple language of the people, thereby allowing the Good News to be actualized anew within a given assembly.

So how do we go about preparing homilies with language that will be easily understood? I think the first step is one we probably learned at our mother's knee: listen before you speak. To be truly inculturating preachers, we need to listen very carefully to our people as they speak of their faith. How do they express the joys of salvation and the trials of belief? What words do they use when asking for baptism or for the burial of a loved one? What do they say in the waiting rooms of hospitals and at the bars of wedding receptions? One of the ways our respect for the people of God emerges outside the pulpit is by our careful listening to them. Once in the pulpit, we use what we have heard to give the gospel anew as a gift to the assembly.

A second method presents itself, especially to newer preachers. As they make the transition from seminary to parish, novice preachers would do well to share their manuscripts with people who do not have the benefit of a Master of Divinity degree. They should preach their homily to a family member or friend or trusted parishioner—anyone who can be depended upon to give an honest appraisal of the language used. They shouldn't settle for a one-word answer to a closed question either: "Did you understand me?" Rather, they should listen carefully to the response to an open question: "Tell me what you heard me preach."

Two final thoughts on using language easily understood by our listeners. First, neither I nor the Roman documents I cited are talking about "dumbing down" our homilies—unless, that is, the evangelists and Jesus himself could be so accused. The New Testament shows preachers how the most fundamental truths of our salvation in Christ can be expressed in the common language of the people. It has been done, without sacrificing depth and completeness, and it can be done, and it should be done. Second, though, as a lover of the English language, I cannot be a rigorist on this matter. There is something to be said for speaking beautifully as well as powerfully, and sometimes that means that Latin- or Greek-based words will trump good old Anglo-Saxon. If you are quite convinced that a most mellifluous word, a most propitious word, will add beauty to your homily and will be understood in context by most, even if many could not define it, go ahead and use it. The occasional twenty-dollar word can send a good message: "I am not talking down to you, and I care about making your listening an experience of beauty." However, beware that a steady diet of such words sends a terrible message: "I'm smarter than you are."

## The Inculturating Preacher Uses Relevant Illustration

Sadly, it is possible to use language easily understood by our assemblies and still fail to pass the test of relevance. The inculturating preacher's task is not only to speak plainly but also to clothe the gospel in the words and symbols of the gathered community. Jesus, of course, was a master of this aspect of preaching. His parables used familiar cultural materials to speak of the kingdom of God: sowers and seeds, builders and plans, housewives and brooms, fathers and sons. Such an approach is also evident in the earliest preaching of the Church. Think of Peter in Jerusalem, making reference not only to his hearers' past but to a well-known city monument:

Brethren, I may say to you confidently of the patriarch David that he both died and was buried, and his tomb is with us to this day. Being therefore a prophet, and knowing that God had sworn with an oath to him that he would set one of his descendants upon his throne, he foresaw and spoke of the resurrection of the Christ, that he was not abandoned to Hades, nor did his flesh see corruption. This Jesus God raised up, and of that we all are witnesses (Acts 2:29-32).

Think of Paul in Athens, also using native beliefs and monuments to proclaim the gospel:

Men of Athens, I perceive that in every way you are very religious. For as I passed along, and observed the objects of your worship, I found also an altar with this inscription, "To an unknown god." What therefore you worship as unknown, this I proclaim to you (Acts 17:22-23).

The pattern set by Jesus and continued by his followers continues as the pattern for Sunday preaching today—inculturation. The local culture gives us a wealth of material with which to enflesh each particular Sunday message. With his usual precision, David Buttrick wrote that "homiletic thinking is always a thinking of theology toward images."[7] Under the inspiration and guidance of the Holy Spirit, preachers discern each week a message arising from the Sunday Scriptures. But for that message to become an effective homily, we must think toward images. We must find the cultural vocabulary that will allow our message to resonate and achieve relevance.

What cultural materials are fair game for inculturating our homilies? There is almost no limit. Events or trends in the community or nation, the products of popular culture (movies, songs, TV, sports), art in all of its manifestations, from drama to painting to music—all this and more can be used to help our Sunday message achieve relevance.

## The Inculturating Preacher Manifests Empathic Knowledge of Real Life

Of course, to illustrate our homilies in such a way as to be received as relevant, we preachers need to be keen observers of real life—not only keen observers but empathic participants.

I recall an article in a local paper in which a number of priests were interviewed about their opinions on a television series featuring priests. I

7. Ibid., 29.

recall it only because one of those interviewed gave an answer that shocked me, and shocks me still. He said: "I can't comment. I don't own a television." I would guess that he made that declaration with a bit of pride; I think he should have been ashamed. Like it or not, television is arguably the most potent reflector and generator of popular culture that has ever existed. For a preacher to choose to be ignorant of such a powerful force in the life of the world—and of his parishioners—is shocking indeed. That priest will always be a symbol for me of preachers who fail to realize the call to inculturation or who fail to realize that successful inculturation comes only through intimate knowledge of our hearers' culture.

The inculturating preacher knows real life and has empathy for the human condition. And so the inculturating preacher owns a television, although perhaps he doesn't watch it with quite the gusto of the average American (over five hours a day!). The inculturating preacher reads the local paper and keeps up on national and global affairs. Such a preacher sees a good movie from time to time and visits the museum and art gallery and symphony hall, as well as the firefighters' picnic, the school musical, and the occasional wedding reception. The inculturating preacher even does penance by listening occasionally to talk radio. The popular personalities of that popular medium, as well as their callers, have much to teach us—painful as the experience may often be.

Knowledge of real life is key to making our homilies both intelligible and relevant. We gain some of our knowledge by our participation in the cultural realities just mentioned. We gain more of our knowledge by reflecting upon our own real lives. And, as Leonora Tubbs Tisdale argues so well in her book *Preaching as Local Theology and Folk Art,* we gain knowledge of the real lives of our congregation members by concerted effort. Tisdale suggests that a disciplined exegesis of the liturgical assembly is as necessary and as possible as an exegesis of the scriptural texts. She recommends careful attention to the "culture texts" of the congregation: its stories, archives, demographics, art and architecture, rituals, events and activities, and prominent and marginalized people. Tisdale shows how these "texts" can reveal much of the assembly's unique identity, including its views of God, humanity, nature, time, and the Church.[8]

---

8. Leonora Tubbs Tisdale, *Preaching as Local Theology and Folk Art* (Minneapolis: Fortress Press, 1997). See especially chapter 3, "Exegeting the Congregation."

The inculturating preacher is by necessity, then, a cultural anthropologist and ethnographer, although with one key difference. We preachers are not striving for the objective observation of a scientist, but rather for the empathic observation of one who loves the people we observe and serve. Like a lover, we are always hungry to know our beloved better, confident that such knowledge helps us love better and serve better.

❖   ❖   ❖

Lurking beneath the concept of inculturation is interpretation. The effective preacher does not simply repeat the scriptural text, as if by saying the words over and over they would somehow be rendered intelligible and relevant. Mere repetition of the Scriptures would not be preaching at all. As I argued in the last chapter, preaching was born of the necessity of bestowing current intelligibility and relevance to God's Word, once that word had been committed to writing. Remember Ezra, reading from the book of the law of God "with interpretation . . . so that the people could understand the reading" (Neh 8:8). Interpretation is at the heart of preaching.

Before addressing the two directions of this interpretation—text/world and world/text—let me explain what I have in mind when using the word "interpret." Many preachers think of the interpretive task as "connecting" ancient text to present people, and I myself used that terminology for many years. I have come to reject it, however, as inaccurate and even dangerous to our Sunday work. To connect is to join or fasten two disparate things to each other. I connect a hose to a water spigot; I connect a DVD player to a TV. As a preacher, though, I most certainly do not *connect* the Scriptures to God's people, as if the two were separate entities being fastened together by human effort. Rather, I have come to understand the work of homiletic interpretation as a work of *correlation.* To correlate is to set forth a mutual or reciprocal relationship. The inculturating preacher does not connect ancient text to present people but rather correlates the faith experiences of the people of God who gave birth to the Scriptures with the faith experiences of the people of God gathered for Sunday worship. The God who revealed himself to Abraham is the God with us today, and we are the direct descendants of the people whom God first chose. There is no need for preachers to search out connections, then; rather, preachers strive to recognize the already existing relationship between God's people then and God's people now. The work of homiletic interpretation is first of all the work of recognizing and setting forth the continuity of God's relationship to God's people, of recognizing and setting forth the ongoing presence and action of God from the beginning to this very day. This correlation is a two-way street, as we will now explore.

## The Inculturating Preacher Interprets Scripture in Terms of Today's World

The aspects of inculturation that have been discussed so far in this chapter can all be thought of as tools toward successful homiletic interpretation. To interpret a Sunday biblical passage in terms of today's world is first to speak in language easily understood by those gathered. Often enough, this requires a kind of translation from biblical vocabulary to the vocabulary of today. Arguably, there are a few key terms that are irreplaceable, like "God" or "sin." But recall the differential in vocabularies between most preachers and many hearers, and recommit yourself to finding words to speak more understandably of biblical concepts like "covenant," "redemption," and "grace." Beyond such terms, many of our Sunday passages are also replete with geographical, historical, and personal references that will mean nothing to your people without your help. Toward this end, a nice exercise for both proclaimers and preachers of the Bible is to write out a version of the day's passage in your own words. If you are able to tell the story or recount the lesson in familiar terms, you are well on your way to proclaiming it with conviction and preaching from it with accessibility.

Further, a part of interpreting a Sunday biblical passage in terms of today's world is illustrating the central contribution of the text with relevant material. Correlation is the key. As the preacher ponders the faith experience that gave rise to the day's pericope, he or she simultaneously ponders the times, places, and circumstances in which similar faith experiences occur today. From the compact language of image and metaphor, through the everyday example or brief anecdote, to the complexity of a story, illustrative material speaks to the senses and memories of those gathered. Illustrations help the assembly in its own internal correlation, as the familiar reveals God still at work, just as in the Scriptures. If a preacher is having a difficult time finding images, examples, and stories to put flesh to message, it is quite possible that the work of correlating then and now has not adequately been done. If your message defies illustration from real life, how can it be relevant to today's hearers?

A final part of interpreting a Sunday biblical passage in terms of today's world is our bringing to bear on the passage our empathic understanding of real life. For our interpretation to be accessible and relevant, we need to know life as it is lived by the people who have gathered on Sunday. To re-read a biblical passage in the light of current circumstances requires that we know current circumstances and that they resonate in head and heart. Effective homiletic interpretation is always contextual interpretation; hearers must know that the preacher is "on the same page," or at least "from the same planet"!

## The Inculturating Preacher Interprets Today's World in the Light of Scripture

The work of homiletic interpretation is always bi-directional—not only a contextual interpretation of Scripture but also a scriptural interpretation of context. A committee of the U.S. bishops famously captured this second aspect of homiletic interpretation, although unfortunately expressing it in contrast to the first aspect: "the goal of the liturgical preacher is not to interpret a text of the Bible (as would be the case in teaching a Scripture class) as much as to draw on the texts of the Bible as they are presented in the Lectionary to interpret people's lives."[9] Better to say that the preacher's goal is the reciprocal interpretation of scriptural text and real-life context.

How does the preacher go about interpreting the world in the light of Scripture? I will have much more to say about method in chapter 9, but for now I mention the process known as "theological reflection." Theological reflection is a spiritual and ministerial discipline, well known to seminary graduates and Clinical Pastoral Education students over the past three decades. At its heart is the correlation of life experience with our faith tradition—Scripture, creed, doctrine, and worship. Seminarians are taught to reflect on ministerial experiences in the light of faith, thus correlating God's work here and now with God's work throughout salvation history. Pastors who carry the spiritual discipline of theological reflection into their own ministries have a significant leg up when it comes time to prepare the Sunday homily. If one has spent some time each day correlat-

9. Committee on Priestly Life and Ministry, National Conference of Catholic Bishops, *Fulfilled in Your Hearing: The Homily in the Sunday Assembly* (Washington: USCCB Publishing, 1983) 20.

ing the events of real life (events involving parishioners, family and friends, the broader community) with aspects of our Christian tradition, the immediate homiletic task of interpreting the world in the light of Scripture comes most naturally. Theological reflection practiced regularly by the preacher is sermon preparation in its broadest sense, preparation precisely to interpret today's world in light of the Sunday text.

## An Example of a Homily Reflecting Inculturating Characteristics

Second Sunday of Advent, Year A
Matthew 3:1-12
*(Preached three months after September 11, 2001)*

[OPENING]

I had to take my shoes off! I had to take my shoes off! Three nights ago, in the Cincinnati airport, I had to take my shoes off before I boarded a plane. After searching my bag and frisking me, they wanted to make sure that I didn't have any weapon hidden in the soles of my shoes. So . . . I took my shoes off, and I marveled at the heightened security. We Americans certainly are more on guard, watching, alert to what may come.

[FIRST MOVEMENT]

And so, shoeless, it struck me: our country is living its own dark version of Advent. We are a country on the watch, a country vigilant, a country waiting.

After the events of September 11, we've been told again and again that we can expect more terrorism. And three times, most recently last week, Secretary of Homeland Security Tom Ridge has gone before the cameras to declare a state of heightened alert. This time Mr. Ridge told Americans: "Stay on guard . . . Be vigilant, be alert." Of course, since the threats intercepted have not been very specific, we find ourselves on guard for something that is coming, but we don't know what or when or where.

So, we're on high alert. But many of us are a bit confused about what this means. People are asking: "How is my daily life supposed to reflect this period of high alert?" And the answers we've been getting are a bit paradoxical. Our leaders are telling us: "Go about your everyday lives. Work, shop, travel, eat—but do it with an extra special awareness of what is going on around you. Report anything suspicious or out of the ordinary."

So that's our sinister American version of Advent. Watching, waiting, expecting the worst, while at the same time living our regular, old, everyday lives.

[SECOND MOVEMENT]

In many ways our American Advent does resemble the Church's season of Advent. For this is the time in which we are especially called to be vigilant, on guard, alert. We, too, know that something is coming—not terror, though, but grace. Jesus Christ is coming. Now the coming of Christ could be very good news indeed. But still, uncertainty can haunt us. We know who is coming, but we don't know when, we don't know where, we don't know how. And so perhaps we are open to hear that voice that says: "Be vigilant."

For the country as a whole, that voice belongs to Tom Ridge; for us Christians, the voice belongs to John the Baptist. Each Advent John appears anew on the second Sunday with a word of expectation. John was the one sent to prepare the way for Jesus. His ministry was always directed beyond himself and beyond the present day to the "one who is coming after" him. But the people who listened to John originally asked the same question that we ask of Tom Ridge: "What, then, are we supposed to do?"

[THIRD MOVEMENT]

John had a very definite answer: "Repent, repent. Turn your life around and direct your attention to the coming Messiah."

I think that the crux of John's message is a message for me today, and I hope for you. As we hear the call to vigilance, as we experience this season of expectation, we, too, respond by turning our lives around to direct them toward the coming Savior. We place ourselves on heightened spiritual alert, watching and waiting for signs of the Lord's nearness. In all things, we are called to turn our eyes to the one who is coming. But how?

Tom Ridge tells Americans: "Go about your everyday lives, but do it with heightened awareness." I think our Church's Advent message is similar. Advent is not meant to take us out of the ordinary rhythms of our lives, but to imbue those rhythms with a heightened sense of expectation. As we work, as we shop, as we visit with family and friends—and yes, even as we fly—we watch with the eyes of our hearts for signs that the Lord is near.

Each new dawn, each forgiven grudge, each favor from a stranger, each holiday toast—signs that the Lord is near. Signs that can be recognized, if only we are vigilant.

[CLOSING]
We've heard Tom Ridge often enough: "Be alert, for terror is at hand." John the Baptist does not deny that, not at all, but he does top it. "Be alert," John says, "for the very kingdom of God is at hand. Turn your lives and see that the Lord is near."

❖　　❖　　❖

In this homily I have built on the foundation laid by the personal and liturgical characteristics and put into practice some of the techniques of the inculturated homily. Note, first of all, my attempt to preach in easily understandable language. I frequently used contractions, as they sound less stilted and more familiar. My vocabulary was very accessible, with the possible exception of the word "imbue" in the Third Movement. I thought it a beautiful and accurate word that, while not common, would be understood in context, and so I let it go through. In addition, I used synonyms and stealth translation to make the Scriptures more accessible. Be on guard, alert, watchful, vigilant—by using these synonyms, I broadened the imagery associated with the call and hammered it home. The stealth translation came at the beginning of the Third Movement, when I quoted John's message—"Repent"—and immediately followed it with one of the meanings of *metanoiete:* "Turn your life around." Notice that I felt no compunction to use the original Greek word or to point out that I was translating it. That is rarely called for; stealth translation is usually best.

The inculturated homily must employ relevant imagery to illustrate its message. In this case, my message was simple enough: Advent is a time for special alertness to signs of the Lord. I think that this is a valid message, given that Sunday's scriptural text in its liturgical context; however, it is not the most original message. In fact, stated as plainly as I just did, this message is trite and therefore utterly forgettable, true as it is. So I felt a very strong need to inculturate the message, and that is why I turned to the aftermath of September 11 as my central image set. From the concrete hominess of me and my shoes, to the hulking visage of Tom Ridge and his terrifying if confusing admonitions, I tried to use imagery at once power-ful and familiar. I complemented that with some very concrete and famil-iar signs of the Lord's nearness at the end of the Third Movement: dawn, forgiven grudges, favors, and toasts.

Empathic knowledge of real life emerged as well. My anecdote about the shoes placed me in an experiential relationship to the trials of post-9/11. Further, I believe that I accurately captured what was a shared con-gregational reality at that time: the confusion about how to react to the government's warnings. Here, as in every homily, though, the goal is not to show that the preacher reads the newspaper or actually has a life; rather, the goal is a homiletic one. The inculturating preacher uses personal knowl-edge of real life to enflesh the message of the homily, to clothe a declara-tive sentence announcing good news with the shared symbols and images of the gathered assembly.

In this homily I did interpret the Matthean passage in its liturgical context in terms of today's world. I used the familiar figure of Tom Ridge to help my listeners understand the urgency of John's message of alert-ness and repentance. Indeed, I hoped that by comparing and contrasting these two figures throughout the homily, I might yoke them in people's minds. This way the next appearance of Ridge on TV might call to mind the message of John.

I intended as well, though, to interpret an aspect of today's world in the light of the Sunday celebration. The months after September 11 were very difficult times for many people, and I felt it my homiletic duty to shine the light of the gospel on those difficulties. I pointed out that while Ridge and the Baptist both called for alertness in everyday life, only the Baptist called for alertness to good, a goodness that will always prevail in the end. I did not belabor this point, and perhaps did not even develop it enough to be heard, but it was part of my intentionality in this homily.

## The Response to a Homily Reflecting
## Inculturated Characteristics

The preacher who utilizes the strategies discussed in this chapter is one who has embraced the call to inculturation. What sort of response to inculturated preaching might one reasonably expect?

Preaching in easily accessible language leads the listener to avoid such judgments as "too abstract" or "too churchy." Rather, listeners will report that the homily was easy to understand, easy to listen to, concrete. When relevant illustration manifests the preacher's empathic knowledge of real life, the feedback gets even better: the homily was "real," not "pie in the sky"; it spoke of the here-and-now, not of an abstract elsewhere. It was a message for today, not a message from yesterday.

Successful interpretation of Scripture in terms of today's world will garner a response to warm any preacher's heart: "You helped me see how God's Word is relevant." Such a comment should warm our hearts, for we preachers are aware of the heavy hermeneutic task. When we successfully correlate the faith experiences of our scriptural forebears with those of our people, we have truly done our homiletic best.

But in the Catholic vision of the homily, preachers are called also to interpret today's world in the light of Scripture. When we use God's Word to make even a bit of sense of our crazy world, we will be thanked. "Now I can face tomorrow knowing that God is here."

# CHAPTER 7

# The Homily as Clarifying Word: One Good Point, Clearly Made

But Peter said to him, "Explain this parable to us." Then [Jesus] said, "Are you also still without understanding?" (Matt 15:15-16).

Now the apostles and the believers who were in Judea heard that the Gentiles had also accepted the word of God. So when Peter went up to Jerusalem, the circumcised believers criticized him, saying, "Why did you go to uncircumcised men and eat with them?" Then Peter began to explain it to them, step by step (Acts 11:1-4).

As Jesus explained himself on occasion to his disciples, so Peter and the rest went on to explain themselves as the Good News made its progress in the world. Clarity is Christianity's friend.

But, ironically enough, clarity itself is a complex concept. While it might seem a "no-brainer" to insist that preachers be clear, that is not the case. Both mystics and post-modernists would challenge me on this. So at the outset let me be as clear as I can be about clarity.

From the side of the mystics comes the argument that we preach a mystery, the mystery of God's anarchic love manifest in Jesus's salvific life, death, and resurrection, and active still in their Spirit. To try to express this most profound mystery in the black-and-white prose implied by the word "clarity" is to betray the mystery; God will not become a prisoner of our concepts. The divine reality must not be reduced to some homiletic "point."

The avatars of post-modernism would also challenge my call for clarity. They would see in that call a regrettable artifact of the (now discredited)

Enlightenment. The eighteenth-century modern was sure that all could be explained rationally, that scientific inquiry would steadily clarify the nature of the universe, the world, and its people. The twenty-first-century post-modern recognizes rather that ambiguity marks human life much more than clarity and that chaos is as much a part of our universe as order. To stand in a pulpit and claim to bring clarity to some aspect of life, week after week, is to preach as a child of the Enlightenment, as relevant to today as three-cornered hats and medicinal leeches.

So, is clarity the enemy of true and effective preaching? No, it is not. Jesus used stories to evoke the kingdom of God, but he also spoke plainly, helping his followers to better understand his message. Peter and Paul explained themselves frequently, trying to bring clarity to their hearers about the wonderful work of God in Jesus Christ. The New Testament gives witness to many types of language—not only parables, narratives, and hymns, but also analysis and doctrine—all in service of the Good News.[1] So, too, our Sunday preaching uses not only the imaginative language of symbol and story but also the conceptual language of explanation, insight, and clarity.

The mystics, of course, have a point: the subject of our preaching is Mystery itself. If our preaching sounds like a rule book, instruction manual, or freshman theology text, we do indeed dishonor the mystery of redemption. And the post-modernists have a point as well: Church folk have often been all too certain about things that are not certain. If our preaching claims a clarity that exceeds the clarity of real life, we will be dismissed as ideologues, out of touch with the ambiguity all must negotiate each day.

Both positions having been noted, though, the Roman Catholic vision of the homily does include the concept of clarity. Sunday preachers are called to speak clearly and insightfully about Christian tradition, focused in light of the Scriptures and the gathered assembly. Clarifying preachers make a central point clearly, and a central point worth making. They utilize responsibly exegetical and theological scholarship. Clarifying preachers honor the place that their Sunday words have in the greater tradition. Let's take a closer look at these five aspects of homiletic clarity.

---

1. See David Tracy, *The Analogical Imagination: Christian Theology and the Culture of Pluralism* (New York: Crossroad Publishing Company, 1989) 266–268.

## The Clarifying Preacher Makes a Central Point Clearly

Clarity begins with the preacher's written formulation of the one message to be conveyed in that particular homily. Such a formulation gives direction to the composition of the homily, serves as a guide when editing what has been written, and aids the preacher's memory when the homily is delivered.

I will have more to say about the character and role of this formulation of the central point in chapters 9 and 10. For our purposes here, as we ponder the characteristics of the Sunday homily, it suffices to say that this formulation should be a relatively straightforward declarative sentence. The more our central point emerges as a compound and/or complex sentence, the better the chances that we are actually heading down the road of two or three or four "mini-homilies," held together only by conjunctions, semicolons, and hope.

Let me give an example of both a well-formulated and homiletically manageable central point and a more problematic formulation. On the one hand, then, a well-constructed point: "Jesus knows when each of us is ready to respond fully to his call."[2] Such a straightforward sentence could be the basis for a clear and focused homily. On the other hand, imagine a homily constructed around this point: "Because we have seen in Jesus Christ that God is for us, we can be confident that God loves us and cares for us even when our experience seems to deny it."[3] To my ear, this is a homily with more than one central point. "We have seen in Christ that God is for us" strikes me as a great Sunday message. So, too, "We can be confident that God loves us even when our experience seems to deny it" and "We can be confident that God cares for us even when our experience seems to deny it" each strike me as a fine message. But to try to preach a focused homily, a homily enjoying manifest unity yet dealing with all four of these realities, would be quite difficult. "We have seen in Christ that God is for us," "God loves us," "God cares for us," "Our experience sometimes seems at odds with our faith"—great and worthy homiletic ideas all, but too much for one Sunday sermon.

Sticking to one central point per homily is an act demanding two things: acceptance of the idea that in Sunday preaching "less is more" and

2. This is a paraphrase from St. John Chrysostom's Homily 30.1, on Matthew 9:9f.
3. Thomas Long, *The Witness of Preaching* (Louisville: Westminster/John Knox Publishing, 1989) 107 (the focus statement of a sermon on Romans 8:28-29).

great discipline in acting on that idea. Regarding the former, most mainstream homileticians would agree that, in the words of Thomas Long, "sermons should say and do one thing: that is, they should be unified around a single claim from the text."[4] Even the Pontifical Biblical Commission warns preachers that "the explanation of the biblical texts given in the course of the homily cannot enter into great detail. It is, accordingly, fitting to explain the central contribution of texts, that which is most enlightening for faith and most stimulating for the progress of Christian life. . . ."[5] In preaching, less is truly more; one well-developed point will accomplish more than four underdeveloped points.

Unfortunately, believing in homilies with one central point is not enough; preachers must have the discipline to act on that belief. This required discipline rules the preaching process from beginning to end. It first manifests itself when the preacher chooses from among the many insights arising from the preparation process and formulates the Sunday message in one simple declarative sentence. I firmly believe that the dictum of the great homiletician Fred Craddock should be inscribed on a plaque and presented to every preacher: "On a given Sunday, many wonderful Christian things will not be said."[6] The discipline of the central point requires preachers to let go of valid and valuable insights, choosing to develop only one. To reassure yourself that your preparation and inspiration have not gone to waste, file away all the insights you chose not to engage. Three years hence, as the Scripture text reappears in the Lectionary, feel free to check your file and see if the great ideas are still great.

The discipline of the central point next rules the composition process as that single message is developed and illustrated. A good practice for those who have the bad habit of preaching about many things: review your manuscript to ascertain that every sentence is directly related to your central point. Ruthlessly edit out every red herring, excursus, "by the way," and every noble Christian thought not related to your point. Let the red ink flow.

Finally, the discipline of the central point must be maintained in the pulpit itself. Preach what you have prepared, and resist those ideas that

4. Ibid., 89.

5. Pontifical Biblical Commission, The Interpretation of the Bible in the Church (Boston: St. Paul Books and Media, 1993) 128–129.

6. Fred B. Craddock, *Preaching* (Nashville: Abingdon Press, 1985) 156.

pop into your head while preaching. It is rare indeed that such sponta-
neous thoughts are on topic, worthy as they may be. Some preachers take
issue with me on this, claiming that I'm leaving no room for the Holy Spirit.
My response: During the homily, there is simply no time to discern which
spirit put the new thought in your head. Was it really the Holy Spirit or
rather the evil spirit of disjointed, rambling sermons?

## The Clarifying Preacher Makes a Central Point
## Worth Making, Theologically and Pastorally

And now onto the next "no-brainer": Being focused on a central point does
not guarantee an effective homily if that point is on the fringes of Christian
tradition and life. The clarifying preacher strives to develop homiletic messages that are at once theologically significant and pastorally helpful.

When judging the theological value of my Sunday message, I am
guided by the idea that there is a "hierarchy of truths" in Christian tradition. The Second Vatican Council put it this way:

> When comparing doctrines with one another, [theologians] should remem-
> ber that in Catholic doctrine there exists a "hierarchy" of truths, since they
> vary in their relation to the fundamental Christian faith.[7]

The Catechism of the Catholic Church went on to clarify what stands at
the summit of this doctrinal hierarchy:

> The mystery of the Most Holy Trinity is the central mystery of Christian
> faith and life. It is the mystery of God in himself. It is therefore the source of
> all the other mysteries of faith, the light that enlightens them. It is the most
> fundamental and essential teaching in the "hierarchy of the truths of faith."[8]

Our Sunday homilies ought to be concerned with realities that are
higher up in this hierarchy of Christian truth. As we preach God's Word,
we clarify for our people who God is, how God has worked in Jesus to save
us, and how God's Spirit continues this work in our midst today. We clarify
our identity as Church and all that that entails. We reflect on the wonderful

7. Second Vatican Council, Decree on Ecumenism *(Unitatis Redintegratio)* 11. Accessed at
<http://www.vatican.va/archive/hist_councils/ii_vatican_council/documents/vat-ii_decree
_19641121_unitatis-redintegratio_en.html>.

8. *Catechism of the Catholic Church* (Washington: United States Catholic Conference;Vati-
can City: Libreria Editrice Vaticana, 1994) 234. Accessed at <http://www.vatican.va/archive/ccc
_css/archive/catechism/p1s2c1p2.htm#234>.

gifts of Word and Sacrament, Christ-bearers for God's people. Our central homiletic point continually revisits these core beliefs of Christians as they emerge from the Scriptures. The further down the hierarchy of truths we descend, the less likely that our point will be worth making.

The central message of an effective Sunday homily must be not only theologically worthy but also pastorally helpful. From the beginning, the Word of God has been preached in two principal ways, by (traveling) evangelists and by (resident) pastors. Evangelists strive to know as much as they can about those whom they visit, in hopes of inculturating the gospel most effectively. But it is the pastors of established communities of Christians who come to know their people best, through years of ministry to them and life with them. Sunday preachers use their intimate and extensive knowledge of their parishioners to ask and answer this crucial question regarding their central homiletic point: "Who cares?" What difference will this message make in the lives of my youth group members or the elderly? Could this message matter to couples and singles and those searching? Is what I am proposing to say going to help anyone—everyone?—to make progress in their Christian lives? Who cares?

The U.S. bishops' document on the Sunday homily put the case well:

> Unless a preacher knows what a congregation needs, wants, or is able to hear, there is every possibility that the message offered in the homily will not meet the needs of the people who hear it. To say this is by no means to imply that preachers are only to preach what their congregations want to hear. Only when preachers know what their congregations want to hear will they be able to communicate what a congregation needs to hear. Homilists may indeed preach on what they understand to be the real issues, but if they are not in touch with what the people think are the real issues, they will very likely be misunderstood or not heard at all.[9]

## The Clarifying Preacher Utilizes Responsibly Exegetical Scholarship

Scholars can aid Sunday preachers in determining whether our central point is indeed worth making. The first sort of scholarship with which preachers should be familiar is the work of biblical exegetes.

I will have more to say about our encounter with the exegetes in chapter 9. Currently, though, we are considering ways to make sure that our

---

9. Bishops' Committee on Priestly Life and Ministry, *Fulfilled in Your Hearing: The Homily in the Sunday Assembly* (Washington: USCCB Publishing, 1982) 4.

preaching is clear and insightful, and in that context the exegetes are clearly our friends. Biblical scholars help us in three principal ways: they inform us, they inspire us, and they protect us.

Sound, scholarly exegesis of the Scriptures is a dependable source of information for the Sunday preacher. Put simply, exegetes know much more about the passages on which we preach than we ever will. These women and men dedicate their lives to using the tools of scriptural scholarship to plumb the depths of the Bible, and the results of their work are invaluable to the preacher. Through the work of textual critics, preachers learn the most dependable version of an extant text. Through the work of genre critics, we learn the type of literature we are dealing with, while the form critics help us to know the linguistic structures typical of each genre and how best to understand them. Tradition criticism helps the preacher understand how the wording or structure of a literary unit has developed over time, giving us insight into the pastoral situations behind the text. So, too, the redaction critics help us see the role and purposes of the final editors of each text. Beyond these practitioners of the historical-critical method, other scholars come to our aid. Rhetorical analysts study the rhetorical strategy embraced by the author and what we can infer from that about the author's purposes. Narrative analysts help the preacher see what makes each story "work" and what kind of world it invites us into. Other exegetes help us see the place that a particular text has in the Bible taken as a whole (the canonical approach) or how a text was interpreted by Jews and by Christians through the ages. In addition, the results of research in the various human sciences continue to illuminate text after text; preachers benefit from the work of sociologists, cultural anthropologists, and even psychologists.[10]

Without doubt, this battalion of scholars helps the Sunday preacher understand the scriptural text better, therefore promoting our clarity and insight. But beyond clarity, the exegetes are a true source of inspiration. The results of exegesis do no less than help a biblical text come alive in its particularity. Learning the full meaning of some key Greek word in a Sunday text, learning the significance of a particular geographical reference, learning the original biblical narrative being "re-read" in a text at hand—

10. This treatment of the range of exegesis is inspired by The Interpretation of the Bible in the Church, Part I, "Methods and Approaches for Interpretation." The reader is invited to consult that excellent summary and critique of current exegetical methods.

all these insights and so many more are waiting to inspire the Sunday preacher.

Thankfully, though, the exegetes render an equally valuable service: they protect us from eisegesis. *Eisegesis:* one of those twenty-dollar words that does not belong in a homily. Nor, however, does its reality belong in the preparation of a homily. Eisegesis, understood as a groundless and artificial imposition of one's own biases on the interpretation of a text, is to be avoided. The scholarly exegetes help the Sunday preacher discern whether the homiletic direction being considered is in keeping with the reasonable range of meanings of the text.

Avoiding eisegesis, however, is not to be confused with eschewing creativity. The preacher strives to honor both fidelity to sources and creativity in inculturating the message for a particular assembly. As we will see in chapter 9, the Catholic understanding is that interpretation of Scripture can and must involve creativity and that no single interpretation can exhaust the whole meaning of a scriptural text. But at the same time, "one must reject as unauthentic every interpretation alien to the meaning expressed by the human authors in their written text."[11] Exegetes protect preachers from such alien interpretations, as "the principal task of exegesis is . . . to use all of the resources of literary and historical research, with a view to defining the literal sense of the biblical texts with the greatest possible accuracy."[12]

## The Clarifying Preacher Utilizes Responsibly Theological Scholarship

The second sort of scholarship with which Sunday preachers should be familiar is the work of theologians. At the outset, let's acknowledge the special kinship between preachers and theologians. In the early Church, preachers and theologians were the same people. Theology was indeed faith seeking understanding, and frequently that seeking happened in the pulpit. As the pastors of the churches sought to inculturate the gospel in their places and times, issues of faith arose, and Christian doctrine advanced. So much of patristic *theological* literature is actually the record of the *preaching* of the Church Fathers. Doctrinal councils were called to reconcile dueling pulpits. This common ancestry of theologians and preach-

11. Interpretation of the Bible in the Church, 84.
12. Ibid., 82.

ers led Karl Barth to his telling dictum: "Theology as a church discipline ought in all its branches to be nothing other than sermon preparation in its broadest sense."[13] The converse, ideally, is as true today as it was at the beginning: sound preaching aids theological development.

Unfortunately, this symbiotic relationship of theology and preaching is not always honored. I have at least anecdotal evidence that newly minted ordained ministers often suffer a period of theology aversion. A bit burned out from years of theological study and at the same time energized by their new pastoral responsibilities, these newly ordained cease to crack the covers of their theology texts or perhaps even fail to unpack them. This is an understandable aversion, perhaps, but only if it is temporary. The relationship between theology and preaching is an intimate one, and ignoring it in the long term guarantees impoverished Sunday homilies.

Like the exegetes considered above, professional theologians have the time to consider and treat important issues, time that the typical pastor simply does not have. Theologians research and write at the nexus of Scripture, tradition, and the contemporary situation—philosophical, cultural, political, and social. That theological nexus is the very crossroads that meet in the pulpit. Barth was right: theology done well is sermon preparation. Theologians provide a rich resource to preachers.

I think, for instance, of a key cultural development that has profound ramifications in pastoral ministry, and that is the growth in religious pluralism. The days are gone when most saw the United States as a "Christian country" (with a few Jews) or even as a Protestant country. We preach in an environment in which those not belonging to the Judeo-Christian tradition are everywhere. Many "church marriages" are celebrated between people of differing faiths or even between believers and non-believers. What resources does a preacher have in dealing with this sea change in our culture? One of them is certainly theology. It is no coincidence that soteriology is currently enjoying a great renaissance. Theologians are struggling with the place of the Christian claim that salvation comes solely through Christ in a world suddenly aware that Christians are in the minority. Their research into this "technical" question can provide important inspiration and guidance to preachers aware of the heterogeneity of their

---

13. Karl Barth, *Homiletics,* trans. Geoffrey W. Bromiley and Donald E. Daniels (Louisville: Westminster/John Knox Press, 1991) 17.

congregations, of their congregants' significant relationships, and of the wider cultural context.

## The Clarifying Preacher Honors the Great Tradition

The final element demanded by clarity in Sunday preaching is the preacher's recognition of the place of each homily in the wider Christian tradition. We preach the Scriptures, yes, but we preach the canon of the Bible in a context larger than the Bible—indeed, in the context that gave the Bible its canonicity. That context is the fullness of Christian faith, as lived by the apostles, grounded in the Scriptures, built up through the centuries by inspired geniuses, local churches, and ecumenical councils, and celebrated in the liturgy. Catholics happily refer to this fullness as "tradition."

The Pontifical Biblical Commission locates the work of the exegete (and thus the preacher) solidly within this context: "What characterizes Catholic exegesis is that it deliberately places itself within the living tradition of the Church, whose first concern is fidelity to the revelation attested by the Bible."[14] But such a conviction is not foreign to churches of the Reformation. Though *"sola scriptura"* was a critical rallying cry, no less a luminary than Karl Barth insists that "preaching must faithfully adhere to doctrine, that is, to the confession of our faith. . . . Naturally one is not required to preach confessions of faith, but to have as the purpose and limit of one's message the confession of one's church, taking one's stand where the church stands."[15] Though the Sunday homily is necessarily the personal word of the preacher, it is at the same time an "act of living tradition"[16]—standing where the Church stands.

The clarifying preacher is clear about the role tradition plays in preaching, and it is a dual role.[17] On the one hand, "tradition" is a convenient label for recognizing that the preacher does not stand alone, but rather "in explicit continuity with the communities which gave rise to the Scripture and which preserved and handed it on."[18] Our immediate context on Sun-

---

14. Interpretation of the Bible in the Church, 88.
15. Karl Barth, "The Preaching of the Gospel," in Richard Lischer, *Theories of Preaching: Selected Readings in the Homiletical Tradition* (Durham: The Labyrinth Press, 1987) 346.
16. Congregation for Clergy, General Catechetical Directory, 13. Accessed at <http://www.vatican.va/roman_curia/congregations/cclergy/documents/rc_con_cclergy_doc_11041971_gcat_en.html>.
17. See Interpretation of the Bible in the Church, 118.
18. Ibid.

day is the community of faith gathered in this time and place. But our particular community of faith belongs in turn to a broader context—all those who have worshiped the Lord before them. Christianity, like its forebear Judaism, is a historical faith. We are who we are because of who we have been; our identity lies in the unbroken continuity from Jesus and his first followers to each contemporary gathering in faith.

The clarifying preacher recognizes this continuity and gives thanks for it. It is the continuity of tradition that has preserved the Scriptures to this day. It is the continuity of tradition that guarantees that today's recipients of the inspired Word are the sisters and brothers of those who first heard it spoken, and thus rightful recipients. As we prepare our homilies, we can benefit richly by learning how the text at hand has echoed through the Church's history. Examine the wake left by the Word, from its early redaction, to patristic preaching and the development of doctrine, through the subsequent preaching of pastors in every time and place. Thank goodness collections of sermons and doctrinal sources make such an examination quite possible. Sunday preachers must honor the place their homilies hold in the greater tradition.

On the other hand, tradition is a guardian, or better, a judge. If tradition doesn't tell us what to preach on a given Sunday, it can certainly tell us what not to preach. Above all, tradition tells us not to preach heresy. "Heresy"—the word may have a dusty, dated quality to it, but it captures nicely the fact that Christians have worked out an orthodoxy over the centuries, and positions outside of that orthodoxy work against the true preaching of the gospel. In my years as a seminary professor of homiletics, I learned weekly that the grand old heresies are alive and well, aching to be preached. You thought Pelagianism was settled by the Council of Ephesus in 431? Then why do we hear sermons that insist that in salvation, we must take the first step? Or what of Semi-Pelagianism? Dead and buried in 531? I can't number the times I've heard Catholic preachers suggest that we merit grace by our good works. Certainly Donatism disappeared into the sands of fifth-century North Africa—or did it? Across denominations, one can hear sermon after sermon portraying the Church as an exclusive company of saints, with room only for those following God's rules as understood by a particular pastor. I could go on, but I don't have the stomach for it. Heresy lives, and knowledge of Christian tradition is the only sure way to make certain we do not preach what is not orthodox.

## An Example of a Homily Reflecting Clarifying Characteristics

Thirteenth Sunday of Ordinary Time, Year A
[Revised Common Lectionary, Proper 7]
Romans 6:3-4, 8-11

[OPENING]

We Americans are known for our denial of death. Our culture bids us to be forever young, and when the time comes for death, our culture wants us to pretend as best as we can that death didn't really happen. American culture strives to deny the reality of the grave.

[FIRST MOVEMENT]

Luckily, we've got a multi-billion dollar death industry to help us with our denial. In the old days the dead body was prepared by the family and laid out at home. Now the funeral industry takes care of all of that and tries its hardest to make sure the person in the coffin looks alive.

And then, think about what happens at the cemetery. Or better, what doesn't happen. Most times we go for prayers and leave. The burial itself happens out of sight, and while we're in the cemetery, the grave is carefully hidden. The dirt is covered in festive Astroturf, and so is the opening to the hole. Apparently the American death industry has decided that we shouldn't face that stark, haunting symbol that is a six-foot-deep casket-shaped hole.

[SECOND MOVEMENT]

And that's a shame. It's a shame in the way that any denial of reality is a shame. Death, after all, is real—and it is a most significant part of life. The open grave is a powerful reminder of that reality.

But the "hidden grave syndrome" is a shame also from the perspective of our faith. Hiding our graves is a shame because the grave has something very important to say about our Christian faith. Listen again to St. Paul, as he wrote to the church in Rome:

Do you not know that all of us who have been baptized into Christ Jesus were baptized into his death? Therefore we have been buried with him by baptism into death, so that, just as Christ was raised from the dead by the glory of the Father, so we too might walk in newness of life.

In baptism, we were buried with Christ. We share his very grave, that's how close we are to Jesus. No cloaking Astroturf, no hidden hole. Just union with Christ in his grave.

But, of course, in baptism we are raised out of that grave, with Christ. The new life that he took up on Easter morning becomes our life force as well. Jesus in us and we in him, risen from the grave. And that's how close we are to Jesus.

St. Paul uses the image of the grave as a metaphor for our union with Jesus Christ in baptism. Baptism is not the beginning of a nice friendship, a meeting over coffee with a new acquaintance. No, baptism is intimate union with Jesus. His life, his suffering, his death, and his resurrection are now ours. Or, in shorthand, we go down into his grave with him, and are raised up out of his grave with him.

Believing in this intimate union with Jesus is a source of comfort and strength for me. I love knowing as I face struggles that Jesus is with me in time of trial. As I face the deaths of everyday life—the death of a relationship, the death of a job, the literal death of family and friends—as I face these deaths, I find strength in my union with the one who conquered the grave.

[THIRD MOVEMENT]

Some of the very early church buildings had a great way of symbolizing St. Paul's metaphor of the grave. They built their baptismal pools in the shape of a grave: a casket-sized hole in the floor. And at the Easter Vigil, the early Christians enacted the words of St. Paul to the Romans. Those to be baptized were led down into the casket-shaped hole. They were buried with Christ, although buried under water instead of dirt. And then they were raised back up and led away from the grave to be clothed in white.

Our cathedral here in Milwaukee has replicated that early baptismal pool. And believe me, there is a power in seeing that casket-shaped hole in the floor. It is a powerful reminder of what Jesus suffered on our behalf and a powerful reminder of the reality of death that faces us all.

But that pool was most powerful at the moment of baptism during the Easter Vigil. I stood there and watched the elect being led down into the grave, buried with Christ. And you should have seen the beatific smiles on their faces as they were raised up out of the grave, now in the deepest of unions with Jesus himself. It was as if they knew that their lives had changed, indeed that their old lives of

alienation and fear had been buried. Their faces glowed with the
knowledge that they had been lifted out of the grave and into a new
life of union with Jesus and his followers. Alienation and fear buried,
and a new life of conviction and hope in the love of Christ raised up.

[CLOSING]
For Christians, the grave is a symbol of our union with Christ. The
grave reminds us that we are one with him. We are one with him in
our life's journey toward that hole in the ground. We are one with
Christ when we rest in the grave. And most of all, we are one with
Christ as we are finally raised up at the end.

❖    ❖    ❖

In this homily I built on the personal, liturgical, and inculturated foundations discussed previously, and went on to utilize some of the strategies
involved in clarifying. The homily featured some first-person-singular language, as I shared my faith at the end of the Second Movement and gave
a firsthand account of baptism in the Third. The homily is suffused with
a liturgical spirit, as I reflected upon the Church's baptismal practices. It
also strives toward inculturation by recognizing and exploring the American denial of death.

Regarding clarifying characteristics, note first that I have a clearly
discernible central point: "The grave is a symbol of our baptismal union
with Christ." I don't suppose that I would have to argue too strongly that
this is a point worth making from the theological perspective. Baptism is,
after all, the door to the Church. And one of the central mysteries of the
Christian faith is our union with Jesus Christ in baptism.

However, the next judgment may not be as clear—was this a point
worth making from the pastoral perspective? Any homily may be judged
on this score, but a homily whose central purpose is a clarifying one must
especially answer this pastoral question: "Who cares?" In the present homily
I believe that I passed the "Who cares?" test in the Opening and the First
Movement. The reality of death is a fairly universal concern, and my language was blunt and vivid. I suspect that my listeners were with me through
that part of my preaching. But as I moved into consideration of baptism,
my gut tells me that on its face, most people don't care. Baptism is ad-

verted to when babies are baptized; in most people's lives, it's not much on the radar screen after that.

Aware of this, but also convinced of the theological value of my central point, I tried to leverage that universal concern about death and the emotionally powerful symbol of the grave into caring about the reality of baptism. Indeed, I used personification to highlight and strengthen that powerful symbol: "The grave has something very important to say." In addition, I tried briefly in the Second and Third Movements to give some concrete examples of the difference that our baptismal union with Christ can make. Arguably, I could have done more in the way of concrete illustration, as that always helps listeners to better understand why they should care.

The scholarly community was my friend in preparing this homily. Learning from the exegetes about the purposes of Paul's letter to the Romans helped inspire me to do what Paul himself was attempting: to explain the Christian faith clearly and powerfully to a local church. Paul utilized an image very much at hand: burial. My judgment was that the grave remains a symbol that can speak to Christians today, just as it did to the Romans. In addition, theological scholarship assisted me. The history of baptism and of early fonts played a supporting role in this homily, as did the reflections of theologians on American culture's attempts at denying the reality of death.

Finally, this homily is well aware of its place in the greater tradition. Baptism is the foundational sacrament in every Christian denomination. From the beginning, that foundational importance has been clear: "one Lord, one faith, one baptism, one God" (Eph 4:5). The Lectionary as it stands provides ample opportunity for clarifying various aspects of our faith; on this particular Sunday, the Pauline text was the perfect inspiration to consider baptism. I was true to the passage and used its central symbol. But I also used more conceptual language to unpack some of the significance of that great sacrament.

## The Response to a Homily Reflecting Clarifying Characteristics

The homilist who prepares and preaches a central point—one worth making, informed by exegetical and theological scholarship, and true to the tradition—is a clarifying preacher. What sort of response might such a preacher expect from the assembly?

Clarifying preachers are likely to be affirmed as being, well, clear: "I understood you." "I get it." Particularly if we have successfully passed the "Who cares?" test, our listeners will say things like: "That spoke to me" or "That was a great insight" or "You hit the nail on the head." Of course, the vast majority of worshipers are not in a position to give feedback on how well the preacher has utilized exegetical and theological scholarship or how true the homily was to the tradition. Those contributions remain unseen, supporting the preaching that ultimately emerges. But when we've got one good point worth making, our listeners will certainly respond positively.

Unfortunately, tact probably keeps us from hearing honest feedback when we fail to be clear. But I know what they're saying to themselves: "I couldn't quite follow that." "What does this have to do with what was said two minutes ago?" "Get to the point!"

Clarity is the preacher's friend; even more, it is the listeners' friend.

# CHAPTER 8

# The Homily as Actualizing Word: Written Text Becomes Living Word

For as the rain and the snow come down from heaven,
   and do not return there until they have watered the earth,
making it bring forth and sprout,
   giving seed to the sower and bread to the eater,
so shall my word be that goes out from my mouth;
   it shall not return to me empty,
but it shall accomplish that which I purpose,
   and succeed in the thing for which I sent it (Isa 55:10-11).

At the very heart of Judeo-Christian belief about the Word of God is the conviction that God's Word is efficacious. We continue to proclaim the Word of God in the sure knowledge that the divine Word has power. It has touched lives, and will continue to touch lives in very real ways. It shall not return to God empty.

At the very heart of the Roman Catholic vision of the homily is a similar conviction about preaching. The homily is no mere commentary on the Word but is itself a living word, capable of bearing the saving presence of Christ himself. The scriptural Word in itself is powerful, but the well-preached homily increases the efficacy of the Word.[1]

The shorthand term to describe this homiletic goal of increasing the Word's efficacy is "actualization." The Pontifical Biblical Commission put

---

1. Congregation for Divine Worship, General Instruction of the Roman Missal, 9, in *Documents on the Liturgy: 1963–1979* (Collegeville: The Liturgical Press, 1982) 208. International Committee on English in the Liturgy, General Instruction of the Roman Missal, rev. ed. (Washington, D.C.: USCCB, 2003) 29.

the matter straightforwardly: "The homily, which seeks to actualize more explicitly the Word of God, is an integral part of the liturgy."[2] The Commission describes the why and how of actualization this way:

> Actualization is necessary because, although their message is of lasting value, the biblical texts have been composed with respect to circumstances of the past and in language conditioned by a variety of times and seasons. To reveal their significance for men and women of today, it is necessary to apply their message to contemporary circumstances and to express it in language adapted to the present time.[3]

The actualizing homily reveals the significance of God's Word, and it is no less than this: through the proclaiming and preaching of the Scriptures, God speaks to us today.

The Bible itself gives ample testimony to the conviction that God continues to speak to every age and place. As I describe my understanding of the actualizing preacher, I will highlight some of the more important biblical precedents for my claims. We will see that the actualizing preacher communicates a sense of urgency, while proclaiming a lived truth grounded in experience. The actualizing preacher acts on the belief that God's Word is addressed to people here and now, and indeed the preacher elicits an encounter with the living Christ through the homily. At its summit, the actualizing homily does what the entire liturgy does: it signifies and effects our salvation in Christ.[4] Let's take a closer look at this highest goal of Sunday preaching.

## The Actualizing Preacher Communicates a Sense of Urgency

> For I am longing to see you so that I may share with you some spiritual gift to strengthen you . . . hence my eagerness to proclaim the gospel to you also who are in Rome (Rom 1:11, 15).

St. Paul was "longing" to preach to the Romans, yearning with "eagerness" to bring the Good News to another community. We Sunday preach-

---

2. Pontifical Biblical Commission, The Interpretation of the Bible in the Church (Boston: St. Paul Books and Media, 1993) 125.

3. Ibid., 117–118.

4. Second Vatican Council, Constitution on the Sacred Liturgy *(Sacrosanctum Concilium)* 2 (". . . the liturgy, 'through which the work of our redemption is accomplished'") and 7 ("In the liturgy the sanctification of the man is signified by signs perceptible to the senses, and is effected in a way which corresponds with each of these signs"). Accessed at <http://www.vatican.va/archive/hist _councils/ii_vatican_council/documents/vat-ii_const_19631204_sacrosanctum-concilium_en.html>.

ers need to manifest an analogous sense of urgency, eagerness, and longing to break open the Word for our people.

The first and most important element in manifesting such urgency is our feelings about the message we have chosen to preach. I mentioned in the last chapter my conviction that the central point of a homily needs to pass my listeners' "Who cares?" test. But it is at least as important that the homiletic message first pass the preacher's own "Who cares?" filter. A message about which I have no passion is unlikely to be a message preached with power. Famed homiletician Henry Mitchell, in arguing that preaching must reach both head and heart, put the case bluntly: "We are obliged to avoid a message unless we feel deeply about the subject. If a preacher does not care *greatly* about the text and its meaning for the hearers, then why should they?"[5]

Feeling the urgency of our Sunday message is necessary but not sufficient to actualizing preaching. We must also have the ability to communicate that urgency. The content of the message is part of that communication; we choose to preach about things that really matter to our people and ourselves. But the manner in which we preach is equally important. As was noted when considering the homily as personal word, sincerity in public communication entails a congruence of content, gesture, and affect. So for our preaching to communicate urgency, our faces, bodies, and voices must reflect the significance of our content. Our people must be able to see and hear the urgency contained in our words. Preachers not naturally gifted with expressive faces and voices must work to overcome their flat affect if actualizing preaching is their goal.

There is an ascetical dimension of preaching with urgency. Simply put, it is not easy to develop messages we feel deeply about Sunday after Sunday, year after year, decade after decade. Any professional, after a certain number of years, is prone to the temptation to "phone it in," to place oneself on autopilot and do what we've always done. To give in to this temptation is disastrous for the preacher, though. So one of the principal asceticisms of the preacher's life is resisting this temptation, resisting the "SSDD" syndrome—same sermon, different day. We resist this temptation with all the weapons of Christian asceticism: prayer, meditation, immersion in the Word, and the support of the Christian community. A prolonged

---

5. Henry H. Mitchell, *Celebration and Experience in Preaching* (Nashville: Abingdon Press, 1990) 33.

period of inability to feel deeply about our Sunday message is often enough a signal that a break is in order. Thank goodness for vacations, retreats, and sabbaticals. They are gifts from the community that allow us to recharge and return to the pulpit with deeply felt urgency.

## The Actualizing Preacher Communicates Lived Truth

We declare to you what was from the beginning, what we have heard, what we have seen with our eyes, what we have looked at and touched with our hands, concerning the word of life—this life was revealed, and we have seen it and testify to it, and declare to you . . . what we have seen and heard (1 John 1:1-3).

How do we know what we know? That is, of course, the concern of epistemology. But that question is equally the concern of the actualizing preacher. Especially in these days of rampant skepticism and suspicion of absolutes, most mainstream Christian listeners expect to know the basis of their preachers' truth claims. "Because the Bible told me so" is rarely sufficient these days.

So if an appeal to authoritative books—the Bible or a catechism—is insufficient, how does the actualizing preacher demonstrate the truth of what is preached? Almost forty years ago, Pope Paul VI read the signs of the times and said: "Modern man listens more willingly to witnesses than to teachers, and if he does listen to teachers, it is because they are witnesses."[6] To preach with effect, we must preach as witnesses. We must preach "what we have heard, what we have seen with our eyes, what we have looked at and touched with our hands, concerning the word of life." Preaching's experiential life force did not die out with the apostle John, but remains. Indeed, because of the post-modern times in which we minister, this preaching of lived truth is perhaps as important as it has ever been.

Mere "book knowledge" dutifully rehearsed is not likely to light the fire of faith in the hearts of our people. Scriptural and doctrinal "facts," true as they may be, are not in themselves life-giving or life-enhancing. At the heart of actualizing preaching are not facts but people—Jesus Christ and his followers. Effective preaching is at its core a person of faith speaking faith. The faith that we preach is the faith we struggle to live and to understand. It is the faith that wears the faces of real people, made in the image and likeness of God. It is the faith that speaks in the voices of those

---

6. Paul VI, apostolic exhortation on Evangelization in the Modern World *(Evangelii Nuntiandi)* 41. Accessed at < http://www.vatican.va/holy_father/paul_vi/apost_exhortations/documents/hf_p-vi_exh_19751208_evangelii-nuntiandi_en.html>.

in our lives, and especially in the voice of the poor. We preach the faith that touches us in countless ways as we minister and are ministered to.

The call to preach lived truth means that at certain points in the life of any preacher, there will be messages we should not attempt to deliver. If I am actively nurturing a grudge, it will be difficult for me to deliver an actualizing homily on the beauty and joy of forgiveness. A more credible homily at that point in my life would speak of the difficulty of living up to Christ's invitation to forgive. Actualizing preaching demands that we have experiential knowledge of the grace of which we speak or of the struggle with which we struggle. And that means that on any given Sunday there will be some messages that I am not "qualified" to preach.

Perhaps this element of actualizing preaching strikes you as over-limiting in terms of homiletic content or even in terms of who can right-fully preach. I don't mean to suggest that only a living saint can preach well about love or that the less-than-perfect can't preach well about perfection. I only mean to say that Pope Paul VI got it right: people do listen more willingly to preachers who are witnesses. We preach more effectively when we have experienced in our real lives the things we are preaching about. In the pulpit, lived knowledge trumps book knowledge every time.

## The Actualizing Preacher Expresses God's Word as Present Address

But the LORD said to me,
". . . you shall go to all to whom I send you,
and you shall speak whatever I command you. . . ."
Then the LORD put out his hand and touched my mouth;
and the LORD said to me,
"Now I have put my words in your mouth" (Jer 1:7, 9).

As I noted above, Christians believe that God continues to speak to us today, through the proclamation and preaching of the Scriptures. The Pontifical Biblical Commission reminds us that "the Church . . . does not regard the Bible simply as a collection of historical documents dealing with its own origin; it receives the Bible as Word of God, addressed both to itself and to the entire world at the present time."[7] Consequently, it is the preacher's task to ensure that the scriptural Word "appear as something

---

7. The Interpretation of the Bible in the Church, 117.

addressed to Christians now."[8] This conviction was at the very heart of Karl Barth's understanding of the sermon: "Preaching is the Word of God which he himself speaks, claiming for the purpose the exposition of a biblical text in free human words that are relevant to contemporaries."[9]

Although the Sunday homily is the personal word of the preacher, then, it is also one of the means that God uses to speak to believers. In some sense, God continues to put words into the mouths of preachers, just as he did for Moses and Isaiah and Jeremiah. And so our preaching should reflect that God's Word is addressed to us here and now. I find two techniques to be important toward this end.

First and most important, there is room in preaching for the preacher to use direct address. Just as use of the first person singular helps to personalize a homily, and just as use of the first person plural helps to bolster ecclesial unity, so also use of the second person plural helps manifest the "address" character of the homily.[10] Hans van der Geest contrasts these two sermon sentences to show how simple it can be to transform a bland "we" statement into a more vibrant and personal direct address: "We have trouble because we have to live in faith and never in seeing" versus "I have trouble because I have to live in faith and never in seeing. Do you have the same trouble?"[11] Addressing our listeners directly by use of the second person plural can increase the power of our words and serve as a reminder that God addresses us still.

A second technique to honor the homily's character as present address by God is the use of verbs in the present tense whose subject is God or Christ or the Spirit. Because the Sunday Scriptures are records of what God *did* for the Hebrews and what Jesus *said* and *did* (past tense all), it is easy for the preacher to be trapped in the past. But consistent use of the past tense when referring to divine activity is a sure way to relegate God and the Son of God to a display case in the museum of faith. Sunday preachers should be inspired by the Deuteronomist, who has Moses say to the second and third generations after the Exodus: "The Lord our God made a covenant with us at Horeb. Not with our ancestors did the Lord make this

8. Ibid., 128.

9. Karl Barth, *Homiletics,* trans. Geoffrey W. Bromiley and Donald E. Daniels (Louisville: Westminster/John Knox Press, 1991) 44.

10. Hans van der Geest, *Presence in the Pulpit: The Impact of Personality on Preaching,* trans. D. W. Stott (Atlanta: John Knox Press, 1981) 46.

11. Ibid., 46–47.

covenant, but with us, who are all of us here alive today" (Deut 5:2-3). As the Word of God was taking written form, it was crucial to insist that the God of Abraham, Isaac, and Jacob, the God of the Exodus, was still active in the present moment. Hence the saying of the elderly Moses just cited and the words of the Pontifical Biblical Commission above: the Church "does not regard the Bible simply as a collection of historical documents"; rather, it receives the Bible as the Word of God addressed to us today.

So, for every past-tense reference to what God *said,* actualizing preachers will want to explore what God *is saying* here and now. Christianity is a historical faith, and there is nothing wrong with preaching about the words and events that are our origin. But actualizing preaching can never stop there. God continues to address us today. Our preaching must reflect that present reality.

Now clearly there is a fine line here. We must strive to avoid putting words in God's mouth, rather seeking to have God put words in our mouths. But actualizing preaching is willing to take risks as it strives to be the medium for God's present address. As the Pontifical Biblical Commission reassured: "The risk of error does not constitute a valid objection against performing what is a necessary task: that of bringing the message of the Bible to the ears and hearts of people of our own time."[12] So each Sunday speak boldly of the message God has for us that day.

## The Actualizing Preacher Elicits an Encounter with Christ

> Then beginning with Moses and all the prophets, [Jesus] interpreted to them the things about himself in all the scriptures. . . . Then their eyes were opened, and they recognized him; and he vanished from their sight. They said to each other, "Were not our hearts burning within us while he was talking to us on the road, while he was opening the scriptures to us?" (Luke 24:27, 31-32).

For Christians, the Word of God is first and foremost a person—Jesus Christ, the Word made flesh. It is natural, then, that preachers of that Word should seek to bring their listeners to an encounter with the Risen One. The Pontifical Biblical Commission wrote that in preaching—analogously to catechesis—the "presentation of the Gospels should be done in such a way as to elicit an encounter with Christ, who provides the key to the whole

---

12. The Interpretation of the Bible in the Church, 121.

biblical revelation and communicates the call of God that summons each one to respond."[13]

Such a conviction about preaching has echoes throughout Christian history, of course. As early as the late first century, the *Didache* urged: "My child, thou shalt remember, day and night, him who speaks the word of God to thee, and thou shalt honor him as the Lord, for where the Lord's nature is spoken of, there is he present."[14] Although the Fathers of the Church shared the same conviction, the Middle Ages saw a diminished recognition of Christ's presence in preaching. Such presence, however, was foundational for Luther and many other Reformers.[15] And as we saw in chapter 2, the teaching on the presence of Christ in the preaching of the Church re-entered Catholic doctrine with Pope Paul VI in 1965. For two generations, then, mainline Christianity has been united in its belief that in preaching, we meet Christ himself. What implications does this belief have for the Sunday preacher?

The first implication concerns our own experience with the Scriptures we preach. We will look at our encounters with the text in greater detail in the next chapter, but in the present context it must be said that actualizing preachers themselves must first be open to encountering Christ in the Word. From the first moment of our contact with the Sunday texts, we should be prayerfully open to meeting Christ anew and hearing his voice. This means at least constantly monitoring our approach to homiletic preparation to ensure that it never becomes a mechanical process or a merely intellectual exercise. As we open the Lectionary early in the week, we must make an act of faith that through his Spirit, Jesus can open the Scriptures to us and manifest himself to us. We preachers are perennially the disciples on the road to Emmaus, meeting the Risen One in the interpretation of Scripture. In some sense, our hearts must burn first if we are to enkindle the hearts of our listeners. Or to put it another way, it's hard to introduce to others a person you haven't met yourself.

A second implication of our belief in Christ's presence in preaching concerns the bearing of the preacher, the attitude toward preaching that

---

13. Ibid., 128.

14. *Didache*, 4:1. Accessed at <http://www.earlychristianwritings.com/text/didache-lake.html>.

15. Hughes Oliphant Old, *The Reading and Preaching of the Scriptures in the Worship of the Christian Church*, vol. 4: *The Age of the Reformation* (Grand Rapids: William B. Eerdmans Publishing Company, 2002) 40–41.

we communicate in tone, affect, and content. The preacher must manifest a profound reverence for the preaching event, a reverence that is the same as the reverence with which we approach the Eucharist. Hughes Oliphant Old reminds us that such parallel reverence was a key in Martin Luther's thought: "Luther insisted on the eucharistic real presence, and in the same way he insisted that Christ is truly present in the reading and preaching of the word."[16] And since the Second Vatican Council, Catholics have been reminded that "the Church has always venerated the divine Scriptures just as she venerates the body of the Lord, since, especially in the sacred liturgy, she unceasingly receives and offers to the faithful the bread of life from the table both of God's word and of Christ's body."[17] Such veneration, such respect for the real presence of Christ in both Word and Sacrament, must be evident as we preach—just as evident as when we handle the eucharistic bread and wine.

So what does this reverence look and sound like? It's easier for me to say what it does not look and sound like. Communicating our recognition of Christ's presence precludes a "preaching as entertainment" approach. Joke-telling, insipid badinage with the assembly, over-reliance on props (which as inanimate objects are not good bearers of Christ's presence)— all these seem to me to be out of character with our homiletic reverence for Jesus. Now don't get me wrong. Reverencing the Lord in our preaching does not rule out homiletically justified humor nor a conversational style. What it does demand, though, is acting as if Christ is in the room—because he is.

Finally, preachers help elicit an encounter with Christ when they seek to do in their homilies what Jesus did in his ministry. Jesus helped people come to know God better, he healed their infirmities, he forgave their sins, he reconciled the alienated, he reached out to those excluded from community, he challenged entrenched doctrine and the functionaries who benefited from it. The actualizing preacher helps people meet Jesus when the homily does these very things. By our words we can inform and heal and forgive and reconcile and challenge. Here, too, the use of present tense is key. For every reference to what Jesus *did* for the sick in A.D 30, actualizing

---

16. Ibid.
17. Second Vatican Council, Dogmatic Constitution on Divine Revelation *(Dei Verbum)* 21. Accessed at <http://www.vatican.va/archive/hist_councils/ii_vatican_council/documents/vat-ii_const_19651118_dei-verbum_en.html>.

preachers will have examples of what Jesus *is doing* here and now. In his Spirit, Jesus continues to act, and our use of the present tense and contemporary illustration helps our listeners encounter the Risen One.

## The Actualizing Preacher Evokes an Experience of Salvation

> When [Jesus] came to Nazareth, where he had been brought up, he went to the synagogue on the sabbath day, as was his custom. He stood up to read, and the scroll of the prophet Isaiah was given to him. He unrolled the scroll and found the place where it was written: "The Spirit of the Lord is upon me, because he has anointed me to bring good news to the poor. He has sent me to proclaim release to the captives and recovery of sight to the blind, to let the oppressed go free, to proclaim the year of the Lord's favor." And he rolled up the scroll, gave it back to the attendant, and sat down. The eyes of all in the synagogue were fixed on him. Then he began to say to them, "Today this scripture has been fulfilled in your hearing." All spoke well of him and were amazed at the gracious words that came from his mouth (Luke 4:16-22).

When Jesus preached in that synagogue in Nazareth, he rose to the homiletic pinnacle that remains to this day the goal for all Sunday preachers: he announced that salvation was a present reality. His preaching was so effective that his listeners were amazed. They marveled at the words of grace they heard. (Yes, I remember how that story ends! We'll get to that later.)

"Fulfilled in your hearing"—a phrase so apt, so evocative of the goal of Sunday preaching that the U.S. bishops used it as the title for their 1982 document on the Sunday homily. In preaching, the Scriptures are to be fulfilled, not merely restated or explained. The model that Jesus laid down for us is that preaching is meant to have an effect, and that effect is fundamentally a salvific effect: good news of release, recovery, freedom, and favor. Actualizing preachers seek no less than to evoke an experience of salvation in their listeners, an experience aided by announcement of good news and naming the reality of grace.

***Homiletic Experience of Salvation Demands the Announcement of Good News.*** St. Paul revealed the evangelical heart of his preaching in the emotional words he spoke before his departure from Miletus: "But I do not count my life of any value to myself, if only I may finish my course and the ministry that I received from the Lord Jesus, to testify to the good news of God's grace" (Acts 20:24). At the heart of Paul's ministry was always news that was good: we are saved by God's grace in and through

Jesus Christ. Such good news must always be at the heart of our Sunday preaching. As the Pontifical Biblical Commission put it, in preaching "the biblical message must preserve its principal characteristic of being the good news of salvation freely offered by God."[18]

As we saw in the Lukan pericope above, "good news" is a phrase from Isaiah 61:1. For the prophet, as for Jesus, the good news was not some vague assurance of pie in the sky by and by. No, this good news is that God's salvation has real and specific effects in our lives; we preach "release to the captives and recovery of sight to the blind, to let the oppressed go free, to proclaim the year of the Lord's favor." Actualizing preachers announce concretely how this good news is news today.

Of course, for our Sunday news to be good, it needs to be, well, good. Perhaps a trip to the dictionary would be helpful in this regard. Webster's lists forty-one shades of meaning for the adjective "good," and reading through that list could perhaps refocus our homiletic mission. As we ponder the meaning of "good," we once again pledge ourselves to preach as Jesus and Paul and Luther, to preach as the Roman Catholic documents envision: to preach the Good News.

If your listeners regularly leave the Sunday service feeling depressed and guilt-ridden, anxious and despairing, chances are you are not preaching news received as good.

***Homiletic Experience of Salvation Demands Naming the Reality of Grace.*** Once again, I appreciate the words of St. Paul in the Miletus harbor. He suspects that he will not see the Ephesians again, and he leaves them with his most deeply felt benediction: "And now I commend you to God and to the message of his grace, a message that is able to build you up and to give you the inheritance among all who are sanctified" (Acts 20:32). At the heart of the experience of salvation is grace—the very love of God, the very person of God. The Catechism of the Catholic Church describes grace this way:

> Grace is favor, the free and undeserved help that God gives us to respond to his call to become children of God, adoptive sons, partakers of the divine nature and of eternal life. Grace is a participation in the life of God. It introduces us into the intimacy of Trinitarian life. . . . The grace of Christ is the gratuitous gift that God makes to us of his own life, infused by the Holy Spirit into our soul to heal it of sin and to sanctify it.[19]

18. The Interpretation of the Bible in the Church, 129.
19. John Paul II, The Catechism of the Catholic Church, no. 1999. Accessed at <http://www.vatican.va/archive/catechism/p3s1c3a2.htm#II>.

The actualizing preacher who wishes for the Sunday assembly to be an experience of salvation will name the ways that God's grace is at work here and now. Indeed, Mary Catherine Hilkert argues that the act of preaching itself is best characterized as "naming grace."[20] The phrase is felicitous shorthand for the task of the actualizing preacher. As we have seen in this chapter, we are called in many ways to achieve the actualization of the Sunday Scriptures: communicating urgency and lived truth, giving voice to God's present address and eliciting an encounter with Christ so that salvation can be experienced anew. At the core of each of those ways to actualization, though, is naming the current work of the Lord, naming the graces that flow in our daily lives. What favors is God bestowing today? What help does the Lord give us? How do we experience our adoption as children of God? How are we healed of sin and brought to holiness? Grace is real, but often not "on the radar screen" of busy twenty-first-century Americans. And so the actualizing preacher does what Shakespeare said the poet does:

> The poet's eye, in fine frenzy rolling,
> Doth glance from heaven to earth, from earth to heaven;
> And as imagination bodies forth
> The forms of things unknown, the poet's pen
> Turns them to shapes and gives to airy nothing
> A local habitation and a name.[21]

The actualizing preacher gives God's grace "a local habitation and a name" so that its effects can be known and felt.

## An Example of a Homily Reflecting Actualizing Characteristics

Easter Vigil, Year B
Mark 16:1-8[22]

[OPENING]

We celebrate tonight our union with Jesus in his dying and rising. In baptism we have died with him and have been raised up with him to new life. We are one with Christ.

---

20. See Mary Catherine Hilkert, "Naming Grace: A Theology of Proclamation," *Worship* 60 (1986) 434–448, and her fuller treatment, *Naming Grace: Preaching and the Sacramental Imagination* (New York: Continuum, 1997).

21. *A Midsummer Night's Dream,* 5.1.

22. Mark 16:1-8 is the appointed lection in the first Lectionary for Mass published after the Second Vatican Council in 1969. It is also the lection appointed in the Revised Common Lectionary.

But on this Easter night, I wonder if some of us do not in fact feel closer to the women at the tomb than to Jesus, more completely united with the trembling mourners than with the one who has died and risen?

[FIRST MOVEMENT]

I'm convinced of it: sometimes we resemble the two Marys and Salome, and their approach to Easter becomes ours. For instance, what about the way we honor Jesus? These three women were moved by a deep respect and affection for Jesus, whose memory was fresh in their hearts. And so they left the warmth of their beds that first Easter morning to honor Jesus. Well, that's not quite accurate: they came out that morning to pay final tribute to a dead body, to bathe and anoint it for its eternal rest. Sometimes, I suspect, that's about the extent of the honor that many can muster for Jesus: the honor due a beloved corpse. "He was a wonderful man," we all admit that. Indeed, we should try to be more like he was. We should treasure his memory and never use his name in vain. And on Easter we should put lots of pretty flowers by his grave, because he really was a very nice man.

We resemble the women at the tomb whenever the respect and honor we pay Jesus is the respect and honor due a great man, long dead.

Of course, we may identify with the two Marys and Salome on another level as well. As we join them before the empty tomb, we, like they, may not fully grasp—may not grasp at all—what has happened. The women, St. Mark tells us, were "bewildered," "amazed." In fact, Mark uses a rare Greek word to capture their emotion; beyond bewilderment or amazement, it means the strongest possible feeling of awe and agitation: "a shuddering awe."

Perhaps some of us join these women in that emotion: aware, this Easter night, that something has happened, something awe-provoking, even world-changing; aware, but unsure of what has happened or what it all means. "He is risen," the young man in white said. "What does he mean?" the women wondered. "What does that mean for *me*?" we muse.

---

However, in 1981 the revised Lectionary for Mass dropped verse 8 ("So they went out and fled from the tomb, for terror and amazement had seized them; and they said nothing to anyone, for they were afraid"). This omission strikes me as a shocking disrespect for the plan of Mark's Gospel. It would also have cost me an important image for the present homily had I honored the omission.

We may even resemble these women in their fear. They were, Mark tells us, not only amazed but afraid. They were afraid at finding an empty grave where they thought their friend's body would be.

That which is not logical, that which is violently, surprisingly contrary to our expectations—that is frightening.

And *fright* is paralyzing: "Because of their great fear, they said nothing to anyone." [PAUSE]

So, perhaps some of you are with me and the women of the Gospel: ready to honor Jesus, the great (albeit dead) man; bewildered and agitated about the significance for me of the words "He is risen"; even afraid, silently afraid to discover the resurrection's power.

[SECOND MOVEMENT]

Mark originally ended his Gospel with this fearful silence. And here let me make a little confession: fearful silence is the very way that I have often left the resurrection. Whether in mere bewilderment or in abject fear, I've often put off wrestling with the reality of the Risen One. I've been—here's the confession—an agnostic on the resurrection. First I was an "intellectual agnostic"—you know, saying stuff like "since resurrection is about life beyond this world, there's simply nothing to say about it. I just don't know." Then I got a couple of degrees in theology, and I became a "theological agnostic." That means that I can give you lots of reasons founded in tradition and the human sciences why we can know nothing about resurrection!

Little by little, though, I'm discovering that my agnosticism is a house built on sandy ground, and this Easter night that house has been shaken. My resurrection agnosticism was built on sandy ground because its only foundation was the intellect—and there's a lot more to life than thinking, thank God! Little by little I'm beginning to sense that maybe Christian experience knows more about resurrection than theology does. Maybe the full human range of thinking, feeling, and acting is a better route to the Risen One.

For instance, at the beginning of this service we experienced one of the finest moments the Church's liturgy has to offer. The sight of the Easter flame, divided but undimmed, bathing your faces in light; the smell of the incense as it rose heavenward; the voice proclaiming the mystery of our faith—this moment was for me a foretaste of resurrection, when we will be embraced by the Light, when we will become light from Light. Tonight I saw it and heard it and smelled it: the resurrection is real! Christ is alive!

But it's not just in liturgy that we meet the Risen One. A few months back I experienced something many of us have faced: a falling out with a dear friend. I do not overstate the case by saying that something died that day. And yet I came to learn that death is not the end. When we forgave each other in Jesus's name, we experienced new life. In fact, we experienced not a resuscitation of what had been, but a resurrection. Our friendship was not merely restored, but brought to new birth. I lived it: the resurrection is real! Christ is alive!

A few weeks back I attended the funeral of a priest friend's father. As I experienced that gathering of the faithful, as I heard my friend preach about his father and about our faith, I felt in my heart the reality of the resurrection. Evidence be damned—death is not the end! Jesus's death was not the end; the deaths of family and friends are not the end; our deaths are not the end. The end is life; the end is love; the end is God. The resurrection is God's promise to each of us tonight: "My all-powerful love will not be defeated; my loving embrace is what awaits you on the other side of the grave." At that funeral I felt it: the resurrection is real! Christ is alive!

[CLOSING]

When experiences like these enter our lives, we can feel anew the reality of resurrection. We are empowered by the Spirit of the Risen Lord to move beyond the fearful trembling silence and more deeply into the new lives we have been given at baptism, united with Christ. We are empowered to meet the Risen One in all that is good and true and beautiful. Agnostics no more, we can proclaim from the depths of our hearts: Christ is risen, to the glory of God the Father!

❖   ❖   ❖

In this homily I built on the personal, liturgical, inculturated, and clarifying foundations discussed previously and went on to use some of the strategies involved in actualizing. This homily was a personal word, especially since I chose to share my own experiences of confusion and insight into the resurrection. The homily was deeply infused with the spirit of the liturgy of which it was a part. Indeed, the first illustration in the Second Movement was a mystagogic one, drawing out the power of what had just been celebrated. The principal way in which inculturation marked this homily was my wrestling with the post-modern mind and its agnosticism toward the miraculous. Though I used the first person singular in "confessing" agnosticism, this was meant to be a use of the "representative I"—listeners were implicitly invited to identify their own agnostic leanings by hearing me speak of mine. The homily was clarifying, I think. It did have a central point—"the resurrection is real"—and that was a point worth making, especially on Easter!

Building on those four characteristics, I further sought to create and preach an actualizing homily. Regarding urgency, you will somewhat have to take my word on this, since urgency emerges more in sight and sound than words chosen. Nonetheless, I did structure my message to become increasingly urgent as it progressed. The first burst of excitement came in the first illustration of the Second Movement, when I exuberantly exclaimed for the first time, "The resurrection is real!" This was repeated two more times, with vigor. Another burst of enthusiasm came in the third illustration of the Second Movement, when I practically shouted, "Evidence be damned—death is not the end!" (In fact, I must confess, a few little old ladies jumped out of their seats at the sound of a mild expletive.) Finally, the closing section was delivered quickly and strongly, building to the final doxology. I believe I succeeded in communicating urgency.

I placed great value in the homily on preaching lived truth. My conviction in preparing it was that if the mystery of Easter cannot be experienced, it will not be valued by most. And so each of the three illustrations in the First and Second Movements were grounded in experience. I wanted the doubt and fear to be drawn from real life, and I wanted the experience of resurrection to be drawn from real life. I succeeded at this better in the Second Movement, I believe, because the three illustrations were particularly concrete and accessible.

In terms of honoring the role of preaching in allowing God to address us here and now, I reworked a section to help make this clear. Originally, I ended the funeral illustration with these words: "The resurrection is not an exception, it is an exemplar. God's all-powerful love will not be defeated; the loving embrace of God is what lies on the other side of the grave." As I edited my draft, though, I sensed an opportunity for a more actualizing way of saying this. I explicitly stated that Easter is God's promise. I then made bold to speak as God directly to my listeners, and so that passage became this: "The resurrection is God's promise to each of us tonight: 'My all-powerful love will not be defeated; my loving embrace is what awaits you on the other side of the grave.'"

One would not want to overuse this technique of having God speak, but if used judiciously and done well, it can be extremely effective. The preacher using this technique, though, must be as sure as possible that God's "message" is compatible with the God of Jesus Christ whom we come to know in the Scriptures. In this case I felt on solid ground as I poetically expressed what is at the heart of Easter.

I sought to help elicit an encounter with Christ for my listeners in a few ways. First, I hope that even though you were only reading my words on a page, my reverence for the presence of Christ in the liturgy emerged. The Easter Vigil is such a powerful liturgy in so many ways, and I tried to honor the manifold presence of Christ there in my words and in my bearing. In addition, the three illustrations in the Second Movement were precisely illustrations of meeting Christ here and now. My hope in sharing my experiences of the Risen One was that listeners would recall analogous experiences, and in that recall meet Jesus anew. Finally, I played a bit with my verb tenses. The first illustration of the First Movement was all about the past: Jesus was good, Jesus died. Then, in the Second Movement I shifted to present tense: "Christ is alive," "We are empowered by the Spirit of the Risen Lord. . . ," and so on.

In the liturgy "the work of our redemption is accomplished."[23] How did I honor this in the preaching part of the liturgy—how did I strive to help my listeners experience salvation? First, I was firmly convinced that my message was "good" news—in fact, it was arguably *the* Good News: Christ is raised and death is not the end. The entire Easter Vigil signifies and effects this good news in Word, in baptism, in Eucharist. I strove to preach in such a way as to help the assembly feel the reality of our salvation in Jesus as manifest in the resurrection. Secondly, I was quite conscious of my role in naming grace, specifically the grace of the resurrection here and now. The second half of my homily was an attempt to do just that. In my three illustrations I named the grace of the Risen One at work, in hopes that listeners could join in that naming from their own experiences.

23. Constitution on the Sacred Liturgy, 2.

## The Response to a Homily Reflecting Actualizing Characteristics

As every preacher knows so well, there are no guarantees about the effect our words may have. A homily that is personal, liturgical, inculturated, clarifying, and actualizing in the preacher's mind may still leave at least some hearers cold. Indeed, remember Jesus at the synagogue in Nazareth. He gave what I judge to be the quintessentially actualizing homily. At first his hearers were favorably moved, but later they tried to throw him off a cliff! Accepting the fact that we, too, will have our occasional "cliff Sundays," what kinds of responses can the actualizing preacher normally expect?

If your urgency is manifest, people may well comment on it. You'll hear things like, "Boy, you were really on fire this morning," or "I appreciate your zeal." The more you preach lived truth over book knowledge, the more you'll hear people say, "That homily really rang true," or "I felt that you were on the journey with me, and not just preaching at me." When we honor the homily as a means for God to speak here and now, we can expect positive reaction. "I heard God this morning." "God really spoke to me." So, too, if we have successfully elicited an encounter with Jesus: "I felt the Lord here with me," or "I know that Jesus will be walking with me this week." And if all our ducks are in order, and if the Spirit wills, our people will experience the salvation that the liturgy signifies and effects. Redemption becomes more real, and our people can say, "I feel freed, forgiven, and loved." No preacher could ask for anything more or aim for anything less.

# CHAPTER 9

# Arriving at the Sunday Message: Three Necessary Encounters with the Word

In the last five chapters we've explored the vision and practice of Sunday preaching. Building on the contributions of thirty years' worth of Roman Catholic documents, I have shared with you the five characteristics of the Sunday homily: it is to be personal, liturgical, inculturated, clarifying, and actualizing—PLICA for short. We have looked at the components of each of those characteristics and how to enflesh them in our Sunday preaching. In the present chapter and the next, I will concentrate on the process of preparing a PLICA homily. In taking two chapters to discuss the homiletic preparation process, I am honoring the classic distinction articulated by Fred Craddock in his book *Preaching:* "The process of arriving at something to say is to be distinguished from the process of determining how to say it."[1] In this chapter we will examine a process for arriving at our Sunday message, that is, arriving at the single, declarative sentence that will be the focus of our homily. The following chapter will examine a process for moving from that message to an effective Sunday homily.

## Interpretation: The Road to a Sunday Message

At the heart of arriving at our Sunday message is the act of scriptural interpretation. As we have seen earlier, Roman Catholic officials figured out

1. Fred B. Craddock, *Preaching* (Nashville: Abingdon Press, 1985) 84.

(in stages) that actualizing the Word of God required more than what was being done on Sundays. The liturgical reform of the Second Vatican Council finally allowed for the proclamation of the Sunday Scriptures in the vernacular—a mere four hundred years after the Reformers had! But translation to an understandable tongue is not alone sufficient to inculturate the Word. "Translation has to be followed by *interpretation,* which should set the biblical message in more explicit relationship with the ways of feeling, thinking, living and self-expression which are proper to the local culture."[2] Such interpretation is the preacher's task.

The Catholic understanding of this necessary interpretation embraces many of the tenets espoused by the modern discipline of hermeneutics, that is, the study of the interpretation of texts. Three key principles make the preacher's effective interpretation of the Bible possible.

***The Text's Plurality of Meaning.*** The first hermeneutical principle is that literary texts are open to a "plurality of meaning." This principle stands in marked contrast to the position shared by biblical fundamentalists and early practitioners of the historical-critical method, namely, that a scriptural text has only one meaning. For fundamentalists, that meaning is immediately obvious to the reader; for historical-critical purists, that one meaning is discoverable through scientific analysis. Current Catholic understanding of biblical interpretation rejects this "single meaning" hypothesis. As the Pontifical Biblical Commission noted,

> A written text has the capacity to be placed in new circumstances, which will illuminate it in different ways, adding new meanings to the original sense. This capacity of written texts is especially operative in the case of the biblical writings, recognized as the Word of God. Indeed, what encouraged the believing community to preserve these texts was the conviction that they would continue to be bearers of light and life for generations of believers to come.[3]

This first hermeneutical principle accounts for the fact that even after two thousand years of Christian preaching, new things are still being said every Sunday. If there were only one fixed meaning of a scriptural text—a meaning fixed across ages and cultures—then preachers would have run out of things to say long before now!

2. Pontifical Biblical Commission, The Interpretation of the Bible in the Church (Boston: St. Paul Books and Media, 1993) 122–123.

3. Ibid., 83–84.

***The Preacher's Subjectivity.*** The second hermeneutical principle under-lying the preacher's ability to interpret the Bible is that subjectivity is not a bad thing, but rather natural and necessary. Hermeneutical theory re-jects the Enlightenment ideal of the unbiased, purely objective interpreter, recognizing instead that it is simply impossible for a human being to be a *tabula rasa.* We can never approach any text innocent of our own life ex-periences, biases, loves, and faith. By the very nature of the enterprise, "exegesis of the accounts of these [biblical] events necessarily involves the exegete's own subjectivity."[4]

But beyond recognizing the reality of the interpreter's subjectivity, hermeneutics insists that this very subjectivity is a necessary precondi-tion to textual interpretation. Two ways of expressing this precondition emerge from the literature: the interpreter's "pre-understanding" and the interpreter's "affinity" with the text. Each has significance for the preacher as interpreter.

A first aspect of subjectivity is the interpreter's "pre-understanding." Adopting the work of Bultmann, Gadamer, and others, the Pontifical Bib-lical Commission recognizes the important place of the interpreter's own understanding of self and world.

> Modern hermeneutics has made clear . . . the impossibility of interpreting a text without starting from a "pre-understanding" of one type or another. Catholic exegetes approach the biblical text with a pre-understanding which holds closely together modern scientific culture and the religious tradition emanating from Israel and from the early Christian community.[5]

When interpreting the Bible, "particular presuppositions, such as the faith lived in ecclesial community and the light of the Spirit, control its inter-pretation."[6] This aspect of subjectivity is necessary for authentic interpre-tation, but not sufficient nor absolute. That is because the interpreter must be open to being interpreted by the text itself. "To avoid subjectivism, how-ever, one must allow pre-understanding to be deepened and enriched— even to be modified and corrected—by the reality of the text."[7]

The Sunday preacher, then, enters the interpretive process fully aware of the presuppositions brought to the text. Some are fixed, such as belief

4. Ibid., 79.
5. Ibid., 88.
6. Ibid., 80.
7. Ibid., 77.

in God, the incarnation, the paschal mystery, the ongoing work of the Spirit, and the Bible's status as Word of God. Other elements of pre-understanding vary from preacher to preacher, based on personal experience, age, denomination, culture, and so on. But all aspects of our pre-understanding affect our interpretation of the Sunday texts.

A second aspect of subjectivity is the necessity for affinity between interpreter and text. "Access to a proper interpretation of biblical texts is only granted to the person who has an affinity with what the text is saying on the basis of life experience."[8] This affinity "constitutes, in fact, one of the conditions that makes the entire exegetical enterprise possible."[9] As we shall see, this principle means that an important part of preparing the Sunday homily is identifying the affinities that exist between the world of the text and the world of the Sunday assembly. This hermeneutical principle, by the way, underlies my claim in the last chapter that preachers preach most effectively when preaching lived truth. When something in the text corresponds with something in the preacher's life, there is affinity and there is homiletic power.

***The Biblical Mandate.*** Plurality of meaning, subjectivity, pre-understanding, affinity—all are concepts from general hermeneutical theory adopted by current Catholic thinking. But one final hermeneutical principle is particular to biblical interpretation, and it is this: The interpretation of the Bible is demanded by the Bible and modeled in the Bible.

> The Bible itself and the history of its interpretation point to the need for a hermeneutics—for an interpretation, that is, that proceeds from and addresses our world today. The whole complex of the Old and New Testament writings show themselves to be the product of a long process where founding events constantly find reinterpretation through connection with the life of communities of faith.[10]

The Bible models for its interpreter the interpretation of scriptural events by "re-reading" accounts of past faith experience in the light of new faith experience. The Interpretation of the Bible in the Church describes this well:

> One thing that gives the Bible an inner unity, unique of its kind, is the fact that later biblical writings often depend upon earlier ones. These more re-

8. Ibid., 79.
9. Ibid., 89.
10. Ibid., 79.

cent writings allude to older ones, create *"re-readings" (relectures)* which develop new aspects of meaning, sometimes quite different from the original sense. A text may also make explicit reference to older passages, whether it is to deepen their meaning or to make known their fulfillment.[11]

The same document gives many examples of the phenomenon of re-reading. For instance, take Nathan's prophecy of a "house" for David. The Bible gives witness to re-reading this prophecy, as its meaning develops from dynastic succession to a return of Davidic kingship over Israel to a universal kingdom, to—in the New Testament—fulfillment in Jesus. Of course, for Christians the most common and important scriptural re-reading is that of the New Testament. For "it is in the light of the events of Easter that the authors of the New Testament read anew the scriptures of the Old."[12]

When preachers engage the interpretive process, then, they are fulfilling a biblical mandate. Even more, a preacher's preparation continues the pattern established by the Bible itself. In their interpretation of the Sunday texts, preachers "re-read Scriptures in the light of [their] new context, which is that of life in the Spirit"[13] who animates both preacher and assembly, here and now.

***Characteristics of Sunday Interpretation.*** Preachers who adopt the three hermeneutical principles sketched out above will find their biblical interpretation marked by three things. The first is creativity. The preacher as interpreter acts upon the belief that the plurality of meaning in the biblical texts allows those ancient texts to speak to us in our very concrete circumstances. As the Bible itself re-read events in the light of ongoing experience, so the "interpretation of the Bible should likewise involve an aspect of creativity; it ought also to be able to confront new questions, so as to respond to them out of the Bible."[14]

The second characteristic is a respect for pluralism. The Pontifical Biblical Commission couldn't be clearer on this point:

> The Bible is a repository of many ways of interpreting the same events and reflecting upon the same problems. In itself it urges us to avoid excessive simplification and narrowness of spirit. . . . [I]nterpretation must necessarily

11. Ibid., 90.
12. Ibid., 93.
13. Ibid., 85.
14. Ibid., 95.

show a certain pluralism. No single interpretation can exhaust the meaning of the whole, which is a symphony of many voices.[15]

A final characteristic marking the preacher as interpreter is fidelity to gospel values. The preacher interprets the Sunday Scriptures with the goal of actualizing them in the homily. But this interpretation happens always and only in the context of the teachings and life of Jesus Christ. "Clearly to be rejected," then, "is every attempt at actualization set in a direction contrary to *evangelical justice and charity,* such as, for example, the use of the Bible to justify racial segregation, anti-Semitism or sexism whether on the part of men or of women."[16] Not every text in the Bible is of equal merit, nor is every interpretation fair game. The record of Jesus's call to justice and love always controls the preacher's efforts to interpret other texts.

The current Catholic understanding of scriptural interpretation, then, walks the middle road between fundamentalism and historical-critical absolutism. On the one hand,

> the basic problem with fundamentalist interpretation . . . [is its] refusing to take into account the historical character of biblical revelation. . . . It refuses to admit that the inspired Word of God has been expressed in human language and that this Word has been expressed, under divine inspiration, by human authors possessed of limited capacities and resources.[17]

Indeed, fundamentalist interpretation

> accepts the literal reality of an ancient, out-of-date cosmology, simply because it is found in the Bible; this blocks any dialogue with a broader way of seeing the relationship between culture and faith. Its relying upon a non-critical reading of certain texts of the Bible serves to reinforce political ideas and social attitudes that are marked by prejudices—racism, for example—quite contrary to the Christian gospel.[18]

In short, "fundamentalism actually invites people to a kind of intellectual suicide."[19] Intellectual suicide is not a good road to a Sunday message.

15. Ibid., 94–95.
16. Ibid., 121.
17. Ibid., 73.
18. Ibid., 74–75.
19. Ibid., 75.

On the other hand, though, the current Catholic adoption of modern hermeneutical principles means that the tyranny of the scientific approach to the Scriptures is likewise to be rejected. "Contemporary hermeneutics is a healthy reaction to historical positivism and to the temptation to apply to the study of the Bible the purely objective criteria used in the natural sciences."[20] The purist version of the historical-critical method directs all its efforts into defining "the" one sense of a biblical text. But this purist version "has now run aground on the conclusions of theories of language and of philosophical hermeneutics, both of which affirm that written texts are open to a plurality of meaning."[21] Neither, then, is "objective" science the road to a good Sunday message.

It is my conviction that to walk the middle road described above—to interpret the Sunday Scriptures with accuracy and power—three encounters with the Word are necessary. The preacher must have an initial encounter, an exegetical encounter, and a hermeneutical encounter. Each of these has its own unique nature and method, and yet they work together to make biblical interpretation possible for the Sunday preacher. Let's take a closer look at these three encounters with the Word and how together they lead to the formulation of a Sunday message.

## The Initial Encounter: Experiencing the Word

The preacher's initial encounter with the Sunday Scriptures is first of all noteworthy for what it is not: it is neither exegetical nor hermeneutical nor even an attempt to figure out what to preach about. No, the preacher's initial encounter with the text is simply and profoundly an attempt to hear the text as the Sunday assembly will and to open one's head and heart to the inherent power of the Word. Our initial encounter is an effort to experience the Word.

Many preachers find it conducive to this first encounter with the Sunday Scriptures to spend time with the Word away from the usual office setting. We need neither library nor computer at this stage, but only a place of quiet and prayer. Perhaps the place where you pray best would be a good place for this initial encounter. What is needed when we arrive in this place is a Lectionary (and perhaps a Bible), pen and paper, and an open heart.

20. Ibid., 79.
21. Ibid., 81.

I would suggest reading the four scriptural passages (first reading, psalm, second reading, gospel) in their liturgical order. Although it is often the case that the gospel passage has influenced the choice of one or both of the earlier readings, the liturgical order is the order in which the Sunday assembly experiences these Scriptures. And from the very outset of the preacher's encounters with the Word, we must have our congregants along with us. The preacher encounters the text as a person of faith seeking the Lord, but also always as a representative of the Sunday community. So it seems best at the very beginning to hear the texts as our people will.

After some time in quiet meditation, it is not too early to pick which of the four texts you feel you might like to engage further. Although the Lectionary provides preachers with a great feast of scriptural images each Sunday, it is my conviction that a clear and focused homily almost always demands sticking with one text.[22] The preacher who seeks the "golden thread" to tie all the readings together into a single, coherent insight is the preacher on a fool's mission. Almost always, preaching on three or four texts means three or four mini-homilies. So, having heard the Sunday readings and prayed with them, pick one to engage further. You may ultimately change your mind, but a choice at this point is important.

Next, one could reflect on the chosen text using the five characteristics of the homily: PLICA. I find that keeping the homiletic end in mind, even at this early stage, helps keep me focused and on task. So perhaps the following reflection questions could be of help to you in this initial encounter.

***Personal: What immediately strikes me about this text, in head or heart?*** Having pondered the Word, what happened inside of me? Perhaps a word, or a phrase, or an image caught my attention. Maybe an emotion was stirred or a memory fired. At this early stage, be aware of any intellectual or emotional movement within—and jot those movements down.

***Liturgical: How did the juxtaposition of the texts affect my hearing of them? How does the liturgical season impact my hearing?*** Although one is concentrating on only one text, that text will be proclaimed in the context of the other readings. Was there something from the first reading that helped me connect with the gospel, for instance? Additionally, the liturgical season may color my initial reactions. Perhaps the ex-

---

22. For more on this topic, see Stephen V. DeLeers, "More Than One Text? No!" in *PREACH: Enlivening the Pastoral Art* (May/June 2004) 35–36.

pectant hope of Advent revealed a layer of meaning I would otherwise have missed in my chosen text.

***Inculturated: What might immediately strike my community about this text?*** As I noted, the Sunday assembly needs to accompany the preacher down the road of preparation, so it is not too soon for the preacher to speculate on how a passage might be heard. Is there an image sure to resonate or a character sure to engage? Hear with the ears of your people, and jot down some of those insights.

***Clarifying: What would my people have problems with in this text?*** Part of clarifying a Sunday text is anticipating the assembly's resistance to the Scriptures. As with those who heard Jesus in Capernaum, many today find the Lord's words hard: "When many of his disciples heard it, they said, 'This teaching is difficult; who can accept it?'" (John 6:60). In our initial encounter, we note what we find difficult about the text and what we suspect our people will object to.

***Actualizing: How is God speaking to me in this initial encounter?*** Christians trust that when we come to the Bible in prayer, with faith and openness, God will be with us. As this initial encounter with the text draws to a close, it behooves us to jot down any stirrings of the Spirit of which we have been aware.

In each of the preacher's encounters with text, there are temptations to be resisted. In this initial encounter, I am aware of several that never cease plaguing me. First on the list is the temptation to skip this encounter entirely and move on to exegesis. As we will see next, exegesis is a crucial part of the interpretive enterprise, but at this initial encounter, it is simply too soon to invite the scholars into the room. This first meeting should involve only the preacher, the assembly, and the Lord.

A second temptation is to let the demands of other aspects of ministry dominate my calendar, thus squeezing out the time needed for a prayerful first encounter or delaying that encounter until very late in the week. Preachers could benefit from how organizational experts differentiate between what is "urgent" and what is "important." Without careful analysis and conscious choice, the urgent always dominates the important—and that is bad. A phone call from a known pest, demanding to speak to the pastor, may seem urgent, but it is certainly not important. My conviction is that Sunday homily preparation is among the most important tasks of every pastor. My experience tells me, regrettably, that other tasks seeming more urgent often impinge on the preacher's preparation.

A final temptation during this initial encounter is to move right into homiletic mode. In other words, our first read-through of the Sunday Scriptures finds us casting a homilist's eye at the texts, waiting for a sermon topic to present itself. Or even worse, we make a quick skim of the texts and a decision to preach "what I always talk about when this text comes up." If our goal is to develop a PLICA homily, such early moves into the homiletic mode are disastrously premature.

The preacher's task in the initial encounter, then, is simply this: to hear the Sunday texts as our people will (sans preparation, sans commentary) and to note initial reactions and stirrings of the Spirit.

## The Exegetical Encounter: Understanding the Word

Having spent some reflective time with the Sunday scriptural text, the preacher next invites the biblical scholars to join in the journey toward a Sunday message. Such scholars are irreplaceable allies, as the preacher's second necessary encounter with the Word is an exegetical encounter. The preacher seeks through this encounter to understand what the scriptural text meant in its original context.

In chapter 7 I briefly sketched the range of biblical scholarship available to the preacher. From the current Catholic perspective, however, the starting point for a preacher's exegetical encounter is familiarity with the results of historical-critical analysis of the Sunday text.

It was not always so. As was noted in chapter 1, early in the twentieth century various popes condemned the newly emergent historical-critical method of biblical exegesis. By the mid-1940s, though, some tolerance on the part of Catholic officialdom began to be evident. And by 1993 the Pontifical Biblical Commission could write:

> The historical-critical method is the indispensable method for the scientific study of the meaning of ancient texts. Holy Scripture, inasmuch as it is the "Word of God in human language," has been composed by human authors in all its various parts and in all the sources that lie behind them. Because of this, its proper understanding not only admits the use of this method but actually requires it.[23]

23. Ibid., 35.

The preacher's second encounter with the text, then, takes place in our study or library—wherever we have access to the work of biblical scholars. A good place to begin the work of coming to understand the text in its original context is to read commentaries that explain the results of historical-critical research into the passage at hand. Such research helps the preacher to understand how the text came to reach its final form, and the pastoral realities of both the first hearers and the early churches that had an impact on that final form. Scholars help us to hear the text as its first recipients would have—attuned to historical, cultural, and linguistic nuances that no twenty-first-century American would catch without help. Luckily for the preacher, there are many excellent biblical commentaries available. We are deprived of the results of historical-critical research only by choosing to be.

Of course, the wealth of exegetical insight does not end with the historical-critical method. Narrative analysts, rhetorical analysts, cultural anthropologists, and more all contribute to our knowledge of the text. Some very fresh work has been done in the last twenty years by exegetes exploring the role of women in the Scriptures, and that research has deepened our knowledge. The best gift that preachers can give themselves—and their congregations—is a constantly expanding library of the best available biblical scholarship. We come to know our Sunday texts better only through study.

I mentioned in chapter 7 that the professional exegetes inform us, inspire us, and protect us. I'd like to expand on that last contribution. On the one hand, exegetical scholarship helps protect us from eisegesis—reading meaning into a text rather than drawing its meaning out. The Interpretation of the Bible in the Church put it well: "To avoid, then, purely subjective readings, an interpretation valid for contemporary times will be founded on the study of the text and such an interpretation will constantly submit its presuppositions to verification by the text."[24] On the other hand, though, exegetical scholarship can protect the preacher from elements of the text that are no longer valid for Christians. Cultural anthropology can help the preacher greatly in this regard, as it "allows one to distinguish more clearly those elements of the biblical message that are permanent, as having their foundation in human nature, and those which are more contingent, being due to the particular features of certain cultures."[25] For instance, "Slaves,

---

24. Ibid., 80.
25. Ibid., 63.

obey your earthly masters with fear and trembling" (Eph 6:5) is no longer taken by Christians as indication of God's approval of human slavery. Neither do mainline Christians require that women hide their hair or keep silent in church, St. Paul notwithstanding. Exegetes, then, both protect the text from the eisegetical preacher and protect the preacher from culturally contingent elements of the text.

Since our ultimate goal is to develop a Sunday homily manifesting the PLICA characteristics, those can once again guide our interaction with the exegetes. Perhaps the following reflection questions can help you bring your exegetical encounter to a focused and fruitful conclusion.

***Personal: What exegetical insights am I choosing to engage? Why?*** When we've read through a number of commentaries and jotted down some notes, almost inevitably some of what we've learned interests us more than the rest. It is helpful to be aware of this and to take the next step of exploring why. My finding something to be interesting is not alone reason enough to share it on Sunday.

***Liturgical: How will my proclamation of this text be affected by what I have learned about it?*** Good preaching begins with good proclamation of the text to be preached on. The more we learn about a text, the better we are able to understand and express its nuances when we read it aloud.

***Inculturated: How might my people hear the exegetical insight I have engaged? What effect might it have on them?*** Once again, our Sunday assembly must be with us in this second encounter with the text. As we seize on some new insight garnered from the scholars, we must be anticipating how that insight might affect our people. I remember well when a biblical professor of mine failed in this task. He was speaking to a gathering of Catholic school teachers and decided to share with them some of Bultmann's program of demythologization. Shock and panic ensued. The next day the front page of the local paper featured this headline: "Jesus did not walk on water, priest says"! The professor failed to anticipate the kind of effect scholarly exegesis can have; preachers must not fail in this regard.

***Clarifying: What do my people need to know about this passage? What must they grasp?*** For the most part, the work we do in the exegetical encounter will not show up explicitly in the homily. Sunday worship is not the time for Bible study per se, but rather the time for actualizing the Scriptures so that their power becomes real in the lives of those gathered. That having been said, however, there will be times in which our preaching will contain information—Bible facts, if you will. This becomes necessary when some life-giving aspect of the text is obscured or hidden from the average listener. For instance, many contemporary worshipers miss the power and beauty of Ephesians 5:21-33 because they can't get beyond the admonition "Wives, be subject to your husbands." A preacher preaching on this text would almost certainly need to spend a bit of time explaining how the author of the epistle was using standard—now outdated—household codes as a way of making a powerful point: that "out of reverence for Christ" we Christians are to carry one another's burdens.

***Actualizing: How will this new knowledge help them to be grasped by the God of Scripture?*** Though our exegetical homework may at times find a place in the homily, the sharing of Bible facts is never an end in itself. The results of scientific exegesis are only tools the preacher uses to help the Sunday assembly experience anew the saving love of God. So as we come to the end of our second encounter with the text, we should be explicit in asking ourselves how what we have learned about the Sunday lection can be used to help actualize that text.

This exegetical encounter with the text has its own set of temptations to be resisted. The first is the same temptation that confronted us with the initial encounter, that is, the temptation to skip this encounter completely. Particularly as the years of exegetical study roll by, we might be tempted to read a Sunday lection and think that we already know everything we need to know about the passage. But the scholarly work of exegesis goes on, and there is always more to learn. Of course, this implies ongoing investment in the work of scholars of quality. If you still have the same set of commentaries you had ten years ago, then it might well be a waste of your time re-reading them yet again. Rather, one of the great sources of freshness in our preaching work is being exposed to new ideas, new research, a new way of looking at all those old, familiar texts.

A second temptation in the exegetical encounter is settling for secondhand or thirdhand scholarship. The opportunity to give in to this temptation arises out of the popularity of subscription "sermon aids" and "homily helps." The majority of subscription sermon aids are not written by exegetes. Their exegetical content (if any) is secondhand or thirdhand at best. Rather than reading C. H. Dodd or Raymond Brown on John's Gospel, some preachers are reading Pastor X's thoughts on Dodd or Brown—or even worse, Pastor X's thoughts on the recycled commentary that drew on Dodd or Brown. Preachers are always better off reading the exegetes directly. Opt to buy a commentary written by a recognized scholar rather than subscribing to a service whose scholarship is dubious at best. At the very least, preachers should commit each year to buying a commentary on the Gospel that will be preached on during that cycle of the Lectionary. Over the years their library will grow, and they will remain fresh.

A final temptation in this second encounter is the same as in the first encounter: moving too quickly into the homiletic mode. The goal of the exegetical encounter is not to come up with a homily, but rather to understand the scriptural text in its original context. Such exegesis informs, inspires, and protects preachers, as we have seen. But exegesis in itself is insufficient preparation for arriving at a Sunday message. One final encounter is needed.

### The Hermeneutical Encounter: Actualizing the Word

The last encounter with the text on our way to arriving at a Sunday message is a hermeneutical encounter—interpreting the text in its present-day context. The exegetical encounter helped the preacher understand the text in its original context, but such understanding is not enough for actualizing preaching. Rather,

> all exegesis of texts is . . . summoned to make itself fully complete through a "hermeneutics" . . . overcoming the distance between the time of the authors and first addressees of the biblical texts and our own contemporary age, and of doing so in a way that permits correct actualization of the scriptural message so that the Christian life of faith may find nourishment.[26]

As in the first two encounters, the preacher may find it helpful to let the PLICA characteristics guide the hermeneutical encounter.

*Personal: What excites me most about this passage? Why?* Back in the initial encounter, we noted our first feelings about the text. Now, however, having prayed with the text and studied the text, it is time to discover the source of the passion that will allow us to preach with urgency. Perhaps an exegetical insight gave the text new life for us, or perhaps a

26. Ibid., 78–79.

phrase spoken by Jesus has echoed in our heart. Maybe a character in a parable struck us as someone we'd love to know, or one of the disciples reminded us of ourselves. Whatever the way, God does speak to us through the biblical texts, and that should excite us.

***Liturgical: What aspect of the assembly's identity as Church is strengthened by this text?*** As we discussed earlier, one the purposes of liturgy is confirming our people's identity as the Body of Christ. The Word proclaimed and preached has the potential to upbuild that ecclesial identity. But the Christian life embraces a wide gamut of beliefs, attitudes, and actions, and one can't preach about everything all the time. So, in this hermeneutical encounter, preachers might like to reflect on the aspect of Christian identity that is highlighted by the text at hand. The Prodigal Son might remind us of the place forgiveness plays in the lives of Christ's disciples, while the Good Samaritan might remind us of the importance of charity. Almost any biblical text can suggest an answer to the question: How am I to live out my baptismal union with Jesus Christ?

***Inculturated: What affinities can I identify between people in the pericope and/or original audience and my people? What cultural realities are on my mind as I encounter this text?*** The inculturated character of the Sunday homily requires that preachers have the ability to correlate and interpret Scripture and present experience. It is in this third encounter with the text that we tackle that correlative task. We saw above that hermeneutical theory holds that interpretation of texts is possible only when affinity exists between text and interpreter. Now is the time to identify that affinity. Having prayed with the text and studied it, we ask what the people of God in the pericope or the people of God for whom the biblical author wrote have in common with the people of God who will gather this Sunday. Affinities can be found on many levels. Perhaps the text is wrestling with a perennial problem of human nature or religious faith, a problem still grappled with by the preacher and the congregation. Maybe one of the characters in a biblical story manifests traits or concerns that most could identify with. Perhaps the action that drives a biblical story is an action that drives Christian life today—doubt resolved, fear allayed, forgiveness given, for instance. Maybe emotions present in the text resonate with the emotions currently dominating your community. In all these ways and more, the preacher identifies the affinity of text and people.

This work of identification will always take into account the cultural realities of the congregation and of the world in which they live. A text that warms the heart of one culture might leave another cold. And world events can inspire a preacher to draw meanings from a text never before imagined. To give a gruesome example, I remember preaching the Sunday after the arrest of Jeffrey Dahmer, whose obscene serial killings shocked my hometown of Milwaukee. The story was so omnipresent and so disturbing to everyone that I could not imagine failing to preach about it. The crafters of the Lectionary, of course, cannot and have not anticipated the course of history. But one of the texts appointed for that Sunday spoke with power to me as I confronted the Dahmer story. I was not guilty of eisegesis, but I certainly did preach the text in a way that had never before occurred to me. I experienced the grace reflected in modern hermeneutical theory: old texts can speak powerfully in new contexts. The key to this power is identifying the affinities between text and our Sunday assemblies.

***Clarifying: In light of my three encounters with the text, what one central point is worth making this Sunday?*** Having had my initial PLICA encounter with the Sunday lection, having used the PLICA characteristics to focus my exegetical research, and now having identified what excites me about this text and the affinities between it and my people, now I am ready to decide on a Sunday message. As was mentioned in chapter 7, I plight my troth with those homileticians who believe that preachers should be able to state the central concern of their homilies in one declarative sentence, the simpler the better. Drawing on the work of his peers, Paul Scott Wilson offers a set of synonyms for that sentence: "focus statement, unifying theme, sermon-in-a-sentence, central idea, controlling idea, major concern of the text, what the text says."[27] Call it what you will—I like "message"—but now is the time in our preparation process to create one. Actually, "create" is probably an inaccurate word choice, since this crucial moment in homily preparation is the moment of inspiration. We have done our homework, and now the Lord works through our imaginations and heads and hearts to grant us a Sunday message.

***Actualizing: How has God manifested himself to me through my encounters with the text? How is my message good news?*** The PLICA preacher seeks to create a homily that will do no less than facilitate an en-

27. Paul Scott Wilson, *The Practice of Preaching* (Nashville: Abingdon Press, 1995) 150.

counter with Christ, an experience of salvation. But as the old saying goes, we can't give what we don't have. At this final moment of our preparatory work with the Sunday text, we should look back over the three encounters and name and give thanks for the ways in which we have experienced God through our work. The consolations, the challenges, the insights—we give thanks for all the ways in which God spoke to us through the text. Such explicit naming and gratitude will help us in our task of actualizing the scriptural text, as it fuels our urgency (God is speaking!) and confirms our interpretation as lived truth. Furthermore, I think it is good practice to fig-uratively place ourselves in the pews, listen to the Sunday message we have arrived at, and ask bluntly: Is this good news? As I hear it, am I sup-ported in my faith, overwhelmed by amazing grace, reassured of salva-tion in Christ? If so, your message has passed the final test. The three encounters with the Sunday text have yielded a message that can be de-veloped into a fully PLICA homily.

As with the previous two encounters, though, there are temptations lurking during the hermeneutical encounter. They are all forms of one temptation, that is, the temptation toward inadequate interpretation of the Sunday text. Through my own experience and through the research of Barbara Reid and Leslie Hoppe of Catholic Theological Union,[28] I've iden-tified four flawed, though common, attempts at interpretation.

***Mining and refining the nugget.*** Here the assigned Scriptures are treated by the preacher as one big idea mine. The preacher puts on a miner's hat and searches around until finding an attractive nugget. The preacher then mines the nugget, refining and shaping it to fit some favorite agenda. For example, on the Third Sunday of Lent (B), the preacher reads the Gospel passage—the cleansing of the Temple (John 2:12-25)—and the word "signs" jumps out (as in "they could see the signs he was performing"). The preacher then goes on to preach about the sign of Jesus's healing ministry and how that continues today in charismatic laying on of hands. See what hap-pened: the preacher mined a single word and then removed it from its scriptural and liturgical context, using it instead as a pretext for "ferverino no. 472" on faith healing. Missing in action are the significance of the cleans-ing of the Temple and the season of Lent. This is flawed interpretation.

28. Barbara E. Reid and Leslie J. Hoppe, *Preaching from the Scriptures: New Directions for Preparing Preachers* (Chicago: Catholic Theological Union, 1998).

***Have I got a story for you.*** This is a model closely related to the first. It's found most in preachers who have the entire "Chicken Soup for the Blank" series. You love to tell stories, and you think people like stories, and so the Scriptures in the context of the liturgy serve not as ancient texts speaking modern grace but rather as prompts for the latest story you heard or read. There's nothing wrong with a judiciously chosen story in support of your scriptural message, but it is no interpretation at all to use the Sunday readings as mere cues for a story.

***Paging Dr. Freud.*** Here the assigned Scriptures are a jumping-off point for a psychological commentary on human experience. One of the preachers in the Catholic Theological Union study, for instance, when preaching on the Third Sunday of Lent (A), proclaimed John's story of the Samaritan woman at the well (John 4:5-42) and went on to give a homily on sexual addiction (her multiple husbands was apparently the jumping-off point). Jesus was a good psychologist, and so must the homilist be, but we must be cautious about leaving Scripture and liturgy behind as we share the latest psychological theory. This is flawed interpretation.

***From "is" to "ought."*** This is a very common dynamic in preaching whereby the preacher takes whatever text the liturgy offers and turns it into moralizing. I never cease to be amazed at how we can take a text of pure blessing like the first beatitude, "How blessed are the poor in spirit," and turn it into a moral imperative, "You must be poor in spirit." I hate to speak for our Lord, but I think that if Jesus had wanted on that Mount to issue a new set of commandments instead of a set of blessings, he would have done so. Nonetheless, how quick we preachers are to go from the "is" of grace to the "ought" of moralizing! I very much resonate the Pontifical Biblical Commission on this matter. It warns that "good hermeneutical principles are necessary," as is adequate preparation. Indeed,

> want of preparation in this area leads to the temptation to avoid plumbing the depths of the biblical readings and to being content simply to moralize or to speak of contemporary issues in a way that fails to shed upon them the light of God's word. . . . Preachers should certainly avoid insisting in a one-sided way on the obligations incumbent upon believers. The biblical message must preserve its principal characteristic of being the good news of salvation freely offered by God. Preaching will perform a task more useful and more conformed to the Bible if it helps the faithful above all to "know the gift of God" (John 4:10) as it has been revealed in

Scripture; they will then understand in a positive light the obligations that flow from it.[29]

I conclude my meditation on homiletic temptations with a warning about skipping any of the three encounters with the text described in this chapter. When a preacher stops after the initial encounter and skips the exegesis and hermeneutics, what the people get is how the pastor *feels* about the Scriptures. That *may* be interesting, but I'm not sure how it is life-giving or life-changing!

When a preacher stops after doing the exegetical homework, what people get is a lot of Bible-study facts. You know you've skipped the hermeneutical moment when a parishioner comes up after a homily and says, "Pastor, that was fascinating. I never knew about the annual rainfall in the Jordan Valley!" Again, it's good to be interesting, but it's not quite enough.

On the other hand, when a preacher attempts to interpret the Scriptures for today without having had a personal encounter with the text, the interpretation will lack warmth and lack the witness character it so needs.

Or, if a preacher attempts to interpret the Scriptures for today without having done the exegetical homework, then very often we get the models I mentioned earlier: mining and refining the nugget, have I got a story for you, paging Dr. Freud, or the simplistic move from "is" to "ought." Or worse, we speak foolishness or even heresy.

The three-stage journey to arriving at a message represents the first half of the process of creating a Sunday homily. These three encounters with the text represent the irreplaceable interactions required of every preacher. In his letter on the importance of Sunday, Pope John Paul II put it well:

> Clearly, much depends on those who exercise the ministry of the word. It is their duty to prepare the reflection on the word of the Lord by prayer and study of the sacred text, so that they may then express its contents faithfully and apply them to people's concerns and to their daily lives.[30]

In our initial encounter with the Sunday text, we pray. In our exegetical encounter, we study the sacred text. In our hermeneutical encounter, we interpret the text, in fidelity to its original meaning and its significance for the lives of our people.

---

29. Interpretation of the Bible in the Church, 129.

30. John Paul II, apostolic letter On Keeping the Lord's Day Holy *(Dies Domini)* 40. Accessed at <http://www.vatican.va/holy_father/john_paul_ii/apost_letters/documents/hf_jp-ii_apl_05071998_dies-domini_en.html>.

# CHAPTER 10

# From Message to Homily: Content, Structure, and Delivery

Having had our three encounters with the Word, we arrived at our Sunday message—our sermon-in-a-sentence. We have thereby completed the first phase of the process of preparing to preach, namely, arriving at something to say. Now it is time for the second phase, which Fred Craddock names "the process of determining how to say it." Clearly, one sentence will be insufficient to feed our people on Sunday morning! So the preacher needs to determine more fully both the content of the homily and its structure. This determination involves a series of decisions about what must be said and how it must be said, in order that our message be received with clarity and power. In this chapter we look at the decisions involved in moving from message to homily.

## The Place of Writing in Preparing to Preach

To begin, though, let me weigh in on the place that writing has in this process of determining how to preach our message effectively. My short answer: writing plays a critical role in every step of the process, from initial note-taking to completed manuscript. For those preachers who already believe this to be true, bear with me as I try to convince those who do not that writing makes us better preachers.

In a very real way, of course, the phrase "written homily" is an oxymoron. A written text is an object, produced in private, fixed in space. A homily is an oral event, the product not of a single agent, but of the interplay of preacher, hearer, and the Holy Spirit. A homily is not a text. So what role could ink on paper play in effective Sunday preaching?

In a nutshell, writing forces us to create a complete work, which can then be improved prior to its delivery. When we write, we confront directly how we will begin our preaching, how the homily will develop, and how it will conclude. The discipline of working through a sermon sentence by sentence can be accomplished only by writing those sentences down. Once the homiletic manuscript exists, it can be evaluated and changed to improve clarity and effectiveness.

I fear that many preachers have gotten into the practice of moving from Sunday message to sketchy outline to the pulpit. Especially for those with the gift of gab, it is not difficult to take a brief outline and spin it into a ten- or fifteen-minute homily. However, I daresay that such preaching is prone to two of the complaints most often heard from the pews: "The preacher rambles" and "The preacher did not know when to stop." When we have not done the hard work of thinking the homily through, sentence by sentence, it is only to be expected that its development will not be entirely logical, its transitions unclear, its endings manifold. Now, is it possible that a rambling, three-ending manuscript underlies such a problematic homily? Yes, I suppose it is. But the odds of catching and correcting such problems before they happen are much greater when a written version of the homily exists.

There is another benefit to composing our homilies on paper. Ken Untener makes this very good point: "Writing frees us to go beyond the repetitive phrases we customarily use in conversation. . . . 'Writing frees the preacher from the tyranny of his own clichés.'"[1] Again, this benefit of writing is not guaranteed, but we are more likely to catch and eliminate stock phrases, jargon, and commonplace banalities when we have the chance to look over a manuscript than we do "on the fly" during an extemporaneous homily.

Before leaving this topic, it is important to note that homiletic writing differs from most other forms of writing in which we regularly engage. When preachers write, we write with the intention of our words being reconstituted into sound. Or as Fred Craddock put it, preachers write with "anticipated oralizing"[2] as our goal. This implies first that writing a

---

1. Ken Untener, *Preaching Better: Practical Suggestions for Homilists* (New York: Paulist Press, 1999) 49. Untener cites John J. Hughes, *Proclaiming the Good News* (Huntington, Ind.: Our Sunday Visitor, 1983) 1:12-13.

2. Fred B. Craddock, *Preaching* (Nashville: Abingdon Press, 1985) 214.

homily will involve speaking what we write as we write it and again as we review it. Unlike the process of writing an article for a church bulletin, writing for speaking must always be aware of what the words on the page will sound like. In addition, as we write our homiletic manuscript, we must utilize what we might call oral grammar: structures that communicate effectively when heard. Compound-complex sentences, for instance, though elegant on paper, are difficult to understand when heard, since there are no sounds for colons, semicolons, and dashes. I won't dwell on this, as others have written helpful books on writing for speaking.[3] Suffice it to say that pen and paper (or keyboard and monitor) are the preacher's friend and natural ally in the war against rambling, cliché-ridden homilies that don't know when or how to conclude.

## Content: A Homily Has Parts

An effective homily is not just an undifferentiated string of words filling the time available. No, an effective homily has parts; the Sunday message must be analyzed to discover the discrete but related components that bear its content. In turn, these components must be developed using both conceptual and image-based language. To demonstrate what I mean by such discovery and development, let me take a sample walk through this first phase of the process of determining how to express our Sunday message.

***Discovery of Components.*** The first step in the process of determining how best to communicate the message is to consider what areas need to be covered in order for the fullness of the message to emerge.[4] So let's say I am preparing to preach on Matthew 15:21-28 (Twentieth Sunday in Ordinary Time [A]; RCL, Proper 15 [A])—the story of Jesus and the Canaanite women seeking his help for her ill daughter. After my three encounters with that Word, I arrive at this Sunday message: "As Jesus himself did, we, too, strive to practice what we preach." By the grace of God working through my own encounters with the text, I now know the core of what I hope to preach.

But what content does this message really contain? In this case I look closely at my message and discover that I am really talking about three

3. I think especially of G. Robert Jacks, *Just Say the Word: Writing for the Ear* (Grand Rapids: William B. Eerdmans Publishing Company, 1996).

4. Cf. Thomas Long, *The Witness of Preaching* (Louisville: Westminster/John Knox Press, 1989) 107, who speaks of "breaking down" the focus and function of the sermon "into a set of smaller undertakings."

interrelated realities. My message claims that Jesus practiced what he preached. It further claims that Jesus "strove" to practice what he preached—implying some effort was involved. Finally, it claims that we are like Jesus in that we, too, strive to practice what we preach. Given this analysis, I might then conclude that my message requires me to develop three ideas:

- Jesus's beliefs were translated into action. (This would develop the "as Jesus did" aspect of my message.)
- Jesus sometimes struggled to translate his beliefs into action. (This would cover the "strive" aspect in regard to Jesus himself.)
- We, too, strive to make our actions match our words. (This would cover the "we, too, strive" aspect of my message.)

These, then, are the three components of my Sunday message.

A good, quick test to determine whether you've accomplished this first step is to check your components to ensure that every word of your message is accounted for. Notice that in my analysis, each word of my message is represented in at least one of the components: "As Jesus himself did, we, too, strive to practice what we preach."

***Development of Components.*** I am now ready for step two. Having determined the components of my message, I must now move forward and develop them. The task facing the preacher at this stage is surfacing the homiletic material needed to flesh out each component in such a way as to ensure its clarity and affinity with its intended listeners.

Such homiletic material can be divided into two types, each of which plays a role in bringing a component to life. On the one hand, our preaching will involve *explanation*. Here my goal is to express clearly to my listeners what I mean. I will use straightforward, everyday language in the hope of clarifying the content of the component at hand. If I wield this type of language well, my Sunday assembly will be clear about what I intended to communicate to them.

On the other hand, our preaching will involve *illustration*. Here the goal is to verify the content of the component by helping the listeners to recognize its truth in their own experience. The language of illustration enables the listener to recognize what the content of a component actually looks, sounds, smells, tastes, or feels like. Or to put it another way, illustration allows preachers to demonstrate "how they know what they know" by bringing forward evidence from real life.[5] Rhetorically, illustrative language is the language of image, example, anecdote, and story. Illustration could be personal, drawing on the preacher's own experience. Or its inspiration could be liturgical, reflecting upon the assembly's experience as it gathers each Sunday. Illustration is often cultural, drawing from the symbols and habits, the customs and taboos, the events and trends of the day. If preachers wield illustrative language well, they will know that the components of their Sunday message will resonate in the hearts of their people. The affinities between text and Sunday listeners will be experienced.

Let me return to my continuing example. Recall that my Sunday message is this: "As Jesus himself did, we, too, strive to practice what we preach." The first component of the message is this: "Jesus's beliefs were translated into action." How might I use explanation and illustration to flesh out this component? I recalled the old adage "Practice what you preach" and thought that that might make a succinct and utterly clear refrain for explaining this first point. Beyond such explanation, though, I wanted to give illustrations of how Jesus did practice what he preached. I brainstormed some patterns of Jesus's ministry and some familiar examples from his life as well. I pictured the kinds of places Jesus preached and the kinds of lives he touched: lepers, sinners, outcasts (including the Canaanite woman of the day's gospel).

My second component is this: "Jesus sometimes struggled to translate his beliefs into action." In terms of explanatory language, I thought of a very straightforward phrase: this is not easy. Practicing what you preach is not easy. In terms of illustrative language, I knew that I wanted to retell the story of the Canaanite woman in terms of the struggle to practice what you preach. I had the images of the pericope at my disposal, especially the dramatic but troubling dictum of Jesus: "It is not fair to take the children's food and throw it to the dogs."

My third component is this: "We, too, strive to make our actions match our words." Here I would need to clarify that what was not easy for the

---

5. See Hans van der Geest, *Presence in the Pulpit: The Impact of Personality in Preaching,* trans. Douglas W. Stott (Atlanta: John Knox Press, 1981) 120–121. Van der Geest rightly holds that "it is not the exegetical or dogmatic correctness of [preachers'] assertions, but rather their own living relationship to the mystery of faith which has that persuasive power." In light of this, preachers must share "evidential experience" with their listeners.

Son of God will, logically, not be easy for us either. Lurking implicitly in this comparison of Jesus and us, though, is not only the struggle but also the success, which is, after all, the climax of the story. In terms of illustrating this point, I immediately thought of my own experience as preacher, called to practice what I (literally) preach. But then I struggled with a key question, one on which the homily's success would rise or fall: How do those who do not literally preach express words that must be translated into action? For good or for ill, most mainline Christians are not very experienced at water-cooler evangelism. Could I come up with illustrations that would help my listeners identify with Jesus's struggle? As I wrestled with this, I turned to the liturgy and thought about the powerful words we all speak when we gather on Sunday. I reflected upon the Lord's Prayer, and the exchange of peace, and especially Communion: "The Body of Christ." "Amen." I was pretty sure that I was on to something.

At this point I have reached the completion of the first phase of determining how to express my Sunday message: I have discovered the components of that message, and I have developed those components with both explanatory and illustrative language. In this process the PLICA character of the homily has emerged once again. My homiletic goal is to actualize the Sunday text, a goal expressed as my Sunday message. I then used the other characteristics to develop that message. I clarified it by identifying its components and by using the straightforward language of explanation. But I also illustrated my components, drawing on personal, liturgical, and cultural imagery.

## Structure: A Homily's Parts Are Interrelated

I said at the beginning of the last section that a homily is not just an undifferentiated string of words. We have seen so far that a homily's principal content consists of the components of the Sunday message, explained and illustrated—far from an "undifferentiated" blob. But now let me tackle the other side of the preparation story, namely, that a homily is not just a "string of words." No, the effective homily consciously attends to its structure—to the interrelationship of its parts. The preacher's task in this phase of the preparation process is to order what will be said in such a way as to maximize the possibility that listeners will be able to follow the homily as it unfolds.

Both the homily as a whole and its constitutive parts need structure. So let's look in turn at the interrelationship of the components (the question of form), the structure of each developed component (what I call a homiletic movement), and the overall structure of the homily (opening, transitions, and closing).

**Form.** The first task of this second phase of preparation is to discover a logical pattern that will enable the listener to follow the preacher from one component to the next, a pattern that many refer to as a homily's "form." Almost every contemporary homiletician has weighed in on the question of form, and, indeed, there is much to be said. There are rhetorical and anthropological dimensions to the question and plenty of good arguments for and against given patterns of homiletic structure. I will leave those debates to others, however, since it seems there is a consensus bottom line: effective homilies depend upon explicit attention to their structure. The preacher consciously chooses to order the parts of the homily in a way that best facilitates active listening.

The centuries of fixed-form preaching—three points and a poem, exegesis-application, or more recently, story-exegesis-application—have left some homileticians wary of suggesting possible forms. David Buttrick, for example, declares: "There are *no* stock patterns into which meaning can invariably be stuffed. . . . Stock sermon 'outlines' are not much help . . .; they invariably distort or truncate fields of understanding."[6] Yet even Buttrick is forced to admit that an effective sermon must have a "logic of movement": "Sermon scenarios must 'travel' in a way that is natural to human consciousness."[7] In contrast, I think that Fred Craddock has got it right: stock homiletic forms are standards precisely because they have proven to provide exactly what Buttrick is calling for, namely, logical movement natural to human consciousness. "These structures have demonstrated repeatedly that they can carry the burden of truth with clarity, thoroughness, and interest. . . ."[8] Craddock goes on to list twelve classic organizational schemes for sermons.

Thomas Long, too, is convinced that there is a "limited set of tried-and-true homiletic forms that can prove serviceable for most occasions."[9]

---

6. David Buttrick, *Homiletic: Moves and Structures* (Philadelphia: Fortress Press, 1987) 308–309.
7. Ibid., 310.
8. Craddock, *Preaching,* 176.
9. Long, *The Witness of Preaching,* 126.

Building on Craddock and others, he lists eleven "frequently appearing sermon forms."

I would like to offer my own list of organizational schemes for the Sunday homily. In this list I adopt or modify the best of the forms given by Craddock and Long and add a few of my own. The brackets indicate possible variants of the given form.

- If this, then this [and thus this].
- Not this, [or this,] [or this,] but that.
- This, and this, [and this,] therefore that.
- On the one hand this, but on the other hand that, therefore we conclude.
- This? That? Both this and that.
- Either this or that.
- This is true in this way, and also in this way, and in this other way too.
- This is the problem, this is the gospel solution [and these are the implications].
- Here is the gospel promise, and here is how it has been fulfilled today.
- Here is a prevailing view, but here is the claim of the Gospel.
- From ambiguity to clarity.
- From the lesser to the greater.
- Major premise, minor premise, conclusion.
- Thesis, antithesis, synthesis.

I offer this list with the same disclaimer offered by the other list-makers: this is not meant to be exhaustive. I simply wish to bring to consciousness some of the patterns that have proven themselves over the centuries as patterns that help people follow an extended spoken word.

In the homily I've been developing in this chapter, remember that I have three components: Jesus's beliefs were translated into action; Jesus sometimes struggled to translate his beliefs into action; we, too, strive to make our actions match our words. Before going on to actually compose these principal sections of the homily, I need to decide how to relate them to each other to best facilitate understanding. In other words, I need to choose an appropriate form. In this case it seemed to me that the logic of my message dictated this form: "On the one hand this, but on the other hand that, therefore we conclude." That is to say, "Jesus translated belief into action, but he sometimes struggled; therefore we, too, can expect to struggle to make our actions match our words." As we shall see, this decision on form helps me in the next two steps.

***Homiletic Movement.*** The next element of structure to consider is the shape of each developed component in the homily. As explanation and illustration come together to make a component live, how should those sentences be structured?

In his classic *Homiletic: Moves and Structures,* David Buttrick named the components of a sermon "moves."

> Sermons are a movement of language from one idea to another, each idea being shaped in a bundle of words. Thus, when we preach we speak in formed modules of language arranged in some patterned sequence. These modules of language we will call "moves." . . . [Moves are] between three and four minutes in length. . . . All moves have an opening "Statement," and some sort of "Closure." In between, moves have some kind of developmental pattern.[10]

Buttrick spends 235 pages spelling out in remarkable detail his theory of moves and how they work. It is profitable and challenging reading for any preacher. As far as I'm concerned, though, the barest bones of Buttrick are sufficiently helpful, and that is what I just cited above.

I prefer to call a developed component a "movement." In this, I am making a symphonic analogy, as opposed to Buttrick's shorthand for his theory of oral communication. Like symphonies, homilies are composed of sections that are distinct but related. Each section opens, develops, and closes, all in such a way as to continually move the composition as a whole forward. And while I wouldn't be quite as rigid as Buttrick in terms of the length of a movement, I think in general he is about right. Three or four minutes seem to be sufficient to develop an idea without losing the listeners' attention. And I also agree that each homiletic movement should clearly open, positioning the listener for what is about to come. Each movement must then develop the single idea that is its focus. Finally, each movement must clearly close, alerting the listener that the preacher has completed a thought. To see what this theory looks like in practice, let's take a look at a sample movement.

---

10. Buttrick, *Homiletic,* 23, 28, 37.

Recall that my first component is this: "Jesus's beliefs were translated into action." I brainstormed explanatory and illustrative language to develop this component, as noted above. I then put pen to paper and composed this movement.

> "Practice what you preach." I cannot imagine a more succinct description of the pattern of Jesus's life. Practice what you preach.
>
> Jesus knew his holy Scriptures well, and he believed what he read. The God revealed in the Bible was real, and Jesus believed in him.
>
> But that belief did not remain only in his head. Jesus was inspired to preach, to teach, to share his belief. To all who would listen, Jesus spoke about his Abba, the Father-God of love and compassion. From the small gathering at Peter's doorstep to the thronged masses who heard the Sermon on the Mount, Jesus preached.
>
> But neither did Jesus stop there; his beliefs and his teachings were translated into action. Jesus preached a God of love, and he lived that love. Lepers felt his touch. Jesus preached a God of mercy, and he showed that mercy again and again. Sinners were welcomed to his table. Jesus preached a God of inclusivity, a God for all, and he ultimately came to embrace all who sought his help—even a Canaanite woman.
>
> Jesus really did believe what he read, preached what he believed, and practiced what he preached.

Note how this movement is structured. It begins with a clear opening. In three brief sentences I orient the listener to the idea that I am going to be developing. Next, I do the work of development. I use explanatory language, mostly in the form of relatively simple declarative sentences: "Jesus knew his holy Scriptures well, and he believed what he read," and so on. But I also use illustrative language, drawing images from the Scriptures that appeal to our senses and thus to our sense of reality. I invite listeners to hear Jesus's words at Peter's doorstep, to see sinners welcomed to his table, and to feel with the leper Jesus's touch. Finally, I close the movement, in this case by restating the principal idea.

I am convinced that homiletic movements structured in this fashion are an extremely effective way to communicate. They provide a format that is tried and true, but also flexible enough to accommodate any sort of rhetorical content. The balance and ordering of explanatory and illustrative sentences can be handled in any way that advances the movement toward clarity and power. But the bare bones remain clear: opening, development of only one idea using both concepts and images, and closing. Even on those (hopefully) rare occasions when the principal content of a movement is a story, there must be an explanatory opening to the movement and a clear closing.[11]

***Overall Structure of the Homily.*** Having chosen an appropriate form for ordering the components of our Sunday message and having developed each component into a homiletic movement, we are now ready to tackle the final step in composing a Sunday homily. And that step is this: assuring that the homily opens, that the transitions between movements are smooth, and that it closes.

I hold with Buttrick and many others that the overall structure of the homily shares significant commonality with the structure of the constitutive movements. In other words, just as a movement opens, develops, and closes, so, too, does the homily itself open, develop, and close.

*Opening.* The Sunday preacher, no matter how limited in talent, does not need an "attention-getter" to begin the homily. No, regardless of past experience, the assembly gives the preacher its attention in that silent moment of expectation following the proclamation of the gospel. We do not need to get their attention, but rather to hold on to what has already been freely given. The best way to do this is to briefly locate the listeners in the general area to be considered that Sunday. By the end of your brief opening section, the assembly should have formed a notion of the subject of the homily. Now, this is not a matter of the old composition dictum, "Tell 'em what you're going to tell 'em, tell 'em, and tell 'em what you told 'em." In fact, that strategy breeds tedium in preaching. No, the opening section is not the laying out of a thesis, but rather an act of orientation, limiting the field of vision, if you will. So, in my example homily, I decided to draw on a sentence from the Roman Catholic liturgy for the ordination of deacons. The sentence, I thought, would help orient my listeners to the direction of my homily, whose focus is: "As Jesus himself did, we, too, strive to practice what we preach." Here's the way I wrote it:

> In just about a month I will mark the nineteenth anniversary of my ordination as a deacon. I remember clearly kneeling before Bishop Sklba as he handed me a book of the Gospels, just like this one. As I took it, he said: "Receive the gospel of Christ, whose herald you now are. Believe what you read, teach what you believe, and practice what you teach."

---

11. I will have more to say about the use of stories in preaching in the next chapter.

Note that I have not revealed my main message. But by sharing this brief anecdote—particularly its final four words, after which I planned a significant pause—listeners would intuit that what they were about to hear was not going to be a homily on marriage or on forgiveness, but rather something to do with living out our faith. And that is enough. When we open well, we give the listeners a "direction" in which to listen.

*Transitions.* If we have chosen our homiletic form well and kept it in mind while writing, our transitions almost take care of themselves. We know the logical relationship of one movement to another, and so it is not at all difficult to make the transition from one to another. Typically, the first sentence of the movement handles the transition task. It must at once look back to what has just been said and make a connection with what is about to be said. But again, if you already know the logical relationship between the parts, finding the right wording is not difficult at all. Indeed, the form itself often provides the language; a homily structured with the "Not this, [or this,] [or this,] but that" form may well have movements that begin "nor is it the case that," or "this is not the case either," or later, "but rather."

*Closing.* Let me assure you that our parishioners intensely dislike Sunday homilies that don't end, or worse, that end several times. I love the analogy between the aborted landing of an aircraft and the multi-ending homily: all the passengers feel the movement slow and the altitude drop; they see the runway and know they are about to land—and then all of a sudden the pilot pulls back the stick and we are airborne again. Whether in the sky or in church, this is a nauseating experience! So we need to plan out our endings well. The close of a homily need not be a recapitulation of the homily—indeed this is usually not called for. On the other hand, our closing is not normally the time to be introducing entirely new ideas, since we will not have sufficient time to develop them. Rather, and simply, the last four or five sentences of our homily need to communicate that the preacher has reached the end of what needed to be said. There are many ways of doing this, but it must be done.

Before presenting and briefly analyzing the sample homily that I have been developing in this chapter, let me review. In the last chapter we looked at the process of arriving at a Sunday message. Our three encounters with the Word—initial, exegetical, and hermeneutical—led us to compose a "sermon-in-a-sentence." In this chapter we have looked at the process of determining how to communicate that Sunday message. We began by discovering the components of the message—those elements that would need to be developed to make the message come alive. We then brainstormed both explanatory and illustrative language to help develop each component. Next, we tackled matters of structure. We figured out what homiletic form would best help our listeners move from component to component. Then we developed each component into a full-fledged homiletic movement, complete with opening and closing. And finally, we composed an opening to the homily and a closing, while at the same time checking to see that the transitions implied by the chosen form were in place. Here's what one such homily might look like.

## Homily

For the Twentieth Sunday in Ordinary Time, Year A
[Revised Common Lectionary Proper 15]
Matthew 15:21-28

[OPENING]

In just about a month I will mark the nineteenth anniversary of my ordination as a deacon. I remember clearly kneeling before Bishop Sklba as he handed me a book of the Gospels, just like this one. As I took it, he said: "Receive the gospel of Christ, whose herald you now are. Believe what you read, teach what you believe, and practice what you teach."

[FIRST MOVEMENT]

"Practice what you teach," or in its more familiar, alliterative form, "Practice what you preach." I cannot imagine a more succinct description of the pattern of Jesus's life. Practice what you preach. Jesus knew his holy Scriptures well, and he believed what he read. The God revealed in the Bible was real, and Jesus believed in him.

But that belief did not remain only in his head. Jesus was inspired to preach, to teach, to share his belief. To all who would listen, Jesus spoke about his Abba, the Father-God of love and compassion. From the small gathering at Peter's doorstep to the thronged masses who heard the Sermon on the Mount, Jesus preached.

But neither did Jesus stop there; his beliefs and his teachings were translated into action. Jesus preached a God of love, and he lived that love. Lepers felt his touch. Jesus preached a God of mercy, and he showed that mercy again and again. Sinners were welcomed to his table. Jesus preached a God of inclusivity, a God for all, and he ultimately came to embrace all who sought his help—even a Canaanite woman.

Jesus really did believe what he read, preached what he believed, and practiced what he preached.

[SECOND MOVEMENT]

But—it wasn't easy.

Turning belief into action is neither simple nor automatic; if it were, our world would instantly be a much better place.

No, practicing what you preach is not easy—not even for Jesus. In fact, as I read today's gospel, it seems that we are glimpsing a moment in Jesus's life in which he struggled to convert his teaching into action.

Just before this story in Matthew's Gospel, we hear Jesus teaching about what truly makes one clean and unclean. It is not the keeping of ritualistic laws that shows one's righteousness with God, but the words and actions that proceed from one's heart. So teaches Jesus.

After that, Jesus withdraws to Gentile territory, an act that no law-abiding Jew would have considered. But with the gospel freedom that he preached, he traveled to Tyre and Sidon. Once there, however, his own self-understanding is challenged by a non-Jewish resident of the place. The Canaanite woman comes forward for a favor, and Jesus's first reaction is one in keeping with the Jewish culture of the day: he ignores her. She is not only a strange woman but a Gentile as well. Jesus ignores her. When his disciples suggest he give her what she wants to get rid of her, Jesus restates his own understanding of his mission: "I have come for the Jews." Period.

The woman persists in her begging, and Jesus responds with an expression common in that day: "I can't give the children's food to dogs." One might imagine that Jesus was speaking as much to himself as to the woman. He had come for the Jews, after all, not the Gentiles—that's how he understood his mission. Then the woman gives her snappy comeback: "Even the dogs get the table scraps."

The gospel doesn't say what crosses Jesus's mind at this point, but I can't help imagining that his own words about clean and unclean, about the law and God's love, came back to haunt him. Here in front of him is a living example of what he taught—a woman who was not in compliance with the law and yet had faith, a Gentile outside his mission and yet trusting in God. He marveled at her faith, and then he practiced what he preached—and the woman's daughter was healed.

[THIRD MOVEMENT]

Jesus's own words about the clean and the unclean prompted him to struggle with his accustomed way of acting, and to change. If this was true for Jesus, how much more true it must be for us! We can't possibly expect any less of a struggle in our own attempts to emulate the Master, to believe what we read, profess what we believe, and practice what we profess.

As a preacher, I can testify to the reality of this struggle in my own life. Believe me, the words I speak from a pulpit or a counseling chair often ring in my own ears or come back to haunt me later on. And that's good. I hope and pray that my preaching helps make me a better person.

But this injunction to practice what we preach is not merely an occupational hazard of those given a pulpit. The struggle of the Master is for all his disciples. Not all of us formally preach, but we all speak some awfully powerful words each time we gather to worship, words that we are called to translate into action. In the Lord's Prayer we ask God to "forgive us as we forgive." In exchanging a sign of peace, we turn to another and say: "Peace be with you."

In Holy Communion we hear the words, "The Body of Christ," and we reply "Amen." We are told that both bread and we are the Body of Christ, to which we say: "Yes, it is, and yes, I am."

Each Sunday we profess with our mouths that we are the Body of Christ, that we are ambassadors of forgiveness and peace. Empowered by that very Christ, we are called to enflesh in our lives the words of faith we speak.

[CLOSING]

The struggle of the Christian life is the struggle to live out the identity we profess, to practice what we preach. Jesus himself struggled to widen his circle of love, and in the power of the Spirit he did just that. We, too, are heirs of the same Spirit, who works within us continually to call us beyond our hypocrisies and into ever greater integrity between our words and our deeds.

❖   ❖   ❖

I've already discussed my strategy for the Opening and the First Movement, so let me continue from there. My transition from the First to the Second Movement reflected my chosen form, although without using the "on the one hand/on the other" wording. The very first word in the movement is "But," thus making it clear that a contrast is being set up. The second word is a very dangerous one: "it." In general, pronouns are not the preacher's friends. This, that, it, she, he—in writing, pronouns add variety, but in speaking they often add vagueness. The noun to which the pronoun refers is hard to remember for more than one sentence when one is listening. However, in this case I wanted to make a succinct statement of the content of the movement: "it wasn't easy." Because the "it" referred to the immediately previous sentence, I took the risk of using the pronoun. But for insurance, the very next sentence begins with the referent for the "it": turning belief into action.

The first four sentences open the movement in such a way as to orient the listener to what is to come. The key idea of Jesus struggling is enunciated; the movement then goes on to develop it by retelling the gospel pericope. My exegesis of the passage led me to the conclusion that I needed to provide context for it, so in three sentences I give the "back story" to the day's lection. I then moved on to retelling the story of Jesus and the Canaanite woman. The key principle to note is that retelling must never be simply repeating the passage that has just been proclaimed. People register their frustration with repetition: "Why is the preacher telling us what we just heard?" No, retelling is a technique that allows the preacher to bring the exegetical and hermeneutical insights to bear on the text. As such, the retelling will never sound just like the passage being retold; something fresh will be added, or better, brought out. In this movement I wanted the listener to understand how Jesus could have said something so seemingly crude as referring to the Canaanite woman as a "dog," and at the same time to appreciate the dramatic change in Jesus's standard operating procedure.

In retelling the story, I used the present tense. My strategy was to have the listeners feel as if they were on the journey of discovery right along with Jesus. In the final three sentences of the Second Movement, I shift to the past tense as I interpret what happened in the story just retold. I closed the movement with a reprise of the opening image of the homily— practicing what we preach.

The transition to the Third Movement is accomplished by referring back to what had just been said (Jesus's words about clean and unclean), followed immediately by the "how much more for us" phrase that moves listeners from Jesus as focus (Second Movement) to us as focus (Third Movement). Once again, the first three sentences orient the listener to what is to come. I developed the Third Movement with a personal example and then several liturgical examples. I brought it to a close with a different way of saying "Practice what you preach": enfleshing in our lives the words of faith we speak.

The transition from the final movement to the Closing restates the central idea twice in its first sentence. Then, in the next sentence, I restate the content of the Second Movement and make explicit that what happened in the story was the Spirit at work in Jesus's life. Finally, I make explicit the fullness of the analogy that drove the homily—Jesus struggled and succeeded in the Spirit, and so can we.

One final note on the Closing. Given that a Sunday homily is ultimately to be an experience of Good News, I think it appropriate to avoid endings that place burdens or leave listeners in despair. I could have said, "We must move beyond our hypocrisies and strive for integrity of word and deed"— a way of putting things that seems to me to be placing a burden. Instead, I crafted the final sentence to come across as a word of grace. The Spirit is at work, and this is Good News. So even with the implicit challenge of the homily, the Good News is the last word that the listeners hear: "We, too, are heirs of the same Spirit, who works within us continually. . . ."

## Delivery: PLICA Strategies for the Act of Preaching

Throughout the homiletic preparation process, we have seen how the five characteristics of the homily can guide and enrich our work. But the importance of these PLICA characteristics does not fade as our manuscript is completed. Rather, PLICA can positively affect the act of preaching itself.

***Personal.*** In chapter 4 we considered the foundational role of the preacher's verbal and non-verbal communication skills. The basics that many of us were taught in high school speech class remain important on Sunday: sufficient volume, good eye contact, appropriate variations in pace and tone, and gestures that support the words being spoken. Such skills are able to be acquired and to be honed, and we owe it to our people to do just that.

Preaching is personal most fundamentally because it is one person speaking faith to other persons of faith. Because of this personal quality, two extremes of public discourse must be avoided. On the one hand, Sunday preaching should not resemble the delivery of an academic paper at a conference. We stand before our people to preach, not to read a manuscript out loud. On the other hand, there is an artificial quality to rote recitation of a manuscript memorized word for word. We stand before our people to preach, not to deliver a painstaking rendition of "Casey at the Bat." Avoiding these two extremes implies an effort by the preacher to know well what has been prepared and to deliver that homily without excessive reliance either on notes or on fixed memorization. Some homileticians are dead set against the use of any written notes, fearing that the personal, even conversational quality of the homily will be harmed. I do not share that fear. I have heard effective preaching by those with a full manuscript in front of them, those with a detailed outline, those with a sketchy outline, and those with no notes at all. The particular *aides de memoir* utilized are neither here nor there; what is important is knowing what you want to say and saying it with an adequate level of verbal and non-verbal skill.

**Liturgical.** In chapter 5 we looked at the importance of ritual presence in preaching. This means that the preacher knows and loves the liturgy and that this knowledge and love manifest themselves in the way the preacher stands, moves, gestures, and speaks. The homily is a part of the liturgy itself, and as such deserves the respect we show to other parts of the liturgy.

So, for instance, it is predictable that our preaching effectiveness will be diminished if the people see that we are uncomfortable in our liturgical vesture or that we race around the liturgical space as if we were on a quick trip to the grocery store. On the other hand, our preaching effectiveness increases when our liturgical behavior reflects the sacredness of the occasion. Our respect for Christ is mirrored in the respect we show for altar and pulpit, for Lectionary/Bible, for bread and cup; such respect enhances the power of the liturgical homily.

Allow me to weigh in on a contentious liturgical issue that is germane to this chapter: the place from which the homily is to be delivered. Following the liturgical reform of the Second Vatican Council, the newly restored homily was to be delivered "at the chair or at the lectern."[12] In practice, most Catholic preachers took the second option and preached from the pulpit (ambo). As the years went on, though, it became more popular to leave the pulpit behind and preach from another place, most commonly in front of the altar or in the aisles. This practice was seemingly blessed by the rubric revised in 2000: "The priest, standing at the chair or at the ambo itself, or, when appropriate, in another suitable place, gives the homily."[13]

I believe that there are strong liturgical reasons to preach from the pulpit. In the reformed Roman Catholic liturgy, it is clear that two principal pieces of furniture visualize the two principal parts of the Mass: the pulpit/ambo (locus for the Liturgy of the Word) and the altar table (locus for the Liturgy of the Eucharist). The homily most strongly emerges as an integral part of the Liturgy of the Word when it is delivered in the place from which the scriptural readings have been delivered. I would argue that the converse is also true: to abandon the pulpit—literally turning one's back on it—is to communicate that the homily is somehow divorced from what has come before.

However, the Roman Catholic Church now recognizes that, "when appropriate," the homily might be delivered from "another suitable place." Thank goodness for the qualifiers "appropriate" and "suitable"! In my judgment, neither propriety nor suitability is determined by the personal preference of the preacher or the feelings of certain parishioners. No, the propriety of leaving the pulpit and the suitability of an alternate location are liturgical decisions, driven by one's understanding of the liturgy and of the homily's place in that liturgy.

If one were to make a liturgically appropriate decision to preach from some place other than the pulpit, though, there are still ways of assuring that the homily's place in the Liturgy of the Word is respected. For instance, one might begin preaching from the pulpit and then move to the

---

12. Sacred Congregation for Divine Worship, General Instruction of the Roman Missal, 97, in International Committee on English in the Liturgy, *Documents on the Liturgy: 1963–1979* (Collegeville: The Liturgical Press, 1982) 208.

13. Revised General Instruction of the Roman Missal, 3rd typical ed., 136. Accessed at <http://www.usccb.org/liturgy/current/chapter4.htm#sect1a>.

other suitable location. In such a case, one might even return to the pulpit to conclude. Or one might take the Book of the Gospels in hand when leaving the pulpit, thus establishing some visual continuity with all that has come before. In any case, effective communication principles forbid preaching from any spot in which the preacher's back is to some of the listeners. Also to be avoided is meaningless movement—nervous pacing and so on. When preaching, all movement is communication, and as such must be coordinated with the words being spoken.

***Inculturated.*** In chapter 6 we considered the critical interrelationship of culture and text when preaching. In terms of delivery, it is helpful to note that different congregations differ in their expectations of the style of preaching. In other words, a congregation's preaching culture must be known and in some way respected. For instance, take the homiletic technique of call and response: "Let the Church say 'Amen.'" "Amen!" In a congregation accustomed to such preaching, a guest preacher who engaged in no moments of dialogue might come across as stiff or even disrespectful, and thus find the homily's power diminished. Conversely, of course, a preacher who tries call and response in an assembly used to sitting stoically during the homily may find some discomfort or even resistance—and thus find the homily's power diminished.

Preaching is always a personal act, and as such the personality of the preacher, including homiletic likes and dislikes, will always play an important role. But preaching is also always the interplay of biblical text and a particular assembly with its particular culture. That means that our delivery style must take into account the modes of communication most effective for a particular congregation.

***Clarifying.*** In chapter 7 I sang the praises of clarity. When it comes to clarity in homiletic delivery, only one thing must be said: Achieve clarity by delivering what you have so carefully prepared. The process outlined in the last chapter and in this one has yielded a manuscript of quality. It is now up to the preacher to review, read over, and rehearse it sufficiently to know well in your head what you have put on paper.

I just finished decrying rote memorization, and that is not what I am calling for. Rather, the preacher goes over the manuscript enough times to be able to tell another person the following:

- Here's how I am going to start.
- Here are the main components of my message and my organizational scheme (form).
- Here are the principal illustrations I'm going to use.
- Here's how I'm going to finish.

If you can do that, you are ready for Sunday.

***Actualizing.*** In chapter 8 I tried to spell out what I meant by the overarching goal of preaching: actualizing the Word of God. The first ability implied by this goal is the ability to communicate a sense of urgency. God is speaking to us on Sunday, and we preachers ought to manifest excitement in the role we play in facilitating this divine communication.

This urgency, this excitement can be communicated. It shows up in our tone, in our volume, in our pace, in our facial expressions, in our gestures. Beginning preachers are sometimes skittish about being "overly dramatic," but I can say that the opposite is much more frequently the problem. A powerful message can fail to be actualized when it is delivered with all of the passion of a grocery list or with the lack of affect that haunts the victims of dementia. Rather, the goodness of our news, and our excitement to be its bearer, must show up in voice, face, and body if we hope for our preaching to be actualizing.

# CHAPTER 11

# Ten Suggestions for Becoming a Better Preacher

Throughout this book, my hope has been to integrate the vision and the practice of Sunday preaching. If I did that effectively for you, you have already absorbed many practical strategies for powerful preaching. In some ways, then, a chapter on becoming a better preacher ought to seem a bit redundant. Nonetheless, my experience tells me that there are very concrete steps that a preacher can take toward improvement, steps I have not yet mentioned or only briefly touched upon. To the extent that you are already employing these ten suggestions, I say "Bravo"—and wish that I were sitting in your church on Sunday! To the extent that these are new ideas or helpful reminders, though, pick one—any one—and commit yourself to working on it for the next couple of months. Then move on to another. In a year you will know you have become a better preacher.

## 1. Get a Life

I pay close attention to "catchphrases" that catch on. Popular wisdom as captured in such sayings can at the very least give a snapshot of where a culture is at during a given period. One of the more enduring catchphrases recently has been "Get a life!" The phrase is usually used as a retort to someone so narrowly focused on the minutiae of one's own concerns as to be out of touch with the broader world. "Get a life" is the call to drop the blinders and engage the fullness of life's offerings. It is great advice for someone seeking to become a better preacher.

We Americans preach in a society where religion is increasingly privatized, and thus marginalized from the decisions and developments of the day. Preachers must resist this trend if God's Word is to be a relevant word. And one of the principal ways of resisting the privatization of faith is to live a full life with one's faith fully integrated into every aspect. Preachers give in to privatized faith when we come across as too narrowly "churchy," focused only on the intra-ecclesial dynamics of organization and doctrine.

For the Word to live vibrantly, our listeners need to know that faith is not just for monks in their cells and the rest of us in the private moments given to prayer. Rather, our preaching must reflect a life fully lived, infused with faith. Over the course of many Sundays, our assembly should come to know us as people with friends and with family, in whose lives our own are intertwined. They should come to know us as people who read literature for its beauty and insight into the human condition and who read the news to stay engaged in the issues of the day. Our listeners can appreciate our struggles to live a balanced life, in which private and public prayer, physical exercise, and festive eating and drinking all commingle into an integrity of mind, body, and spirit. In this way our preaching will be rooted in a real life, a life our assemblies can identify with.

I sometimes worry when I attend social occasions with clergy. It amazes me that even as time is being taken to relax, to eat and drink with friends, the conversation can be dominated for hours by the inner workings of parish life and the supposed machinations of those above us in Church structure. To those among us so afflicted by narrowness, I join with the bold yet plaintive call of the young: "Get a life!" For your own sake and the sake of those who hear you preach, get a life.

## 2. Reflect on Life Theologically

Getting a life is a great first step, but for excellent preachers, it does not stop there. The best preachers inculcate the habit of reflecting upon life by bringing its events into dialogue with Christian tradition.

I earlier mentioned the discipline of theological reflection in connection with the "inculturating" characteristic of the homily. The inculturating preacher is called to interpret Scripture in terms of the world and to interpret the world in the light of Scripture. These homiletic goals are also the goals of theological reflection.

As described by Killen and de Beer in their book *The Art of Theological Reflection,* this practice consists of four steps.

1. Focus on some aspect of experience.
2. Describe the experience to identify the heart of the matter.
3. Explore the "heart of the matter" in conversation with the wisdom of the Christian heritage.
4. Identify from this conversation new truths and meanings for living.[1]

Let me briefly summarize what these authors have in mind.

***Focus attention on some aspect of experience.*** Killen and de Beer warn us about taking the word "experience" too narrowly. They speak of four broad sources of experience: *action* (individual's or community's events and the thoughts and feelings engendered and embedded therein); *positions* (convictions, beliefs, values, statements of meaning); *tradition* (Scripture, liturgy, doctrine, theology); and *culture* (from cultural symbols and mores through social systems to the very physical environment). Experience can arise from any of these sources, and the first step in theological reflection is to focus one's attention on an experience. In focusing, we allow questions to arise or disturbance to emerge or joy to happen or crisis and conflict to erupt.

***Describe the experience as fully as possible and identify from that description the heart of the matter.*** In this second step, the reflector non-judgmentally narrates the experience, considering needs, feelings, intentions, actions, others involved, historical factors, and so on. Reflecting on the experience on its own terms, we allow the heart of the matter to emerge: the question, tension, problem, or wonderment that lies at the core of the experience.

***Explore the heart of the matter in conversation with the wisdom of one's religious heritage.*** The authors suggest a couple of strategies to structure such a dialogue. On the one hand, one could take the "heart of the matter" and ask where we find the same in Scripture, theology, spirituality, Church history, and so on. What in our heritage sheds light on the matter, or critiques it, or offers hope? On the other hand, the theological reflector might explore the classic themes of theology: creation, sin, judgment,

---

1. Patricia Killen and John de Beer, *The Art of Theological Reflection* (New York: Crossroad, 1994/97) 66–67.

redemption, ecclesiology, Christology, eschatology, and so on. I agree with the authors: classic Christian doctrines code the answers to perennial questions about our relationship to God and one another.

***Identify new truths and meanings for living.*** This final step identifies the outcome of the conversation between the experience and Christian tradition. This could be a new perspective or a concrete call to action or a deepening of a conviction or an affective confirmation or more.

It is my conviction that preachers who enhance their own spiritual and ministerial lives by reflecting theologically on their experience are preachers constantly strengthening their hermeneutical muscles. If we adopt the habit of theological reflection—once a day or even once a week—we are constantly involved in doing what every good preacher must do, namely, correlating God's grace in our lives with God's action in Jesus, in the Scriptures, and in worship.

## 3. Share the Word with Parishioners and Peers

In chapter 9 I sketched out what I feel to be the three encounters with the Word necessary as one prepares to preach: the initial, exegetical, and hermeneutical encounters. Many preachers have found that extending these encounters to include dialogue with others is very beneficial in preparing the Sunday homily.

In terms of the initial encounter, nothing can replace the preacher's own quiet, prayerful first reading of the Sunday's texts. But a wonderful complement to that is what could be called a "group initial encounter." Such an encounter could, on the one hand, bring together pastor and parishioners in a prayerful and free-wheeling reaction to the Scriptures. How valuable it would be for a preacher to get a sampling of how parishioners themselves react to the coming Sunday's Word. The stance for the pastor in such an encounter is one of listening: what initial reactions do my people have to these texts? Luckily, parish life is rife with possible times for such a group initial encounter. Perhaps a group might like to stay after morning or evening prayers to engage the Scriptures. Maybe the first fifteen minutes of a meeting might be given over to such an encounter. Meeting with those preparing to be confirmed or the elderly at a card party—almost every congregational encounter could be augmented by discussion of the Sunday Scriptures.

On the other hand, many preachers enjoy extending their initial encounter by a discussion with fellow preachers, either within one's own denomination or ecumenically. In this case, of course, such a discussion might also complement the exegetical and hermeneutical work done by each. The most fruitful discussions among preachers happen when each participant has at least prayed with the text and done some exegetical study already. Hermeneutical sparks can fly when prepared preachers meet.

By the wonders of the Internet, such peer encounters can happen even when physical presence is precluded. I think of a Web site such as <desperatepreacher.com>, which features a weekly threaded discussion of the Sunday texts. Any preacher anywhere can participate. Note well, though: one using such a Web site needs to guard against the temptation of skipping any of the three necessary encounters with the Word. The temptation can be especially strong when a Web site offers not only discussion but complete homiletic manuscripts. Preaching sites on the Web can augment our encounters with the Sunday text, but can never replace them.

## 4. Continue Your Education

I spent six years as a director of continuing formation for clergy. During that period I came to an awful realization, namely, that some of the ordained are natural-born lifelong learners, and the rest are not. Psychology has not yet devised a screening mechanism to identify which group you belong to, but reflection on your own life should suffice. Do you regularly read books and periodicals concerning theology, the Bible, spirituality? Do you take full advantage of the time and the financial assistance (if any) offered to you to continue your education? Is your library alive, always being added to and culled from? If you answered no to any of these questions, you are probably not a natural lifelong learner. And if you are not, growing in your preaching ability will take extra effort, because there is simply no substitute for continuing your education. Whether it comes naturally or not, it must be done, forever.

Exposing oneself to new ideas and new ways of thinking helps prevent staleness in preaching. Ongoing education opens our minds and broadens our horizons. It gives us access to the benefits of professional theologians, professional exegetes, professional homileticians, and so on, access to that corps of scholars who have the time and the skill to do what we cannot do on our own.

Luckily for preachers, the opportunities to continue our educations are myriad. The publishers keep on bringing out worthy titles, and courses helpful to the preaching ministry are available in many localities, not to mention nationally at such places as the College of Preachers in Washington, D.C., and the Aquinas Institute of Theology in St. Louis. The National Organization for the Continuing Education of Roman Catholic Clergy even has a traveling workshop entitled "Renewing Sunday Preaching." Resources are everywhere; we need only reach out.

As a former director of continuing education, I know all the excuses for skipping the reading, studying, and workshops: "I'm too busy," "I don't like theology," "I'm glad to be out of the seminary," "I'd rather minister than read," and so on. In my opinion, though, none of the excuses washes. A vital preacher is one whose knowledge of theology, Scripture, and other disciplines is always expanding.

## 5. Schedule Homily Preparation Time

My fifth suggestion might seem like a "no-brainer," and indeed it is. Most ordained ministers lead rather busy lives—at least as busy as those of most other American professionals! That very pace of life means that activities not committed to on a calendar are unlikely to happen. You know as well as I do that when you tell a friend "Let's get together soon" but fail to set a date, you will not be getting together soon. The same goes for our date with the Sunday Scriptures.

I gather that ministers of the Reformed Churches have generally been much better about scheduling sermon preparation, and I salute that discipline. Admittedly, it might take some Catholics a bit of time to adjust to hearing from the parish secretary, "Father is preparing his homily and can't be disturbed," but adjust they will. As I noted early in this book, the restoration of the homily has been embraced by Roman Catholics in the last three decades. It is long past time for them to realize that good preaching takes good preparation, and good preparation takes time. The only way for them to learn that, though, is from the mouths of the preachers themselves. Roman Catholic priests must help to educate their parishioners about the kind of commitment it takes to be an effective preacher.

## 6. Compose Your Homily with PLICA in Mind

I trust that the five characteristics of an effective homily that I examined earlier proved helpful in fleshing out the vision and practice of Sunday preaching. Of course, not every aspect of each of the PLICA characteristics can be present in every homily. Different homilies will emphasize different aspects. Nonetheless, the five broad PLICA characteristics can be a helpful guide as we prepare.

The homily is to be a **personal** word. So after we have sketched out the movements of the homily, but before we begin to write, we might ask ourselves, "How will I emerge as a person of faith and love in this homily?" By definition, preaching is communication from a person of faith to people of faith. Still, the only way your people will know you as a person of faith is by your sharing your faith. Sunday preaching differs from the "witness talk" of a retreat or revival, to be sure, but the effective preacher finds ways of confirming that it is personal faith that fires the homily.

The homily is to be a **liturgical** word. At its core, this means that the preacher is aware of the context of the homily, namely, it is a constitutive part of the broader act of Sunday worship, which includes scriptural proclamation, prayers, hymns, and in many mainline churches, communion. As such, the liturgical character of the homily should be in our minds throughout our preparation. The preacher is always aware of the coming Sunday's context: its particular readings, the season of the Church year, and so on. While I don't think that every homily must be explicit in its liturgical character, the effective preacher will always ask, "Is this homily an integrated part of this Sunday's worship, or does it feel like a temporary digression?"

The homily is to be an **inculturated** word. I will say much more about illustrations in the next section, but for now it is important to recall that our message must emerge clothed in the language and symbols of the people to whom we preach. This is not just a matter of effective communication, as in speaking the language of your people. The work of inculturation is fundamentally the work of verification. By drawing our images from the real lives of those gathered in worship, we verify for our people the truth of what we speak. As an inculturating preacher, you must "always be ready to make your defense to anyone who demands from you an accounting for the hope that is in you" (1 Pet 3:15). Or to put it in a way someone from Missouri might: "Show me." Show me that what you say about God is true in my life and in the world I know.

The homily is to be a **clarifying** word. In some sense, the first half of preparing to preach—the process of arriving at a message—could be described as the effort to become increasingly clear about what one wants to say on Sunday. We reach that clarity when we have composed the one simple declarative sentence that captures our message. The challenge of the second half of preparing to preach—fleshing out components and structuring them effectively—is precisely the challenge of remaining clear as we move from message to full manuscript. Clarity is a homiletic goal throughout the preparation process and into the pulpit itself.

Finally, the homily is to be an **actualizing** word. The actualization of Scripture is ultimately the work of the Holy Spirit. Preachers strive to remove every roadblock to the Spirit's work, though, and one of those blocks is preaching without having first been touched by the Word yourself. Part of what powers an experience of the God of the Bible for your listeners is their perception that you have encountered that same God in preparing to preach. So as a message becomes clear and as we develop it and illustrate it, we must monitor our own spirits for signs that the Spirit is at work.

## 7. Be Attentive to Your Illustrations

I suggested in the last chapter that each movement in an effective homily ought to be fleshed out with both conceptual language and illustrative language. Each movement would thus both say clearly what it is about and demonstrate how we see or experience that truth in real life. As such, then, illustration is not mere ornamentation—we aren't decorating our concepts with pretty images. We are illustrating from life how we know what we claim to know. I can think of seven pitfalls to be avoided as we seek to illustrate our homilies.

*Lack of illustration.* This is one of the most fundamental failures in preparing to preach—failing to illustrate a point. It is a failure not merely because people "like" to revel in images or hear anecdotes from real life. No, it is a failure because it reveals that the preacher has been unable to identify an affinity between the point being made and the lives of the people to whom it is being made. No image, no example, no anecdote, no story—these are signs that the concept being treated is far off the radar screen. If the preacher cannot show the import of the point in real life, it is most likely a point not worth making.

*Sameness of illustration.* Not every homily can feature illustrative material drawn from the lives of every demographic group in the parish. In fact, a super-inclusive, laundry-list approach to examples winds up being tedious for everyone. However, over the course of the months, it is important that all segments of the congregation experience hearing about their own particular circumstances. Young singles, married with children, widows and widowers, children, recent immigrants, gays and lesbians, teenagers, ethnic and cultural minorities, and so on—all must hear the Good News illustrated in ways with which they can identify. Put another way, any person who feels consistently excluded from the preacher's range of illustrations is a person who may well not experience the inclusiveness of God's love.

***Coercive illustrations.*** I mentioned in chapter 5 my conviction that preachers overuse the first person plural. This is especially true when it comes to illustration. There are problems with stock phrases like "I'm sure that we've all had the experience of . . . ," or "Everyone knows what it's like to . . . ," or "We humans are funny in that . . . ," and so on. Such sweeping formulations often come across as coercive, in that the preacher intends to lump the entire assembly into an example that may well not apply. When shaping an illustration, then, recall my rule of thumb for using the first person plural: Use it only in statements that are theologically or scientifically certain. "We are all sinners"—true; "we need food and water to live"—true; "we are all greedy"—not necessarily true. Don't attempt to corral everyone into your examples, but rather leave the freedom for them to identify or not. "Some of us, I fear, are greedy," or "When I look at my checkbook and see how little I give to the poor, I wonder if I am not a greedy person"—such statements can illustrate and invite identification without coercion.

***Extreme illustrations.*** There can be drama in stories of absolute evil and saintly good, but I'm afraid such stories can at best disedify or edify rather than illustrate. When our illustrations of sin are always on the Adolph Hitler end of the spectrum and our illustrations of grace are always on the Mother Teresa end of the spectrum, we leave out the vast middle ground where most of us live our lives. There is nothing inherently wrong with occasionally seeking to edify our listeners, but I do not think that that is our fundamental goal as Sunday preachers. We seek to actualize the Sunday Scriptures in a way that our listeners experience the reality of God's saving grace here and now. That is best accomplished when our illustrations avoid the extremes and embody daily life, which is always an interplay of sunlight and shadows and ever-shifting shades of gray.

***Breach of confidentiality.*** Intimate knowledge of our parishioners is a double-edged sword. On the one hand, as preachers come to know those whom they serve ever more deeply, their ability to preach the Word in a

powerfully inculturated way increases. On the other hand, the trust parishioners place in their pastors must always be respected, and that will often
enough mean foregoing use of the "perfect sermon illustration" because it
would violate a confidence. Situations in the lives of particular parishioners that are benign and publicly known could be referred to. The birth
of a child, election to a local post, winning the lottery—these kinds of events
could provide matter for recognizable and thus effective illustrations. A
hospital conversation, a family tragedy, grief over a lost job—it seems to
me that knowledge gained in such situations is private and confidential.
The preacher's role as pastor will be greatly hobbled if parishioners get
the sense that every conversation is fair game to be mentioned in a homily.
There is, however, one work-around for using a private moment as a
homiletic illustration. Ask the involved person for permission to mention
the incident (even if anonymously), and then say when preaching: "I asked
one of our parishioners if she would mind my sharing this with you, and
she gave me permission." Normally I don't care for caveats and footnotes
in a homily, but this is one necessary exception.

***Travelogues.*** It matters not how deeply your spirit was moved when you
peered into the Grand Canyon; your people do not want to hear about your
latest vacation. I experienced the most extreme version of homily-as-travelogue a few years ago in Ireland (Oops, now I'm doing it!). The priest began
the homily this way: "Well, St. Paul said some beautiful things about love in
that reading, and Jesus in the gospel really lived that love out in his life. But
it's a wonderful summer day, and I'm sure no one really cares about any of
that, so let me tell you about my recent holiday in Australia." And that is just
what he did. I was flabbergasted. Now, clearly this falls into the category of
an extreme illustration of my point, but the illustration works. How you
spend your disposable income (which many people do not have) and your
leisure time (which many people do not have) is your business, only. So if
your spirit really was moved at the Grand Canyon, why not use a bit of
homiletic license and change the story. Keep the emotion, but change the location to some place close at hand. The illustration will work fine, and people
will be spared the homiletic version of the dreaded vacation slide show.

***Popular culture references.*** There is something to be said for using
touchstones from popular culture as illustrations. Popular culture is in the
business of producing vivid images and catchy slogans, and these can be

put to use homiletically. There are some caveats, however. First, the more universally the reference is known, the better. The title of a popular TV show, for instance, will be familiar to many, while the plot of new movie probably will not. Second, the preacher must always consider how long it will take to explain the reference and whether that amount of time is homiletically justified for that particular illustration. I had a professor in seminary who was an avid movie buff, and he frequently used the movies to illustrate his homilies. I remember the effect negatively though: first, because I often had not seen the film (and thus felt either alienated or envious); and second, because of the inordinate amount of time it took to explain an hour's worth of film to set up the desired illustration. Finally, we need to be ever alert to the subtexts and double entendres present in much of the product of popular culture. For example, a doctoral classmate of mine gave a homily based on the Nike slogan "Just do it," blithely unaware, apparently, of the sexual overtones to the phrase "do it." It made for a rather uncomfortable sermonic experience, to say the least.

## 8. Be Careful with Prescriptions

I have repeated these words of the Pontifical Biblical Commission several times, and now I will again for a final time: lack of adequate homiletic preparation can lead a preacher into "the temptation to avoid plumbing the depths of the biblical readings and to being content simply to moralize." There is nothing easier than telling people what to do, but that is not what preaching is fundamentally about. So let me issue three warnings regarding homiletic prescriptions.

First, I think the Second Vatican Council provides preachers with some helpful caveats. The bishops were treating the need to integrate faith and daily life in all its complexity. And then they wrote this: "Let the layman not imagine that his pastors are always such experts, that to every problem which arises, however complicated, they can readily give him a concrete solution, or even that such is their mission."[2] English translation: It is not the mission of pastors to prescribe solutions to the complex problems of daily life. The council fathers went on to make this very sage observation: ". . . it happens rather frequently, and legitimately so, that with equal sincerity

---

2. Second Vatican Council, Pastoral Constitution on the Church in the Modern World *(Gaudium et Spes)* 43. Accessed at <http://www.vatican.va/archive/hist_councils/ii_vatican_council/documents/vat-ii_cons_19651207_gaudium-et-spes_en.html>.

some of the faithful will disagree with others on a given matter." Given the legitimacy of Christian disagreement, the bishops warned, "It is necessary for people to remember that no one is allowed in the aforementioned situations to appropriate the Church's authority for his opinion."[3] That warning is for all the Christian faithful, perhaps most especially preachers.

Second, communication theory confirms that one of the least effective ways of persuading someone of a certain position is a monologue. One speaker, trying to convince a group of a certain position, usually doesn't. When one adds to that the fact that Americans are increasingly situationalists or relativists when it comes to morality,[4] the preacher as layer-down of moral dicta can be seen as even more impotent. So each preacher must face facts: even if I wanted to convince my people that I know what they should do, I will most likely not be able to.

Finally, I worry that handing down countless moral prescriptions from the pulpit threatens our ability to demonstrate our love for our people—and God's love. The title of an Off-Broadway musical captures my fear: "I Love You, You're Perfect, Now Change." If that is our (mixed) message Sunday after Sunday, I suspect that our people will think that we are fixated on their flaws. We risk being transmogrified in their eyes from proclaimer of the Good News to finger-wagging school marm. My experience tells me that most often people are already fully aware of their flaws and their sinfulness. They know their many failures. What we preachers can and should offer them is not prescription but reassurance that they are loved and saved. It is the grace already secured for us in Christ that empowers us to face our well-known weaknesses and move beyond them. Or as the Pontifical Biblical Commission put it so well:

> Preachers should certainly avoid insisting in a one-sided way on the obligations incumbent upon believers. The biblical message must preserve its principal characteristic of being the good news of salvation freely offered by God. Preaching will perform a task more useful and more conformed to the Bible if it helps the faithful above all to "know the gift of God" (John 4:10) as it has been revealed in Scripture; they will then understand in a positive light the obligations that flow from it.[5]

3. Ibid.

4. See, for instance, "Americans Are Most Likely to Base Truth on Feelings," a report of the Barna Research Group (Feb. 12, 2002). Accessed at <http://www.barna.org/cgi-bin/PagePressRelease.asp?PressReleaseID=106>.

5. Pontifical Biblical Commission, The Interpretation of the Bible in the Church (Boston: St. Paul Books and Media, 1993) 129.

## 9. Be Careful with Stories

Anytime you want to start a fight among preachers or homileticians, just ask, "So, what do you think about using stories in the homily?" and watch the fur fly. This is not a new battle; it is perennial. Recall chapter 1 and Martin Luther's dismissive description of preaching as he experienced it: "The preacher runs through the gospel superficially and then follows it up with a fable about Attila the Hun or a story about Dietrich of Bern, or he mixes in something from Plato, Aristotle, or Socrates."[6] On the other end of the spectrum, I know preaching instructors who insist that their students always begin their homilies with a story, and preachers who follow just that rule. So, aware of the minefield ahead, here are my cautions about the use of stories in preaching.

Let me start with what I mean by story. With a respectful bow to David Buttrick, I've repeatedly distinguished among four general types of illustrative material: the image, the example, the anecdote, and the story. That list is ordered by length and complexity. An image is the shortest and simplest, often appearing as a simile or metaphor: "You are the salt of the earth." An example is a bit longer and consists of material "at hand in the common consciousness of the congregation"[7]: "You know how frustrating it is to misplace your keys." An anecdote is longer still and consists of material that will be new to the congregation: "I was at the grocery store yesterday and ran into an old classmate. What joy I felt in rekindling a relationship that was long 'on hold.'" A story is the longest possible illustration; it has characters, setting, and a plot that resolves. It is to "story" thus understood that I address my cautionary words, for I am convinced that while stories can be helpful to preaching, they can also be harmful.

***Beware stories that are too personal.*** If you ever find yourself writing the words "Let me tell you about my brush with Viagra," you have crossed an important line. I have maintained throughout this book that homilies must be personal to be effective, but the level and quality of self-disclosure must be monitored carefully. Just as the assembly does not want to hear about your vacation, neither does it need to hear about your argument with your spouse or teenager, or your medical woes. Listen to the kids, and avoid the "TMI" faux pas: "Too much information!"

6. Martin Luther, in Hughes Oliphant Old, *The Reading and Preaching of the Scriptures in the Worship of the Christian Church,* vol. 4: *The Age of the Reformation* (Grand Rapids: William B. Eerdmans Publishing Company, 2002) 10–11.

7. David Buttrick, *Homiletic: Moves and Structures* (Philadelphia: Fortress Press, 1987) 128.

***Beware stories that are too impersonal.*** Yes, every coin has two sides. Count me a heretic if you will, but I am convinced that the *Chicken Soup for the Soul* series and its ilk have not elevated preaching. Sunday worship is not "story hour" at the local library, and a steady diet of Sufi stories and Oriental tales and myths of the desert fathers will not nourish our people. It seems to me that the most effective stories are narrations of something that the preacher actually experienced or that has been part of congregational experience. Such stories serve the role that all illustration is to serve: making clear how the claim being made is born out in real life.

***Beware stories that are too long and complicated.*** Unfortunately, one of the dangers of narrating things that actually happened to you is that you share too much. In your excitement over the experience, you give every character a name, every action a place, and every detail you can remember a supporting role in your story. This simply doesn't work in oral communication. Most people will not be able to follow the homiletic equivalent of a Russian novel. A solution to this is writing the story out as part of your manuscript and then editing it ruthlessly to reveal its heart and soul.

***Beware stories that are out of proportion.*** I have experienced homiletic stories that fail the proportionality test in one of two ways. Sometimes this happens when the homilist begins a homily on a short-and-to-the-point gospel text with a long and windy story. In such cases, if one were able to stop the action after the story and ask the listeners, "What was the gospel?" many would be unable to answer. The preached story overshadowed the text it was meant to illustrate. At other times a story can be out of proportion to the point being made. It is never helpful to illustrate a minor insight with a major story. The balance and flow of a homiletic movement are completely thrown off by such a lack of proportionality. A quick example is plenty of illustration for a smaller point.

***Beware stories that are unclear.*** A story can be unclear in two ways. First, it can be narrated in such a way as to make it impossible for the hearer to understand the plot and its resolution. This is always a sign, at least, of inadequate preparation. A preacher might want to practice telling a story to a few people before preaching it to see if people "get it." Second, a story can be unclear when it lacks a context. I have already argued that each of a homily's movements should have an opening that orients the listener. This is true even when—especially when—a story comprises the bulk of the movement. Because of its complex nature, with characters, setting, and plot, stories need to be briefly set in context so that listeners have an idea of what they should be listening for. The preacher need not give anything away; simple orienting remarks like "Jesus's words to the leper remind me of the time that . . ." suffice to guide the listening that is being demanded.

***Beware a story after the story.*** The New Testament is a repository of some of the classic stories of Western civilization. The Good Samaritan, the Prodigal Son, and preeminently the Passion of Jesus Christ—these stories among many others exemplify David Tracy's definition of a "classic": "certain expressions of the human spirit [that] so disclose a compelling truth about our lives that we cannot deny them some kind of normative status."[8] The preacher must beware following a *classic* story with one that begins "I was making coffee Wednesday morning, and the phone rang." Quotidian tales shrivel in the presence of classic religious stories. Perhaps on the Sundays that we preach on the true classics, we should stick to other forms of illustration and let "the" story echo throughout our homily, unencumbered by lesser stories.

## 10. Solicit Meaningful Feedback

"Nice homily, Father." "Thanks for the wonderful words, pastor." I cannot imagine phrases of any less value than these to the preacher striving to improve. As we all know, such phrases are ciphers and can stand for many things: "That was horrible preaching, but you're a great guy," or "I didn't understand a word, but thanks for visiting my mother in the hospital," or "I feel so sorry for you, having to try every Sunday and fail like that." The preacher striving to improve needs ways to get meaningful feedback to his or her preaching. Let me offer a couple of suggestions to that end.

First, recruit a parishioner to videotape you as you preside at worship and preach. Tiny video cameras are as ubiquitous as they are unobtrusive, so capitalize on the technology, for nothing replaces being able to watch yourself in the act of preaching. If all that your ego will allow is the making of such a tape, do it. Review this book and critique your preaching in all the aspects that work and all those that do not.

---

8. David Tracy, *The Analogical Imagination: Christian Theology and the Culture of Pluralism* (New York: The Crossroad Publishing Company, 1989) 108.

Second, though, if ego strength allows, gather a group after a Sunday service, and have someone else solicit meaningful feedback. This, too, ideally, would be audiotaped or videotaped for you. Joan Delaplane, O.P., convinced me as a doctoral student that feedback can be more free and more honest if the preacher is not present, even if the feedback is being taped for the preacher. So have a staff member or parishioner gather a group of parishioners and lead them in a taped discussion of the following PLICA-inspired questions.

*Personal:* The first expectation of a good preacher is that he/she comes across as a real person, manifesting genuineness and sincerity, and communicating a real care and concern for the congregation. How would you describe this preacher's effectiveness in this area?

*Liturgical:* Another expectation of a good preacher is that he/she speak and act in ways that help people worship well. How did you experience this preacher as a minister of the liturgy? Did he/she proclaim the gospel well? Did he/she seem comfortable in the sanctuary? Did he/she help you to pray?

*Inculturated:* A further expectation of a good preacher is that he/she be able to correlate the faith experiences of Scripture with life today. How effective was this preacher in referring to "real life"? Did he/she speak about familiar realities? Did he/she use language you could identify with and understand?

*Clarifying:* Another expectation of a good preacher is that he/she preaches clearly and insightfully. What would you say this preacher's central point was? Was it a point worth making? Was it made clearly?

*Actualizing:* Perhaps the highest goal of any preacher is to help people actually experience the good news of our salvation as a reality in their own lives. To what extent did this happen for you today? Were you touched by his/her preaching? Did this preacher communicate his/her own sense of urgency concerning today's Scriptures? Did he/she seem to communicate his/her own lived experience of faith? Do you feel closer to Jesus Christ after this homily?

If the people of God are asked substantive questions about their experience of Sunday preaching, they will respond with thoughtful and heartfelt answers that can be of immense value to preachers who wish to be all that they can be.

# Appendix

## Official Roman Catholic Documents Concerning Preaching, 1963–1994[1]

[*Format:* Author. Original title. English title (if translated). Original publication information. English publication information.]

Carbone, Vincenzo. *"Dubiorum Solutionum Explanatio. De Commissione Decretis Concilii Vaticani Secundi Interpretandis."* Official Commentary on the 1971 Authentic Interpretation re: General Instruction of the Roman Missal 42. *Monitor Ecclesiasticus* 96 (1972) 323–327. Excerpts in Joseph Fox, "The Homily and the Authentic Interpretation of Canon 767 §1." *Apollinaris* 62 (1989) 123–169 (n. 55).

John Paul II. *Catechesi Tradendae.* Apostolic Exhortation on Catechesis in Our Time. *Acta Apostolicae Sedis* 71 (1979) 1277–1340. Vatican City: Vatican Polyglot Press, 1979.

———. *Catechismus catholicae ecclesiae.* Catechism of the Catholic Church, 2nd ed. Vatican City: Libreria Editrice Vaticana, 1997. Washington, D.C.: United States Catholic Conference and Libreria Editrice Vaticana, 2000.

———. *Christifideles Laici.* Post-Synodal Apostolic Exhortation on the Vocation and Mission of the Lay Faithful in the Church and in the World. *Acta Apostolicae Sedis* 81 (1989) 393–521. Washington, D.C.: United States Catholic Conference, 1988.

———. *Codex Iuris Canonici.* The Code of Canon Law, Latin-English Edition. Trans. Canon Law Society of America. *Acta Apostolicae Sedis* 75 (1983) 1–317. Washington, D.C.: Canon Law Society of America, 1998.

1. For highlights of these documents, see chapter 2. For a complete analysis, see Stephen V. DeLeers, *A Process for the Assessment of Liturgical Preaching Reflecting Official Roman Catholic Understanding of the Homily* (Ann Arbor: UMI [#9708431], 1996) 3–63.

————. *De Tout Cœur.* Address on Interpretation of the Bible. *Acta Apostolicae Sedis* 86 (1994) 232–243. In The Interpretation of the Bible in the Church. Boston: St. Paul Books, 1993. 11–25.

————. *Dominicae Cenae.* Letter to Bishops on the Mystery and Worship of the Eucharist. *Acta Apostolicae Sedis* 72 (1980) 113–48. Boston: St. Paul Editions, 1980.

————. *Pastores Dabo Vobis.* Post-Synodal Apostolic Exhortation on the Formation of Priests in the Circumstances of the Present Day. *Acta Apostolicae Sedis* 84 (1992) 657–804. Washington, D.C.: United States Catholic Conference, 1992.

————. "Priests: Preachers of the Gospel." General Audience Talk, 21 April 1993. *Priesthood in the Third Millennium: Addresses of Pope John Paul II, 1993.* Princeton: Scepter Publishers/Libreria Editrice Vaticana, 1994.

————. *Redemptoris Missio.* Encyclical on the Permanent Validity of the Church's Missionary Mandate. *Acta Apostolicae Sedis* 83 (1991) 249–340. Washington, D.C.: United States Catholic Conference, 1990.

————. *Vicesimus Quintus.* Apostolic Letter on Twenty-Fifth Anniversary of *Sacrosanctum Concilium. Acta Apostolicae Sedis* 81 (1989) 897–918. Vatican City: Libreria Editrice Vaticana, 1988.

National Conference of Catholic Bishops, Committee on Priestly Formation. Mandatory Study of Preaching. *Origins* 3 (1973) 288–289.

National Conference of Catholic Bishops, Bishops' Committee on Priestly Life and Ministry. Fulfilled in Your Hearing: The Homily in the Sunday Assembly. Washington, D.C.: United States Catholic Conference, 1982.

National Conference of Catholic Bishops, Bishops' Committee on the Liturgy. Gathered in Steadfast Faith: Statement on Sunday Worship in the Absence of a Priest. Washington, D.C.: United States Catholic Conference, 1991.

National Conference of Catholic Bishops, Program of Priestly Formation. 4th ed. Washington, D.C.: United States Catholic Conference, 1993. (Promulgated 1992.)

National Conference of Catholic Bishops, Guidelines for Lay Preaching. *Origins* 18 (1988) 402–404. (Approved by U.S. bishops; rejected by Rome.)

Paul VI. *Ecclesiam Suam.* Encyclical on the Church. *Acta Apostolicae Sedis* 56 (1964) 609–659. Vatican City: Tipographia Poliglotta Vaticana, 1964.

————. *Evangelii Nuntiandi.* Apostolic Exhortation on Evangelization in the Modern World. *Acta Apostolicae Sedis* 68 (1976) 5–76. Boston: Daughters of St. Paul, 1975.

————. *Missale Romanum.* Apostolic Constitution Approving the Roman Missal. *Acta Apostolicae Sedis* 61 (1969) 217–222. *Documents on the Liturgy: 1963–1979.* Trans. International Commission on English in the Liturgy. Collegeville: The Liturgical Press, 1982. Doc. 202.

————. *Mysterium Fidei.* Encyclical on the Holy Eucharist. *Acta Apostolicae Sedis* 57 (1965) 753–774. *The Papal Encyclicals: 1958–1981.* Trans. and ed. Claudia Carlen. Vol. 5. N.p.: McGrath Publishing, 1981. 165–177.

————. *Quinque Iam Anni.* Apostolic Exhortation to Bishops. *Acta Apostolicae Sedis* 63 (1971) 97–106. *The Pope Speaks* 15 (1970) 324–332.

————. *Regimini Ecclesiae Universae.* Apostolic Constitution on Reform of the Roman Curia. *Acta Apostolicae Sedis* 59 (1967) 885–928. *Documents on the Liturgy,* Doc. 88.

————. *Sacram Liturgiam.* Motu Proprio Implementing *Sacrosanctum Concilium. Acta Apostolicae Sedis* 56 (1964) 139–144. *Documents on the Liturgy,* Doc. 20.

Pontifical Biblical Commission. *L'Interprétation de la Bible dans l'Eglise.* The Interpretation of the Bible in the Church. Preface by Joseph Cardinal Ratzinger. Vatican City: Libreria Editrice Vaticana, 1993. Boston: St. Paul Books, 1993.

Pontifical Commission for the Interpretation of Canon Law. *Dubium* re: can. 767 §1. Query on Canon 767 §1. *Acta Apostolicae Sedis* 79 (1987) 1249. Fox, "The Homily," 123.

Pontifical Council for the Interpretation of the Decrees of Vatican Council II. *Dubium* re: *Institutio Generalis Missale Romanum* 42. Query on General Instruction of the Roman Missal 42. *Acta Apostolicae Sedis* 63 (1971) 329. *Documents on the Liturgy,* Doc. 215.

Pontifical Commission for the Revision of the Code of Canon Law. *Coetus Studiorum "De magisterio ecclesiastico":* Series I, Session I (23–28 January 1967). *Communicationes* 19 (1987) 246–249. Excerpt in Fox, "The Homily," 156 (n. 60).

————. *Coetus Studiorum "De magisterio ecclesiastico":* Series I, Session VIIa (17–19 January 1972). Unpublished archives.

————. *Coetus Studiorum "De magisterio ecclesiastico":* Series I, Session VIII (13–17 October 1975). Unpublished archives. Excerpt in Fox, "The Homily," 157 (n. 61).

————. *Coetus Studiorum "De magisterio ecclesiastico":* Series II, Session I (4–9 February 1980). Unpublished archives.

————. *Relatio* of meeting of 20–28 October 1981. *Communicationes* 15 (1983) 88–97.

Sacred Congregation for Bishops. *Ecclesiae Imago.* Directory on the Pastoral Ministry of Bishops. Vatican City: Typis Polyglottis Vaticanis, 1973. Ottawa: Canadian Catholic Conference Publications Service, 1973.

Sacred Congregation for Catholic Education. *In Synodo Episcopali (Ratio Fundamentalis Institutionis Sacerdotalis).* Basic Plan for Priestly Formation. *Acta Apostolicae Sedis* 62 (1970) 321–384. *The Pope Speaks* 15 (1970) 264–314.

Sacred Congregation for Clergy. *Directorium Catechisticum Generale*. General Catechetical Directory. *Acta Apostolicae Sedis* 64 (1972) 97–176. Washington, D.C.: United States Catholic Conference, 1972. (Promulgated 1971.)

―――. *Direttorio per il Ministero e la Vita dei Presbiteri*. Directory on the Ministry and Life of Priests. *Notitiae* 30 (1994) 203–246. Vatican City: Libreria Editrice Vaticana, 1994.

―――. *Inter ea*. Circular Letter to Presidents of Episcopal Conferences. *Acta Apostolicae Sedis* 62 (1970) 123–134. *Documents on the Liturgy*, Doc. 333.

―――. On preaching by the laity (Prot. 144823/I). Rescript from C. Wright to C. Döpfner. *Leges Ecclesiae (post CIC editae)*. Vol. V. Ed. Xaverius Ochoa. Rome: *Commentarium pro Religiosis*, 1980. No. 4240, col. 6685–6686. *Documents on the Liturgy*, Doc. 344.

Sacred Congregation for Divine Worship. *Actio Pastoralis*. Instruction on Masses with Special Groups. *Acta Apostolicae Sedis* 61 (1969) 806–811. *Documents on the Liturgy*, Doc. 275.

―――. *Dubium* re: *signum crucis in homilia*. Query on using the sign of the cross at the homily. *Notitiae* 9 (1973) 178. *Documents on the Liturgy*, Doc. 208 (n. R8).

―――. *Dubium* re: General Instruction of the Roman Missal 97. Query on General Instruction of the Roman Missal 97. *Notitiae* 10 (1974) 80 n. 3. *Documents on the Liturgy*, Doc. 208 (n. R24).

―――. *Eucharistiae Participationem*. Circular Letter on the Eucharistic Prayers. *Notitiae* 9 (1973) 193–201. *Documents on the Liturgy*, Doc. 248.

―――. *Institutio Generalis Missale Romanum*. General Instruction of the Roman Missal. Vatican City: Typis Polyglottis Vaticanis, 1969. *Documents on the Liturgy*, Doc. 208.

―――. *Liturgicae Instaurationes*. Third Instruction on the Correct Application of *Sacrosanctum Concilium*. *Acta Apostolicae Sedis* 62 (1970) 692–704. *Documents on the Liturgy*, Doc. 52.

―――. *Misericordiam Suam*. Introduction to the Order of Penance. *Notitiae* 10 (1974) 44–62. *Vatican Council II: More Post Conciliar Documents*. Gen. ed. Austin Flannery. Northport, N.Y.: Costello Publishing, 1982. 35–51. (Promulgated 1973.)

―――. *Ordo Baptismi Parvulorum*. Rite of Infant Baptism. Vatican City: Typis Polyglottis Vaticanis, 1969. *Documents on the Liturgy*, Doc. 295.

―――. *Ordo Lectionum Missae*. Introduction to Lectionary for Mass. *Notitiae* 5 (1969) 240–255. *Documents on the Liturgy*, Doc. 232.

―――. *Publica et Communis (Institutio Generalis de Liturgia Horarum)*. General Instruction of the Liturgy of the Hours. Vatican City: Typis Polyglottis Vaticanis *(ed. non typica)*, 1971. New York: Catholic Book Publishing, 1975.

———. *Pueros Baptizatos.* Directory for Masses with Children. *Acta Apostolicae Sedis* 66 (1974) 30–46. *Documents on the Liturgy,* Doc. 276. (Promulgated 1973.)

———. *Sacris Religionis Vinculis.* Introduction to the Rite of Initiation to Religious Life. *Notitiae* 6 (1970) 114–116. *Vatican Council II: More Post Conciliar Documents,* 190–192.

Sacred Congregation for the Doctrine of the Faith. *Antiquam Causam Reductionis.* Norms on Laicized Priests. *Acta Apostolicae Sedis* 63 (1971) 303–308. *Documents on the Liturgy,* Doc. 317.

———. *Inter Insigniores.* Declaration on the Admission of Women to Ministerial Priesthood. *Acta Apostolicae Sedis* 69 (1977) 98–116. *Vatican Council II: More Post Conciliar Documents,* 331–345.

———. *Mysterium Ecclesiae.* Declaration on the Church. *Acta Apostolicae Sedis* 65 (1973) 396–408. *The Pope Speaks* 18 (1973) 145–157.

Sacred Congregation for Evangelization of Peoples (Pastoral Commission). *Dans le cadre.* Role of women in evangelization. *Documentation Catholique* 1 (1976) 612–618. *Vatican Council II: More Post Conciliar Documents,* 318–329.

Sacred Congregation for Religious and Secular Institutes. *Mutuae Relationes.* Directory for Relations of Bishops and Religious. *Acta Apostolicae Sedis* 70 (1978) 473–506. *Vatican Council II: More Post Conciliar Documents,* 209–243.

Sacred Congregation for Rites (Consilium). *Dubium* re: *Sacrosanctum Concilium* 52. Query on *Sacrosanctum Concilium* 52. *Notitiae* 1 (1965) 137 n. 4. *Documents on the Liturgy,* Doc. 23 (n. R16).

———. *Eucharisticum Mysterium.* Instruction on Worship of the Eucharist. *Acta Apostolicae Sedis* 59 (1967) 539–73. *Documents on the Liturgy,* Doc. 179.

———. *Inter Oecumenici.* First Instruction on Proper Implementation of *Sacrosanctum Concilium. Acta Apostolicae Sedis* 56 (1964) 877–900. *Documents on the Liturgy,* Doc. 23.

Sacred Congregation for Sacraments and Divine Worship. *Christi Ecclesia.* Directory for Sunday Celebrations in the Absence of a Priest. *Notitiae* 24 (1988) 366–378. *Origins* 18 (1988) 301–307.

———. *De Benedictionibus.* Book of Blessings. Vatican City: Libreria Editrice Vaticana *(ed. typica),* 1984. New York: Catholic Book Publishing, 1989.

———. *De Verbo Dei.* Revised Introduction to the Lectionary. *Notitiae* 18 (1981) 361–407. Washington, D.C.: United States Catholic Conference, 1982.

———. *Inaestimabile Donum.* Instruction Concerning the Worship of the Eucharistic Mystery. *Acta Apostolicae Sedis* 72 (1980) 331–343. Boston: St. Paul Editions, 1980.

————. *Variationes In Novas Editiones Librorum Liturgicorum Ad Normam Codicis Iuris Canonici Nuper Promulgati Introducendae*. Emendations in the Liturgical Books Following upon the New Code of Canon Law. *Notitiae* 19 (1983) 540–555. Washington, D.C.: International Committee on English in the Liturgy, 1984.

Second Vatican Council. *Ad Gentes Divinitus*. Decree on the Church's Missionary Activity. *Sacrosanctum Oecumenicum Concilium Vaticanum II: Constitutiones, Decreta, Declarationes*. Vatican City: Typis Polyglottis Vaticanis, 1966. 543–615. *Documents of Vatican II*. Ed. Austin Flannery. Grand Rapids: Eerdmans, 1975. 813–856. (Promulgated 1965.)

————. *Christus Dominus*. Decree on the Pastoral Office of Bishops in the Church. *Concilium Vaticanum II*, 277–321. *Documents of Vatican II*, 564–590. (Promulgated 1965.)

————. *Dei Verbum*. Dogmatic Constitution on Divine Revelation. *Concilium Vaticanum II*, 423–446. *Documents of Vatican II*, 750–765. (Promulgated 1965.)

————. *Dignitatis Humanae*. Declaration on Religious Liberty. *Concilium Vaticanum II*, 511–532. *Documents of Vatican II*, 813–856. (Promulgated 1965.)

————. *Gaudium et Spes*. Pastoral Constitution on the Church in the Modern World. *Concilium Vaticanum II*, 681–835. *Documents of Vatican II*, 903–1001. (Promulgated 1965.)

————. *Lumen Gentium*. Dogmatic Constitution on the Church. *Concilium Vaticanum II*, 93–206. *Documents of Vatican II*, 350–421. (Promulgated 1964.)

————. *Presbyterorum Ordinis*. Decree on the Ministry and Life of Priests. *Concilium Vaticanum II*, 619–678. *Documents of Vatican II*, 863–902. (Promulgated 1965.)

————. *Sacrosanctum Concilium*. Constitution on the Liturgy. *Concilium Vaticanum II*, 3–69. *Documents of Vatican II*, 1–40. (Promulgated 1963.)

————. *Unitatis Redintegratio*. Decree on Ecumenism. *Concilium Vaticanum II*, 243–274. *Documents of Vatican II*, 452–470. (Promulgated 1964.)

Secretariat for Christian Unity. *Ad Totam Ecclesiam*. Ecumenical Directory. *Acta Apostolicae Sedis* 59 (1967) 574–592. *Documents on the Liturgy*, Doc. 147.

Synod of Bishops (Second). *Convenientes Ex Universo*. Synodal Study on Justice in the World. *Acta Apostolicae Sedis* 63 (1971) 923–42. *Vatican Council II: More Post-Conciliar Documents*, 695–710.

————. *Ultimis Temporibus*. Synodal Study on Ministerial Priesthood. *Acta Apostolicae Sedis* 63 (1971) 898–922. *Documents on the Liturgy*, Doc. 318.

Synod of Bishops (Fourth). *Cum Iam ad Exitum*. Message to the People of God on Catechesis in Our Time. Vatican City: Typis Polyglottis Vaticanis, 1977. Washington, D.C.: United States Catholic Conference, 1977.

# Index

accommodating Gospel to cultures, 21–22, 27, 29, 31–32, 46, 88. *See also* inculturation

actualization of the Word, 70, 85, 90
defined, 120
developing concept of, 38–43

adapting Gospel to the times, 20, 21–22, 26, 36, 46, 88. *See also* inculturation

applying Gospel to life, 15, 23–24. *See also* inculturation

assembly, liturgical
identity of, 75–76, 83–84, 93, 151–52
as locus of the Word, 69–70
preacher's relationship to, 72, 73–74, 89, 144–45, 148

Augustine, Saint, 46, 61–62

Barth, Karl, 111, 112, 124
Bergant, Dianne, 80
Bible. *See* Scriptures
Bugnini, Annibale, 6, 17n, 18n
Bultmann, Rudolph, 139, 148
Buttrick, David, 57, 60, 64n, 73–74, 89, 92, 163, 165, 167, 191

Canon Law, Code of, 35–37, 44n
Carrell, Lori, 11
catechesis. *See* preaching, catechesis and Catechism of the Catholic Church

Catechism of the Catholic Church, 40–41, 107, 129
charity, 80
clarity, homiletic, 103–04, 185–86
communication skills, 54–56, 174
contractions, use in preaching of, 66, 99
Cooper, Morton, 54n
correlation
of liturgy and life, 77
of Scriptures and life, 89, 94–97, 151–52, 181–82
of tradition and life, 96–97, 181–82
Counter-Reformation, 3–4
Craddock, Fred, 106, 137, 157, 158, 163–64
Curia, Roman, 13, 18
defined, vii

deBeer, John, 181–82
de Champlain, Mitties, 54n
Delaplane, Joan, 194
DeLeers, Stephen, 78n, 144n, 195n
delivery, homiletic, 173–77
Dulles, Avery, 10

ecumenism, vii, 183
eisegesis, 110, 147
defined, 110
exegesis, 109–10, 146–50

feedback from listeners, 54–55, 68, 193–94

*Fulfilled in Your Hearing,* 47n, 63–64, 96n, 108, 128

fundamentalism, 138, 142

Gadamer, Hans-Georg, 139

grace, 64, 79, 128, 129–30, 187, 190

Greeley, Andrew, 11

heresy, 113, 155

hermeneutics, 143, 150–55

  defined, 138, 150

  principles of, 138–41

hierarchy of truths, 107–08

Hilkert, Mary Catherine, 130

historical critical method

  Catholic acceptance of, 7, 146–47

  Catholic opposition to, 5, 146

  described, 109

  emergence of, 5

  limits of, 138, 143

Holy Spirit, role in preaching of, 54, 61, 87, 92, 107, 136, 141, 145–46, 158, 186

homily

  as act of living tradition, 22–23

  as act of worship, 71

  as actualizing word, 46, 50, 119–136, 187

  central point of, 105–07. *See also* message

  as clarifying word, 27, 46, 47, 50, 103–118

  components of, 159–60

  definitions of, vii, 4, 8, 9, 14, 21, 25, 47, 49–50, 51

  as efficacious, 19, 20, 119

  as explanation, 14, 15, 16–17, 19, 34–35, 36, 46

  as inculturated word, 46, 50, 87–101

  as liturgical word, 45–46, 48, 50, 69–85

  as nourishment, 20

  as part of the liturgy, 8, 9, 14, 17, 19, 34, 36, 46, 175

  as personal word, 46, 48, 50, 53–68

  as proclamation, 15, 16–17, 26, 29, 34

  required on Sunday, 3, 9, 19, 26, 30, 34, 36, 46

  reserved to the ordained, 30–31, 36

  retelling pericope in, 172

  as scriptural interpretation, 46, 50, 69–70

  structure of, 162–69

    closing, 168, 173

    form, 163–64

    homiletic movement, 64n, 165–67

    opening, 167–68

    transitions, 168

  versus sermon, vi–vii

homily helps, 149–50, 183

Hoppe, Leslie, 153

Hughes, John, 158n

humor, use in preaching of, 127

illustration, homiletic, 58, 91–92, 128, 186–89

  described, 95, 160–61, 191

  inclusivity of, 186–87

  popular culture and, 92, 188–89

inculturation, 38–40, 41–43, 88–89, 92, 93

  defined, 31–32

internet, homiletic preparation and, 183

Jacks, G. Robert, 159n

John XXIII, 7

John Paul II, v, 30–32, 35, 37–40, 62, 75–76n, 78–80, 88, 155

jokes, *contra* use in preaching of, 127

joy, 79–80, 81–83

Killen, Patricia, 181–82

language types in preaching

  conceptual/explanatory, 104, 117, 159–60, 166, 186

imaginative/illustrative, 104,
159–61, 166, 186
lectionary, 33, 96, 117, 130–31n, 143–44,
152
liturgical movement, 6–7
liturgical year, 14, 15n, 24, 30, 33n, 34,
36, 80, 185
liturgy
defined, 70–71
full and active participation in, 6, 9,
17–18, 26–27, 46, 76–78
influence on the homily of, 78–81,
120, 135–36, 144–45
renewal of, 6–10, 29, 30, 33, 138
texts of, in preaching, 80–81, 84
Long, Thomas, 105n, 106, 159n, 163–64
Lord's Day. *See* Sunday
love, pastoral, 25, 28, 29, 47, 49, 63–64
Luther, Martin, 2, 4, 126, 127, 129, 191

message (of homily), 137, 152–53, 157,
159
Mitchell, Henry, 121
moralizing, *contra,* 43, 47, 154–55,
189–90

Old, Hughes Oliphant, 2, 3, 4, 126n, 127
Ong, Walter, 56n

Paul VI, 1, 16, 28–29, 31, 38, 51, 61, 63,
79, 122–23, 126
personification, use in preaching of,
117
Pius X, 5
Pius XII, 6, 16, 38
PLICA, 50, 53, 137
defined, vi
exegesis and, 148–49
feedback and, 194
hermeneutics and, 150–53
homiletic content and, 161, 162,
184–86
homiletic delivery and, 173–77

initial encounter with Word and,
144–45
post-modernism, 103–04, 122, 134
prayer, 143–44, 145, 155
preacher
continuing education of, 183–84
faith of, 28, 29, 46–47, 61–63,
122–23, 185
genuineness of, 59–60
respect of, 63–64, 90
responsibility of, 56–59
sense of the sacred and, 71–72, 127,
174
sincerity of, 59–60
subjectivity of, 139–40
transparency of, 60
as witness, 29, 47, 62, 122–23
preaching
catechesis and, 4, 15, 25, 27, 27n,
30–31, 33n
Christ's presence in, 16, 34, 46, 125–28
confidentiality and, 187–88
as craft, vi
as direct address, 51, 59, 124
as God's word, 123–25, 135
as good news, 43, 51, 79–80, 128–29,
153, 154, 173, 190
location of, 175–76
as oral event, 55–56, 66–67, 158–59
as pertinent to needs of listeners,
14, 19. *See also* inculturation
as principal duty of the ordained, 3,
22, 24–25
psychology and, 154
relevance of, 91–92
risk in, 125
stories in, 154, 167, 191–93
as urgent, 121–122, 177
pronouns, use in preaching of
I, me, my, 57–58, 67, 124
it, this, that, 172
we, us, ours, 57, 73–74, 124
you, yours, 74–75, 124

props, *contra* use in preaching of, 127
pulpit (ambo), preaching from, 175–76

Rang, Jack, 71n
Reformation, 1–4, 70–71, 126, 138
Reid, Barbara, 153
repetition, homiletic, 56, 66–67, 134
Rogers, Carl, 63n

sacraments, 2, 61, 117, 127
    relationship to Word of, 2, 8, 10, 17,
        34, 46
salvation, experience in preaching of,
    128–30
Scriptures
    commentaries on, 147–50
    culturally contingent elements of,
        147–48
    importance in liturgy of, 8
    interpretation of, 23–24, 69, 94–96,
        137–43. *See also* hermeneutics
    affinity and, 140, 151–52, 161, 186
    creativity in, 110, 141
    defined, 42
    inadequate, 153–55
    pluralism in, 141–42
    pre-understanding in, 139
    re-reading in, 41, 109, 140–41
    plurality of meaning of, 138, 143
    proclamation of, 71–72, 148
Second Vatican Council
    Constitution on the Sacred Liturgy
        *(Sacrosanctum Concilium)*, vi,
        7–9, 15, 16, 20, 26, 34, 75, 76–77,
        120n
    Decree on Ecumenism *(Unitatis
        Redintegratio)*, vii, 107
    Decree on the Ministry and Life of
        Priests *(Presbyterorum Ordinis)*,
        15, 17, 20, 34
    Dogmatic Constitution on the
        Church *(Lumen Gentium)*, 75

Dogmatic Constitution on Divine
    Revelation *(Dei Verbum)*, 23, 27,
    61, 127
Pastoral Constitution on the Church
    in the Modern World *(Gaudium et
    Spes)*, 21, 87–88, 189–90
sermon. *See* homily
sermon aids, 149–50, 183
sin, 64, 74, 187, 190
stories. *See* preaching, stories in
Sunday
    homily required on, 3, 9, 19, 26, 30,
        34, 36, 46
    nature of, 53, 75, 78–80, 185
    syllabus of preaching topics, 4, 14, 15,
        15n, 27n
synonyms, use in preaching of, 99

theological reflection, 96–97, 180–82
theology, utility for preachers of,
    110–12
Tisdale, Leonora Tubbs, 93
Tracy, David, 104n, 193
tradition, 1, 29, 46, 47, 48
    described, 112–13
    homily as act of, 22–23, 46
    theological reflection and, 96–97, 181
Trent, Council of, 2–4, 5, 22, 24
truth, 122–123

Untener, Ken, 158

van der Geest, Hans, 57n, 124, 161n
Vatican II. *See* Second Vatican Council
verb tense, importance in preaching of,
    78–79, 124–25, 127–28, 135, 172–73
vocabulary, in preaching, 89–91

Webb, Joseph, 54n
Wilson, Paul Scott, 152
writing, role in homily preparation of,
    157–59